For t

AWAKENING
to the
EXTRAORDINARY
YOU!

Thank you for your Radiant Light

KAYITE ASHCRAFT

Love Always,
Kayite

Copyright © 2009 by Kayite Ashcraft
ISBN: 978-0-9841074-0-7
0-9841074-0-1
Published by JimSam Inc.
P.O. Box 3363
Riverview, FL 33568
www.JimSamInc.com

All rights reserved. No part of this book may be reproduced or transmitted in any form or by any means, both known and unknown electronic or mechanical, including photocopying, recording, or by any information storage and retrieval system, without express written permission from the Publisher, with the exception of brief quotes used in connection with reviews written specially for any written, audio or visual media.

1st printing 2009
Printed in U.S.A.

Cover photo by Joshua Possick

Dedication

This book is dedicated to all those who have shined their light for me and to all those who seek to know the light of whom they are.

For all those who show up in my life experience, no matter what form and in what way the participation is, I bask in the presence of your brilliant light.

With Love and Gratitude,
Kayite

Introduction

My name is Kayite Ashcraft and I am here to share my journey with you – the journey of a woman whose ordinary life as a stay-at-home mom was catapulted into the extraordinary life of channeling and communicating with a group of spiritual guides known by the name of Jacob.

It all started a few months ago when I attended a Freedom Retreat with Neale Donald Walsch. Something shifted in me that began an awakening, with a series of incredible events to follow. From there, I was introduced to Abraham – a group of spiritual teachers who dialogue with Esther Hicks. I read *The Law of Attraction* and immediately resonated with Esther Hicks' story about how it all began for her. My first thought was – I think I am supposed to do this too. I was drawn to it. I knew on some level this would be for me.

I began to do the meditation that Esther was given. I thought, why not give it a try? And one day, it worked. Contact was made. They made it clear they were here to stay for as long as I chose the experience. They are here to guide us to a higher consciousness – those who are asking and desire to create this in their life experience.

I shared this experience with a few close friends. Since these friends all live in different states, I requested they please send me questions via email to ask Jacob. I wanted to explore and test out this new thing that had come into my life. Each person shared with me that they connected with the responses and that it was a wonderful and positive experience for them. This gave me the courage to continue. I had been writing down my thoughts as all of this was transpiring in my life. These thoughts, along with many of the conversations with Jacob, are what I will be sharing with you in the pages to come.

You may be wondering why the title of this book is *Awakening to the Extraordinary YOU* rather than *Awakening to the Extraordinary ME* since I have just previously shared that this book is about my own awakening. Although it is about my journey, my journey became about all of us – all those who have been asking and are seeking a greater awareness of who they are.

If you are reading this now, you are one of them. Nothing just "happens." It is all divine creation. Everything unfolds at just the perfect moment. You are here with me in this moment of now. There is great healing here for you. And what is healing? Jacob has said it is the releasing of congested energy that blocks the flow of your natural expression of self. As you share in this experience of others and myself, you open yourself up to release that energy, connect with you, and create a shift in order to grow and expand where you are in this life experience.

This paragraph right here is my final entry in this book. As you read along and join my journey, you will bear witness to my growth process. When the book was compiled and I read back over the material, I could clearly see how much I had shifted throughout this process. Once I opened up to awaken to me, everything flowed in so fast. I was (and am) continually gaining clarity about my life and myself. And I have gained a deeper understanding of Jacob's Message as I experience it in my life. I had several people ask if I were going to change my own personal notes and earlier thoughts now that I have greater clarity about where I was then. I told them the main message of Jacob is about growth and expansion.

This is my journey. I am growing. I wish to share that with you. Not change it to look like I had some greater wisdom than I did at the time. I rejoice in the growth. It is just where I was. And now, here in this moment, is just where I am. Not one is better than the other. It simply just is. I am delighted you have chosen to join me here today. We are co-creating this experience, you and I. Enjoy this journey with me. It is your creation!

The following is the last question I asked Jacob at the very end of this book. It will be shared again then, but I want to share it with you here as well. I want to introduce you to what they are offering and I also feel it will help you have a greater understanding of what they are talking about when they refer to "framing" or "framework" and other such things in their responses. It can also create an opportunity for you to greater expand your perspective (the framework of where you are, as they say) during this experience, if you bring your conscious awareness to understanding the process.

Is there anything else you would like to share with those who are asking, seeking to know more about who they are?
We often say to look within, that the answer is within you. By this we are referring to the awareness of the magnificent being that you are and the power you wield to create and experience the life you desire. There are no real answers. It is not the answers you seek but the experience of seeking the answers.

This is the growth. Explore, observe, create, experience, express, expand. Enjoy the process of your life experience. Our connection with you in this moment is your divine creation. You are seeking to know more about who you are and this desire has led you to us.

We invite you to look within your self, connect with the source of who you are, and experience your world from a greater perspective of where you are. And what we mean by this is that we invite you to consciously choose to expand the framework of your perspective. How does one do that, you ask?

Your perspective is like a picture frame. Envision a small picture frame in front of you. This is the framework through which you view and experience your world. This is just where you are. It is perfection. Everything outside of that frame is not a part of your current life experience.

There are endless possibilities available to you. You have access to all that is. And by consciously choosing to expand your framework, you will invite experiences into your life that will offer you the opportunity to create a shift to expand your current frame. From this expanded perspective, you will experience your world from a greater perspective. And this will now be where you are. It is not who you are but where you are in this life experience. Everything is filtered through this framework. Your view of another is through your own framework. Their view of themselves is through their own framework.

Misunderstandings arise because you are experiencing something entirely different. Many of you feel frustration when others do not view your world the way you do but they do not have your frame. It cannot be. They will always have their frame. And it is never about comparing one frame to another's. It is only ever about the growth and expansion of your own framework.

The purpose of life is growth and expansion. You desire the growth and every experience offers you the opportunity to gain clarity about where you are in order to grow and expand your framing. You are continually growing and expanding. It is for you to enjoy the process. Rejoice in where you are. It is perfection.

My "Story"

As a child, for as long as I can remember, I had been interested in anything metaphysical, out-of-body experiences and channeling. I was always drawn to this type of thing. I knew there was more. I longed to experience it. However, I did have a very stifled childhood that put this on hold for a while. Somewhere along the way, I forgot who I was.

I grew up in a home with a father who was very angry much of the time. He often made me feel I was worthless and not good enough. I never felt like I could do anything right and I finally gave up trying. There was so much chaos. Life was always so serious; I didn't know much about joy or fun. I went through a very rough time and there were many days I no longer wanted to live. I wanted to go to sleep and not wake up again. I just wanted the pain to end. I was tired and rundown. I didn't want to deal with life anymore. It was just too hard.

Things changed some when I met my husband. The relationship gave me a focus. I was nineteen at the time. We dated for five years before we got married and were together for fourteen years. I just wanted someone to love me. I never got the love from my father and I ended up attracting the same situation. A man who was very nice but emotionally shut down. He had a very rough childhood as well and my heart went out to him for that. Of course, I could relate with my own. So we were two people in pain, continuing the cycle.

I felt unworthy and was always seeking his attention and love. He wasn't able to give me the attention and love and that fed his belief that he was a failure and my belief that I was unworthy of receiving his attention and love. I thought I was in love with him but I really didn't know what love was. It was an incredibly lonely time for me and I just continued the cycle of feeling unworthy of anything more – feeling unworthy of the love, the joy and the bliss of life. I wasn't even sure that existed.

At least I felt that until the moment my son Xander was born. He was my only joy at that time. There were many days I still struggled to get out of bed; my son became my reason for living. I got up for him. He reminded me of what love was. I wanted to be a part of his life. Yet, I still felt unworthy even of him.

The first time I told someone "I love you" was to my husband and it felt extremely uncomfortable to say. Even then, it was just words. Over the years I did awaken some. I became more in tune with myself. I often thought of leaving the marriage but didn't know how.

I thought I needed a good reason – a reason that would be acceptable to others so they wouldn't think I just gave up. I thought I was supposed to stick it out. Make the best of it. But I was so absolutely miserable that I often wished he would cheat on me. I thought that would be my way out. I now know he desired freedom too. We both felt stuck not knowing how to free ourselves. No one had ever told us we could just choose to be happy. Not until I got to the retreat.

My Awakening

Who knew that joining Netflix would change my life?

I had been living in a fog so thick I was lost in it. So lost that I didn't even realize there was fog. Or that sunshine existed. One day, I signed up for Netflix DVDs and selected a large number of movies that were of interest. These were all added to my list. Many movies came and went over the course of many months.

And then one day, *Conversations with God* arrived in my mailbox. When I watched this movie, I completely fell in love with this beautiful soul on his journey. The compassion I felt, the love I wanted to give, the tears I cried and the joy that filled my being. I was drawn in. Something had shifted within me.

I immediately got on my computer and found the cwg.org website which listed several upcoming retreats. There just happened to be a Freedom Retreat with Neale Donald Walsch in a location close enough for me to drive to and it was occurring in just a few weeks. I had absolutely no idea how I was going to pay for it or who would watch my three-year-old son while I was gone. I was a stay-at-home mom and had never left him.

Somehow those thoughts of "how" subsided and an overwhelming sense of "I have to be there" flowed through. It was calling me. I felt it so strongly. I had never been to any kind of retreat before. I really had no expectation of what it would be and I hadn't even given it much thought. I just knew I was going. Going for the experience, whatever that may be. In that moment, I signed up.

Everything just beautifully fell into place. My credit card company sent me a letter that they were increasing my limit. I hadn't even requested it. My account had previously been at its maximum limit. And just like that, my payment issue was resolved. Then my sister, Jennifer gladly volunteered to take care of my son for the week while my husband was at work. I felt so incredibly grateful. What had first appeared to be an impossible trip was soon my reality. This was my first big trip driving all by myself. It was an adventure.

For the first time in a long while, I had hope and I actually felt excitement for what could possibly transpire. I was on my way and feeling joy. This was something I had only known from interaction with my son. It was wonderful to feel this for myself and what was possible for me. I enjoyed the beautiful drive through the mountains to arrive at an absolutely gorgeous retreat held in Black Mountain, North Carolina. I could feel the energy.

I had previously requested a roommate but did not know if I were assigned one until my arrival. Sure enough, I was told I had been. I checked into my room and began to unpack as I eagerly waited to meet her. The door opened and a glorious spirit who brought great love into the room greeted me. She was beaming. She had a beautiful smile and I knew instantly she was divine. Or, should I say vibrant as Vibrance was her name. Vibrant she was indeed. She was to be an important part of my process.

Our first session began Monday night. I was so excited to hear Neale speak that I was actually in a state of bliss. His voice was so soothing and I could feel the love. I was feeling absolutely wonderful right up until the moment he asked why we were there and announced he would be passing around a microphone for us to speak.

I quickly went from feeling bliss to feeling petrified. I realized in that moment why I was there (so I thought). I had always had trouble speaking up and here was my grand opportunity. Yet anxiety arose within me. I felt sick. I was too scared to raise my hand. I asked myself, what am I so afraid of? I was afraid that what I had to say was not important and that I would be wasting everyone's time. I felt completely unworthy. That day I just sat there and listened to others share. As they shared, I could feel a small part of me begin to awaken as I connected with their stories, the feelings, insecurities and fears. I felt the pain and I only wanted to love them. I thought, if I want to love them, then possibly, just maybe, they might want to love me too.

Tuesday's session began and I wanted to raise my hand but couldn't seem to get my body to cooperate. Every time Neale asked if anyone had something to share, I just felt paralyzed. The day had passed and I was still sitting there with anxiety. I couldn't sleep. I knew I had to do something. There was no way I could bear another day of feeling like this. I couldn't focus and I felt like I was missing out on the entire purpose of why I was there.

I talked with my roommate and she really provided just what I needed. It was a kind, yet swift kick in the butt. I had tried sharing with her but she didn't want to interfere with my process. She told me I needed to share with the group and to just do it. At first I was hurt as I was trying to connect with someone in the only way I knew how and I felt rejected that she did not want to talk with me. Then I realized what a pattern that feeling of rejection had been for me and how perfect it was for it to be in my face, for me to acknowledge and deal with it. I was grateful to her for helping me bring this issue to the surface. It kind of put a fire under me to really do something about it. And although I was afraid to speak, I was even more afraid of going home and missing the opportunity of a lifetime. This was why I was there. Every part of my being was telling me this. And I was paying attention.

Wednesday's session began. As soon as I heard the request for those who wished to speak, my hand shot up like a rocket. I had to do it quickly before I lost my nerve. In that moment, it was as if time stood still. Everything else disappeared and I only saw Neale.

With a shaky voice, I began to share my greatest fears and my deepest pain. I was fully open. There was nowhere to hide (although I wanted to crawl under the chair). I was out there, exposed for all to see. As we talked through my "story" of unworthiness, it was as if a light bulb came on and I could see things from an entirely different perspective. Then I heard the most beautiful voice singing a glorious song just for me. I looked up and saw Cathy Bolton with her guitar in hand. It was then I began to notice everyone else in the room. They began to sing along too. As I looked around, they were looking right back at me, turning toward me. I realized then they were singing *to* me. I was crying tears of joy.

What had started as the most terrifying moment of my life became the most glorious moment I had ever experienced. I had opened myself up, said this is who I am, and I was immediately embraced by love. That was my healing. And just like that, in an instant, a moment, I was FREE!

I was beaming the rest of the week. I could not get the smile off of my face. I looked in the mirror and I was actually glowing. Glowing, I tell you. And this was just the beginning. I cried along with every person who shared his or her story. I cried for the deep connection I felt. How wonderful it was to see others stand in their truth. To say, "This is who I am." I just wanted to hug them and love them. I wanted to tell them just how magnificent they were. I also felt a deep connection with those who didn't speak. I may not have known that much about them, but I knew we were all a part of something wonderful and that just their presence was of tremendous value.

I was guided out of the fog and immersed myself in the sunshine. I became aware I was a beacon of light shining ever so brightly. *I had awakened.* This was just the beginning. I think how wonderful it is that the girl – who was once too scared to speak into the microphone and felt so unworthy – is now a vibrant woman who is writing a book, sharing all about herself and her experience. Not only writing it, but also knowing there is much to be offered here.

Freedom

I mentioned that in the moment of my healing I was "free" but what exactly does that mean? I knew I felt free at the time, but it wasn't until over the course of my journey to follow that I gained greater clarity of what this meant for me. What I am referring to is being free to be myself, to fully express all of me. That I no longer hold back my expression for fear of judgment or concern myself with what others might think or feel about my decisions and choices in life. I am creating my reality. I am choosing my life experience.

For so long I have allowed others to run my life. To tell me how I should live. To tell me what is appropriate. When I shared all of my fears and insecurities and was embraced by love, I experienced the pure unconditional love of me. I experienced the knowing of the divine being I am (that we all are) and that I am perfection, no matter how I choose to experience life. That life isn't about doing something a so-called "right way." Everyone has a different idea of what the "right way" might be and that is glorious. It is wonderful to have such varied opinions and ideas about what we can experience. But what is right for one person is only right for that person.

Often we try to push our ways upon another. I now choose for myself what gives me joy. And, as I follow my passions and desires, I am simply making a choice of what I wish to experience. There is not a right or wrong choice – only a different choice for a different experience. That's all it is – a different experience. I had finally released myself from the illusion that what others thought of me mattered. What is important is how I feel about me. A weight had been lifted from my shoulders that day. In fact, it felt like it had been lifted from my entire being. I felt so free to live my own life. To create whatever life I desired. To be who I wanted to be and live how I wanted to live. I realized I could just be me. There was tremendous freedom in that.

Time Warp?

We had a lovely final lunch at the retreat and then it was time to get ready for the trip home. We said our good-byes, gave big hugs and felt the love. We knew we would all stay in touch and would be talking again soon. I packed my luggage, put it in my van and was good to go.

Vibrance joined me for the trip. Friends had dropped her off at the retreat and she arrived not knowing how she would get home. She lived in North Carolina and the trip to her house was not that far out of the way. This was just another reason we were perfectly matched as roommates. I offered to take her home the very first day. It took her until the end of the week to accept my offer. I was delighted. I would be heading north to my home in Virginia after that and I rejoiced in this new adventure.

My gas tank was close to empty so we stopped off for gas. She offered me money, and for the first time, I easily received it with gratitude and thanked her for the gift. Before, I would have had a hard time accepting it. Perhaps it was a worthiness thing again. But in that moment, I understood the joy she would feel in giving it. And I would not want to deny another the joy in giving a gift. So I gladly embraced it. I shared this with her and she thanked me and said how glad she was that I welcomed it. We got a couple of drinks for the road and were on our way.

Twenty minutes later we were commenting on how hungry we were. We wondered how that could be as we had just eaten lunch. We checked the time and discovered it had been three hours. Neither one of us could believe it. It definitely felt like we had been driving only twenty minutes. We do not know what happened but we definitely felt like we experienced some sort of time warp. We reached her house in what felt like almost no time at all. It was delightful to see her space. It was then she gave me a CD she thought I would enjoy. I accepted the gift with gratitude and thanked her for her company on the trip. I then headed out the driveway on my journey home.

Shining My Light

I was still hungry at this point so I stopped off at McDonald's for a quick bite. When I left the retreat, I had stated I intended to shine my light to everyone I encountered. This was my first opportunity. I decided to go through the drive-thru as it was getting late and I wanted to keep driving. I ordered and drove up to pay. When a friendly man at the first window gave me my change, I told him what a beautiful smile he had and thanked him for a wonderful encounter. He smiled and said he would see me again at the next window. I laughed all the way to the second window. When he passed me the food, I said "Thank you for honoring me with your presence once again." He had the biggest grin on his face and I was filled with joy. I was having fun. I was enjoying life!

Guidance Home

I was taking a different route home from Vibrance's house that was not on the highway but a back way through the mountains. I got lost twice in the dark with no one around and no cell phone service. It was just the trees and myself. I asked myself, why did I choose this? Before the retreat, I would have been scared, crying and probably would have felt like it was an awful experience and I'd never want to take a trip alone again. But this time, I saw the beauty of it all. It was an opportunity for me to see I really was free, an opportunity for me to experience an entirely different perspective; it clearly made all the difference in my reality.

I looked around at the trees and felt their love. I remember thinking if I had to just stay there with the trees all night, how divine that would be. I was not afraid. I felt nothing but peace. (I have had an incredible connection with trees ever since. I hug them often and just feel their energy, their love.) I said, "God knows the way home. I can always find my way home. I am never alone. All is well." Sure enough, I made some turns and found my way. I truly felt signs appeared just for me, to guide me.

I also had an incredible encounter with a deer along the way. As I came around a winding road, I saw a deer standing just off to the side. He saw my headlights coming and turned around and started to head back into the woods. I was so excited to see this magnificent creature that I said, "You are beautiful! I Love You!" He immediately turned back around and looked right at me. It was amazing. I know in that moment, he heard me. That we had connected. His eyes looked right at mine. It was beautiful. Magical. Incredible. I arrived home feeling like I could do anything. That instead of this whole experience being scary, it let me know how strong I really am. What a gift! I am so incredibly grateful.

Divine Inspiration

Upon my return home, I could feel things continuing to shift in my life. Things were very different. I continued to ask myself what all of this was about. What was to come of my life? About a week after I returned home, I was with my son at the McDonald's Playland. I took a notebook to journal while he played. All of the sudden I began to get this flow of ideas that were coming quicker than I could write them. So I just began writing as fast as I could. Before I knew it, I had written a children's book, although it didn't feel like I was writing it. Something flowed through me. Divine inspiration. It was so exciting. Five more books have since transpired. They are about the adventures of a little boy named Xander (inspired by my son) and the joys of life, the beauty in everything, and the greater depths of who we are. Although they have not been published as of this moment, it was a wonderful experience and my son and I really enjoy them. I know they will be shared with others at the perfect moment.

Message in the Clouds

My life had dramatically changed and I had no idea what was awaiting me. I began to just focus on taking care of my son, envisioning what I wanted for my life, and doing meditations at night. I also spent time going through our massive amounts of "stuff" to prepare for our annual yard sale. This time, I was especially ready to clear it all out. I had the desire to simplify my life.

On a beautiful, sunny Saturday morning, our yard sale began with a bang. Lots of people continually stopped by and we were clearing out so much. I began to eventually just give things away. It felt so good to me. By noontime, there was a lapse in visitors. I was sitting outside in a chair on my front lawn just passing the time. There was nothing going on.

For some reason, I decided to look up at the sky. There were a lot of clouds in the sky that day. But then I noticed a large cloud that was in the center of all the others. All of the sudden, it began to shift quickly and a wolf appeared. It wasn't like when you look at a cloud and say, hey, that kind of looks like something. I mean this was clear as day.

It was very detailed, the eyes, the hair, everything. Then, just like that, before my very eyes, the clouds began again to shift quickly and became a leopard. I couldn't take my eyes off of this. I was captivated. I thought is this really happening? I wanted to go get someone else to look at it too but I wasn't about to miss a moment. It was happening too quickly. It began to shift again and became a woman with a headpiece which looked somewhat Egyptian. And then it shifted again to a panther. I thought to myself, what is this? Is this a sign? What does this mean?

In that moment, it transformed into a large hand and a finger was pointing right at me! I thought it could just reach down and scoop me up. I guess the pointing at me was perhaps a confirmation this message was indeed for me? I hadn't moved an inch. I sat there in amazement as I watched the cloud begin to shift very quickly again and then completely dissipate. There was just this open space of sky in the center of all the clouds. It disappeared right before me.

My mother has a book called *Animal Speak*, which talks about the different animal totems and what they represent. Out of curiosity, I looked them up. I remember thinking it was interesting and the biggest message that seemed relevant at the time was that my life was about to change. I thought perhaps it was about a possible change in my relationship with my husband. I had no clue. And no conscious awareness of what was to come.

Now What?

About a month later, I realized I was continuing to see everything from the new perspective I had opened up to; I could no longer live in the fog and had to acknowledge it was time to create change in my fourteen-year relationship. I realized it was okay for me to be happy. And that wanting to be happy was enough reason to leave, enough reason to create the changes in my life I so desired. My marriage ended because I chose to live my joy; for the first time, I consciously chose preservation of self. Finally, I knew I was worthy to do so. My husband too was choosing this. We had a long talk and we both decided it was best for us to go our separate ways knowing this was a permanent decision; we both felt relief. An overwhelming sense of peace filled the room. It was a beautiful moment as we aligned with what we truly desired. He saw my growth and where I was going with my spirituality. He told me he was not ready to go there with me.

There had been other times I talked about leaving, but he had always asked me to stay, and so I did. (Again, I thought I had no good reason to leave.) This time, he didn't want to hold me back. He was letting me go. In essence, he set me free, at least in releasing the energy he held with me.

Now I know I am the only one who can truly set myself free but it was wonderful he made it so easy for me. That he made it such a pleasurable experience. And now he is happy too because I think he felt like he was always failing me since he knew he couldn't be fully present with me in the way I desired.

What is interesting here is that regardless of how he chose to respond, I was finally prepared to create change this time, I was choosing for me. And as soon as I let go of my concern for his reaction and how that might affect my decision, he let go too. How wonderful! We have great love and respect for one another but we did not desire the same things in life. We simply wanted different things and that was okay. It is more than okay because now we are both living the life that we want for ourselves and it is joyous for everyone.

What About Xander?

Many people understand about my situation with my husband but they often ask me about my son. What about him? There is always great concern from others about how he will handle things. People have told me it's too bad he is in this situation and that it is unfortunate. I would just like to say we are still a family. Where we live does not define a family. How we choose to interact with one another is what it's about for us. And the way we had been interacting was not what we wished to display for him or the environment we desired him to grow up in.

We now choose to share with Xander the joy in following our own passions and desires and let him know he can follow his dreams and greatest desires for his own life. We show him by living this and that feels really good to us.

Xander is a very happy child. And, as we are living our joy, he experiences that joy with us. This is not to say he will not have things come up for him. But this would be the case whether we all still lived together or not. He is growing and exploring life and as things arise, we will talk about it. He likes to share his feelings and he knows he can talk to both his mommy and daddy about anything. So my question is, is this situation so bad? Is it unfortunate? From our perspective, it is pretty wonderful.

Already Set in Place

It would take another two months as we prepared for the transition. I was consciously creating the flow of income for me to afford to move out on my own as we continued to pay for the mortgage on our house as well. My husband was going to stay there until the house sold.

Our house had already been put up for sale a few weeks before the retreat. The value of the homes in our area had increased quite a bit and we had intended to sell it and use the money from the equity to begin anew together. I had already found a lovely townhome complex for us to move to. I had no idea at the time, but it was clear to me I had already set things in motion without even knowing it.

Something as simple as having to sell my house might have prevented me from leaving the marriage. At the time, it didn't seem like a simple thing. It seemed overwhelming and a lot to do. But since we already had it listed, and all the work was done, it became an irrelevant factor. And once we made our decision, I realized the townhome I had picked out was going to be for my son and me, instead of all of us. My higher self had already set it all in place. It was just waiting there for me to step into it. Once I did, once I consciously chose it, the manifestation came to be.

None of My Business

As I continued living with my husband, I noticed things that used to bother me no longer did. It made sense to me. I thought, well, what he chooses to do is now none of my business. Then I had this huge epiphany that wow, it never was! *It never was.* That all this time I thought being in a relationship somehow gave me the right to tell him how he should live his life. That what he was choosing for his life experience was somehow my business. This is exactly what others had done to me that I did not like.

The only thing that would be relevant to me is whether I chose to continue to participate in the relationship based on what he was choosing for himself. Was this an experience I desired? I realized in that moment that I had been trying to change him. I had wanted him to fit into what I was choosing for my life experience rather than allowing it to be what it was. Had I allowed him the freedom to be who he was during our relationship, things could have been tremendously different.

I know it all occurred this way for my growth and for me to be able to come to this awareness now. I rejoice in that. But I also rejoice in knowing that as I move onward and create new relationships, I am gaining more clarity about what a relationship means to me, and how I choose to participate in it. Thank you for this gift.

Showing Up No Matter What

After I returned home from the retreat and during the time I was still living with my husband, I began listening to the CD Vibrance had given me. It was an introduction to Abraham, the group of spiritual teachers who dialogue with Esther Hicks. I immediately felt a connection with her. This led me to purchase the book *The Law of Attraction,* that began my journey of meditations that I mentioned earlier. What is interesting here is that although my roommate had given me this CD, the very next day after I returned home, my sister had also just discovered Abraham and called to tell me all about it.

Right after that, a friend from my retreat called to tell me about a new book she was reading – again it was another book with Abraham. I took notice. I had never heard of them before, but it was clear to me I was now ready to receive this information. And it was going to show up in my life no matter what. It was coming at me in every direction. I got the message! Thank you for this gift.

My New Place

On August 1, I signed my lease for my new apartment townhome. My husband had sold a big job at work, which enabled us the funds for my deposit and a few months' rent. All was unfolding perfectly. I had intended to paint the walls using lots of bright colors that felt good to me. My husband had always nixed the idea of brightly colored paint but I wanted to fully express myself now. I wanted to completely make it my space, for it to represent me. This was a new beginning.

It took the entire month of August to get everything painted and all my stuff settled in. Keep in mind I still had my son during the day. I was continuing to stay at the house with my husband during this time, mainly because of Xander. We had a playroom set up at the house and it was easier for me to be there with him until I was able to set up his new bedroom at my place. I would drive over to the townhome after my husband got home from work and do everything in the evenings.

First Contact

8/26

I have been doing meditations every night to maintain my focus on my desires while still living at the house. I was calling forth and requesting to communicate and channel through me those loving light beings who seek enlightenment through my process. This evening I felt a presence and I asked if I had made contact. Was someone there?

I felt a tingle. I asked, what is your name? I got a vision in my mind of a large rock mountain. Letters began to be etched into the rock and J - A - C - O - B appeared. I asked, Jacob, is that you? I felt heaviness throughout my body that indicated I was not alone and that Jacob was indeed there. I had been trying to communicate and make contact for three months.

Will I be someone who can channel? *Yes.* (This was all asked and answered silently.)

Can I do it now? *You will work through your own process and then help others.*

    I didn't know what all would be involved but I was very excited about it. I felt great joy with the idea of helping others. This was something I was always drawn to. I have always felt great compassion for others and related to where they are. I knew on some level we were all just doing the best we could.

    I began to question my experience. What I felt was so real, yet it was easy to doubt myself and wonder if it really occurred. Was I imagining this? Was it wishful thinking? Am I just nuts? No, it happened. I know it did.

    I decided I would meditate each day and welcome Jacob to integrate with me. I felt the process would get easier and more in depth as I practiced and allowed for it to flow through, whatever "it" was.

Manifesting My Dream Car

    My very first car was a 1971 VW Convertible Beetle Bug. I loved that car. It had virtually no features. There was no heat, no air conditioning, I only got AM radio, and several of the knobs to roll the windows down were broken. But she was beautiful to me. Her name was Zelda. The previous owner had named her and so I kept the name. I eventually traded her in.

    I often thought during the '90s how wonderful it would be to have a VW Beetle with all the power options and features that were available with the technology then. Years later, I began to see commercials that they were coming out with the new Beetles. I was ecstatic! Yet, over the course of many years, I never purchased one. I had always put others desires before my own. Again, it was the worthiness thing.

For several months now I had been thinking about my dream car and had signed up with CarMax to email me if they received any used Beetles with all of the features I desired. I wanted a used one as it would be more affordable and we were already unsure about how I could move. This could just possibly add to the strain of things but I chose not to see it that way. I trusted that all would work out. I knew I would somehow create it to be. In those months, I did not receive one match that had absolutely everything I desired. And even the ones that were only a partial match were usually already sold by the time I got the email.

Things had been in motion with my move and I began to feel that something was in motion with my vision of a new vehicle as well. One day, in early August, I was traveling to Richmond and decided to check out the Volkswagen dealership there. They had a few used vehicles but not with everything I envisioned. The sales associate tried to offer me other vehicles and told me I was never going to find what I wanted. I replied, "Of course I will. I will just create it to be." He just looked at me like I was crazy. I thanked him for his time and was on my merry way.

At this point, I headed to Chuck E. Cheese to catch up with my sister while Xander played with his cousins. While on the way, I got a strong sense to call CarMax in that moment. I explained what I was looking for and the sales associate said he would check and call me back. I was inside sitting at a booth when I got the return call. He told me that they had just received a VW Beetle that was green with tan leather interior, automatic, sunroof, only a year old, and had low mileage. They said it was in like new condition. It had everything that I had desired. I knew in that moment it had arrived just for me. And get this, the vehicle was so recently received by them that they hadn't even officially listed it for sale yet. Thank you for this gift.

All was smooth with the application for credit approval and I was driving home in my dream car the following week. I want to clarify that the manifestation of the car wasn't about my desire for a "material thing." It was about what it represented to me. It was about the joy of knowing I was worthy enough to create it for myself, the joy in the experience of that. The joy of the creating itself is magnificent.

The license plate says it all. It says LVN JOY for living joy. It is a constant reminder to me that I am indeed living my joy. And I can't help but smile whenever I see it. All is coming together. I can feel it. And what is my new Beetle's name? Buttercup. Yes, I know, she's not yellow. My son actually named her. And when her tank is on empty, he tells me she's hungry and needs her tummy filled. How great is that? What a joy he is.

Not Much Happening

I had continued to meditate but not much was happening since that first contact. I was still wondering what I had actually experienced. I know it was a powerful feeling at the time, unmistakable in that moment. Yet nothing had occurred since and it was easy for my mind to talk me out of what I thought had transpired. I chose to remain open, receptive and ready for whatever was to come, although I was a bit distracted by my move. Most of my attention and energy was focused there.

Moving In

I finally officially moved into my apartment the beginning of September. It was really great to be in my own space. It contained a wonderful energy vibration I created and surrounded myself with. I had desired to create a peaceful, joyful space. And so I did. Oh, and did I mention it has a large whirlpool tub?

This is only significant because for years I had wanted one but every time we moved, I would always give in and settle for something else. Again, not feeling worthy of what I truly desired. And my husband and I had many moves together, eleven to be exact. Then, as I was off on my new journey of joy, I had finally manifested my bathtub. Yes! (And I am delighted to say I have since been in it every night and it is my place of meditation and a sanctuary for me.)

Something Big
9/14

As I am living in my new environment and enjoying every moment, things have begun to shift for me again. I have experienced continual joy and excitement rather than sadness and depression from a lack of hope of a better life. I have created the most fantastic friendships I know will last a lifetime. This is the happiest I have ever been or known possible. I am living my joy. As I look back upon my life, I can clearly see the millions of stepping-stones that have guided me to this very moment. I feel something really big is waiting for me.

I am on the edge of a cliff and ready to take the leap. Ready to soar as my wings expand. I shared with a close friend about this intense feeling I have been getting that something really big is about to happen. It is the only way I know how to describe it – an overwhelming sense that something huge is about to transpire. I don't know what, but I sure am excited about it. Something is happening. I can feel it.

We Are Here
9/17

It is 10:00 p.m. on the eve of my thirty-fourth birthday. For the first time in my life I am truly celebrating my life and rejoicing in who I am. I decided I would spend the evening with a relaxing bubble bath. I lit some vanilla candles and filled the tub. I sank down into the water and basked in the warmth.

I thought this might be a good time to meditate so I asked again to communicate with Jacob. I began to feel tingly all over, almost dizzy but not. I felt heaviness on my chest and eyes. My breath increased as almost gasping for air. Then I began taking deep breaths.

I felt as though I couldn't speak. My arms were numb. My mind was clear. All of the sudden *We........Are........Here* came out of my mouth. The dots….. indicate a pause in the communication. I was amazed, surprised, elated. I thought, is this real?

Yes…..We……..Are……..Here. This was the beginning of a two-hour conversation that was to change my life completely.

First Conversation

I began asking questions in my head and then they would answer speaking through my voice. I felt as though I could not speak myself. I was still just trying to breathe and maintain focus.

Or perhaps a more accurate way to describe it would be "non-focus." I had no thoughts whatsoever when the information was flowing through. I felt clear, a blank slate. I did not hear the words until they came out of my mouth. It was a very slow process.

You said we are here. Is there more than one? Who is Jacob?

Many more than you can comprehend. It is unimportant as we are all here working together with you as one. We are source expressed in this form to offer the guidance you have been seeking. We are and have always been. We are many….excited for you.

Why was I chosen to experience this?

You were not chosen……you chose us. We are here because you called us forth and then we chose to participate in your process. It is exciting for us to observe and to interact with you. It is exciting for us when we speak and the words flow through. We have connected. We are communicating. We are thrilled.

Why am I choosing this path?

You wanted to experience this communication and you surrounded yourself with those who have many questions and greatly desire answers…..guidance…...understanding. You have very few questions for us yourself. You are open and a great receiver. You allow us to flow through you with ease. (This I knew to be true.)

I began to question if all of this was really happening. I believed it could be. It was so surreal. It is hard to even describe it but I am trying.

Am I crazy? Is this really happening?

You are not crazy. It IS happening.

It seems too good to be true.
That cannot be. We are here…..communicating with you……so you must have believed this in order for it to occur. You do not doubt us….doubt this experience. You doubt whether others will believe your experience.

After an hour in the bathtub, I was becoming a prune. I wanted to get out but was afraid I would lose this incredible communication. The moment I thought this out came – *do not be concerned. This is just the beginning. We are here. We will always be here for as long as you choose. You can call upon us anytime. Simply ask – Jacob, are you here? We will be. In an instant. There is no need for concern for we have many discussions ahead.*

I got out of the tub and I continued to feel their presence, heaviness in my eyes and deep breaths. I felt so relaxed. Like in a trance-like state (although I don't know exactly what a trance is like but it seems to fit). When I looked in the mirror, my eyes were different. They were with me. It was not scary at all but rather blissful. I felt such an overwhelming sense of peace and love that I could not possibly think it to be anything else but what was being felt. I went in the bedroom, grabbing a pen and paper to write down all I could remember, and then lay down on the bed to be comfortable. *We are still here*, they said.

What about my family?
Your family is irrelevant. You are moving into a path of greatness. We refer to greatness in the sense that you will experience great expansion in this process. Not in the sense that you are above or better than any other.

Why now?
You are ready. This is why you have been asking so often and calling us forth. You shifted into a greater awareness of self and as you experienced the harmony and joy of full expression of self, you opened yourself to receive us. Everything in your life has prepared you for this. You have been awakened. The healing has just begun. You will be guiding others. You ARE guiding others. You chose to participate in creating great change for your world in this manner. This is the experience you seek.

What About War?
There is only harmony. That which appears different is simply your manifestation of your reality and not what is actually so. There is no need for concern, as only harmony truly exists.

Is this really real?
You know it to be so. You are looking for physical, concrete proof but the answer is within you. You feel us. You feel our presence. You know what we speak is true. And yet you doubt. The doubt comes from your concern for what others will believe. This is your confusion and discomfort.

I am feeling tired but I am also intrigued. It is almost midnight. How can I sleep when I have this incredible opportunity?
We will always be here for as long as you choose. Sleep….rest. We will continue. We will continue until you are fully comfortable. Then you will share us with another….and another…and another. And then you will share us with…..EVERYONE. Sleep. There is much to come. We are here. We love you.

In awe I thought I would try to sleep. I couldn't wait to get up and try it again the next day. I thought – I know this IS happening. It really IS. I know my higher self understands this but the rest of me is still trying to adjust.

Birthday Celebration

I have never made a big deal about my birthday. In the past, most of my friends usually didn't remember it anyway. Of course with my feelings of unworthiness, why would they? I certainly created that. I didn't feel that I was worth celebrating. And I looked to others to give me value. I thought if they remembered, it meant I was somehow worthy. But now, from my new perspective, it is only about how I feel about myself. I don't need others to remember it. I know my own value and I choose to celebrate how magnificent my life is, that all life is. This is the joy.

I woke up with the feeling of exhilaration. Here it was my birthday, and I had just had this incredible communication. I could barely contain myself. Wow! I still had to take my son to school for a half day. I dropped him off and then headed for the gym. I started my day with a personal training session. Then I picked up my son and took him out to lunch. I watched him play at the playground for the afternoon. It was blissful. I found myself thinking about Jacob, the process, and what was to come. I couldn't wait to explore this further.

My former husband (I refer to him as my former husband because in this moment of now, we are no longer living together and he is no longer participating in my life experience in this way) took off work early in order to pick up Xander and give me some free time to enjoy myself. I went to a spa and had a Swedish massage and facial. All of these things were things I had never done before. Things I felt unworthy of. Things I thought I would not have been worth spending the money on. It was glorious to enjoy this wonderful day all about me knowing I am a magnificent being (we all are) and I felt tremendous joy in that.

Freedom Circle

My Freedom Circle began on July 31. Many of us from the retreat had kept in contact through emails and called ourselves the Freedom Family. From that group, someone came up with the idea of creating a small mastermind group of five to seven people to support one another's desires and to discuss different topics of life each week. There ended up being enough interest that two groups were formed.

There were five of us, all women, in the Tuesday night group. We set up a conference call time for 9:00-10:00 p.m. The first two calls went so well that we ended up extending the time until 10:30. We all ended up getting so much more out of this connection than we had envisioned when it began. We live in different states yet distance is not even an issue when we share so openly and deeply with one another. It all seemed to flow so perfectly.

We had a general guideline of the amount of time for each of us to speak and share. However, when someone needed to share more, there was always someone else who was feeling she had less to share that day. It always worked out to perfection. We were all excited about this and we all found it interesting how we all ended up together, just the five of us.

What did we have in common? For one, we all – at some point – had trouble speaking our voice. Three of us had a blockage on our thyroid (which clearly indicated to me the physical manifestation of not speaking up). We didn't know where we were all going but we knew we were drawn to one another. We had chosen this path together in this moment.

Our call was scheduled for the night of my birthday as it fell on a Tuesday. Normally we have a topic we discuss but for some reason the leader of our group decided we would just talk about whatever we wanted to. I did not know what I was going to share, but I knew I felt safe with my group.

When my turn came, I just blurted out about Jacob. They were all very excited and supportive. They wanted to know more.

We talked and decided they will all send me questions so that I can continue to expand this communication at a deeper level. My group also decided to sing me happy birthday. It was gloriously bad. No one was singing together. We all started laughing so hard that I am amazed they were able to get through it. It was absolutely delightful and I will definitely remember it for a long time. We all got a kick out of it.

Questions and Privacy

I bought a tape recorder with a microphone and started to tape the sessions with Jacob. Many of those sessions will be in the pages to follow.

I have not included the names of those asking the questions in order to respect their privacy, as this is what they are comfortable with. I honor that. Who is asking is unimportant with regard to this book. The responses are what will be relevant to you, as they will create an opportunity for growth and expansion. With some of the questions, I have included email discussions with the asker and with others, there is just the date. These are still questions asked by other individuals and the only questions asked directly by me will state this. I am grateful to those who chose to participate in this process and I thank you all for your many gifts.

First Questions from Others

9/19
Is moving my son's highest choice?
It is for you to live your own life. You do not need to concern yourself with what others are choosing. They will always choose their path. Their highest path is always whatever they choose. There is no higher path. What one chooses is what it is. They will choose and follow and experience and expand.

What would be a fair charge or resolution with my current customer issue?
It does not make any difference. It is how you feel. How you feel in this interaction with others. Is it good for you? Does it feel good? The money is irrelevant. You want interaction that feels good. What do you choose? How do you want to experience this? What is the growth in this for you?

Is there anything else that will help her in this process? (I added this question.)
Find your own way. Live your life. Let go of concerning yourself so much about what others are doing. You often worry and there is no need to do so as they will live their own path....their own journey. Release them and in doing so you release yourself.

End session

9/20
This was an email I sent to a friend about my recent experiences:
Did I tell you a butterfly landed on my shoulder last week? I was at the park with my nephews. They were on the swings. All of the sudden, a butterfly came and landed right on my shoulder.

It sat there for a few minutes. It's the closest I have ever been to one. I tried to get my nephews' attention in order for them to take a look, but when they turned around, the butterfly flew away. I have been seeing them every day now. Fluttering around me. Isn't that interesting?

I have much to share with you now. After we spoke last night I was really excited to get home and do a session. I remembered that when I had asked your first questions it was late and I was so tired when I was done that I never got a chance to play back the tape.

At the time, I felt like I didn't get enough information and I had planned to ask again. I finally played the tape back to write it down in my notebook and I was truly amazed at what came through. I was like "wow, this is really good stuff here." Some responses were longer than others but I realized a lot could be said with just a few words. I was so thankful for whoever recommended I get a tape recorder because I was not aware of all that came through at the time and there was no way I could have remembered it all. This has just been the most amazing experience.

Thank you for your in-depth questions. It is so incredibly helpful to me as I am figuring it all out and adjusting to this new thing in my life. It is so surreal. I am so glad you are just as excited about Jacob as I am. I wrote everything down and was so thrilled by it that I went right into another session to ask your second set of questions. It was phenomenal. I got done at 2:30 a.m.

I wanted to call you but it was too late. I didn't think I could sleep. I couldn't wait to share this with you. This was the first time I was really missing access to a computer. I hope to purchase a new one soon as my former husband is keeping the one we had. I drove to my old house this morning to type it up because I wanted to get this to you right away. I can't wait to talk to you and hear what you think.

Here it is, word for word. When you see these dots...... this means a long pause as they were scanning for the next word. At least that's what it feels like to me. Fascinating!

Where are we going as a human race?

Wherever you choose to go. There is not a defined outcome. There are endless possibilities. Endless expansion. It all is for the purpose of expansion. You are going wherever you choose. Creating whatever you choose. And therefore, humanity will be as it is created.

How is Jacob helping us meet our purpose here?

We are here to observe....to guide...the only purpose is growth and expansion. You have an opportunity to grow and expand with every experience. We are here to guide you back to you, to awareness of self.

How long before we will see our earth planet make spiritual changes?

Spiritual transitions are happening all of the time whether or not you perceive them. A collective shift is occurring. Time is irrelevant. It does not matter since the continual process that we are all ever experiencing is the expansion. We will all experience it. All of us. It does not matter when it will be. The only moment is this moment of now.

How do you go about greater expansion?

Seek it. Look within. Ask to connect with your true self......relax... feel....feel open to EVERYTHING and take notice as who you are emerges.

What does that mean? (I added this question to clarify.)

Allow yourself to FEEL the source that is you, expressed. Consciously acknowledge the divine being that you are and all that you create as an expression of self.

What will life be like for Xander's generation?

Xander's generation is a time of healing. Peace, love, tranquility, a collective shift in consciousness. We are all one source. More will come to this awareness.

(I sensed that it will be toward the later part of Xander's current lifetime.)

9/21
Am I on the right track with my book about beliefs?
On the right track is an interesting way to phrase it. There is not a right track.....a wrong track.....it simply is. Your book about beliefs is simply your belief and sharing it with others is always uplifting. Beliefs are ever changing but your current perspective can help to shift others regardless of the ever-changing beliefs. Your words will flow and you will know them to be your truth. Then you will have your answer.

Am I on track with other books to come?
All books are from your perspective. All books will be as you write them. No track is even necessary. It simply is....where you are ...now.

How will I know who to choose to help me with publishing the books?
You need not concern yourself with who will help you....who is the right one. They will arrive in the perfect moment as you set your intentions. Allow them to flow into your life......they will appear for you.

What do I need to do to allow some extra cash flow into my life?
You are already creating abundance in your life. Your writing and belief in yourself has begun energy in motion. You will have great impact on others. The income will flow as you open yourself to receive it.

How do I let in a fulfilling relationship?
You are already allowing in fulfilling relationships. You will continue to do so as you continue to open yourself to those in your life now. When you are ready, it will be. Manifested instantly. You are not a match for that which you currently desire.

You are transitioning. You are moving through that process. You are defining where you are and what you want. When you know the answer.....you will be ready to invite someone in....and your intention will be clear to manifest it.

(I sensed they were speaking of relationships such as our friendship that are currently fulfilling.)

What do I need to do to allow the new direction of my business to flourish?

The direction you are moving is already flourishing.....blooming....blossoming...so many things occurring without even your awareness to them. Just know that it is in motion, that all is coming to fruition. Trust in that. Believe in that. And follow what your inner source is telling you. THAT is all you need.

What is the role of the Freedom Circle in regards to Jacob? Is there a common purpose among us?

Your freedom circle has come together because you all seek a deeper understanding of life, you seek more, you want more, thrive for more. The combination together creates an opportunity for tremendous growth and expansion. Your vibrations draw one another. You will all work together....in creating great change.....for humanity.

How can we rise to that purpose? How do we embrace this expansion?

You will help in this process simply by seeking to know.... to understand.....and sharing....sharing it with others one by one – expansion occurs. That is the embracing. It simply occurs. Everything will unfold. Just allow yourselves to be in the moment, open yourselves to the possibilities....the ideas....open yourselves to what can be....expansion occurs....for you....for everyone.

What are the most important things for humanity to now know as we seek to live the ultimate life?

You are love…...You are the creator of your life experience…….That the only end to what is possible is that which you believe in your mind it to be…There are endless possibilities.

How do we embrace the truth of who we are while managing our daily and family needs?

There is no separation of the two except for that which you create. Embracing the truth of who you are is simply choosing to be consciously aware your life experience is an expression of source. Your search to manage these daily needs is also a divine expression of source. Understand the only needs are that which you define for yourself. Observe yourself and how you feel, as you desire to understand the balance of the needs you have created and your search for self-awareness. Allow yourself to express all that you think and feel. Full expression of self IS the joy of living. It is in this process that growth occurs. Be the observer of your life experience. This will guide you to a higher consciousness, a greater awareness, into the realm of peace, love and joy.

What do we need to do and know now?

Know that you are love. Know that there is nothing to do but simply be.... experience... .express... .expand.

What is the role of pain or sadness or any negative emotion?

Emotions help you to know more about where you are. Know where you are in relationship to yourself, to the life you have created, to everything around you. They are responses to the current thoughts you hold about what is transpiring in your reality. Use them as a tool to guide you to a greater awareness of self. As you shift your thoughts, an event that once brought forth a painful emotion can bring forth a joyful emotion. It is not the event that changes. It is how you choose to experience that event. Your thoughts can shift your experience not only of what is occurring in your life experience now, but what has already transpired for you. In this shift, that painful energy can be released.

How do we do that?

Allow yourself to feel all that comes to you. Become aware of what these emotions are telling you. Understand that all emotions are beneficial and are serving you well for where you are. Utilize them to guide you. Do not resist what comes forth but allow yourself to feel what surfaces for you and BE in the experience of it. It is in the experience itself that an opportunity is created for shifts to occur, for releasing the energy held. Feel it and then ask yourself – what is the source of what I am feeling? What thoughts do I hold about this situation? What is this really about for me? – When you can identify the source, you then wield the power to create change. But you must first feel the emotion and allow yourself full expression. Emotions are your friend. Embrace them. They will guide you to a greater awareness of self.

How and when will the wisdom of Jacob be shared with others?

We are already being shared with others. We are being shared with you right now. As others are ready to receive us, as they are continually seeking and asking, the sharing will occur. There is no set way. It is being created by you and by all of those who choose to participate in this process.

End Session.

The following is an email I sent my dear friend who asked the previous questions:

This is so incredible. I have only been doing this a few days and I am already getting so much flowing through in response. Not only that but I feel as though I am learning to interpret better. I sense the meanings. It is really neat I can know what they are intending to say. And the words in all caps come across clear to me in that way. Wow, isn't that something? Just imagine the depths we can go to once I adjust and really get in the flow of things. I can't wait.

Another interesting thing occurred last night. When I was all done and trying to go to sleep I made a simple comment like "Thanks, Jacob, this has been something" and in an instant I felt their presence envelop me. I wasn't even trying but clearly they are always with me as they told me they would be. It was amazing to experience such easy access. What I am wondering about now is if I will be able to do it in the presence of the person asking the questions?

9/22

The following is part of an email sent to another friend who had some questions:
Hello, you beautiful being you!

I am excited for you and all that is transpiring in your life. You will know soon enough just how magnificent you are. Great things are happening. I also wanted to tell you I don't normally laugh so much on the phone but there is something about you that just makes me giddy and I just can't help but giggle.

It is truly a wonderful thing but I really can have a deep conversation. So if I am laughing, just smile and know it is magical. I did a session last night and asked your questions. I actually added quite a few more just based on the conversation that we had. I sensed there was more for you to know.

When will the love of my life come into my life?
You are asking a question that many wish to know. You must first look at where you are in your life experience. Are you open to receive what you have been asking? You have been seeking a need to be fulfilled. When you are fulfilled within yourself then you will open yourself to attract and come together with another that is fulfilled. This is what you seek. You are eager. You want more. Focus on you and it will unfold.

What can I do to help me get through my impatience?
Focus on you, your writing, and expression of self. In this process you will help others...but ultimately yourself. This will help to guide you. Follow what you are feeling. What you know to be so. It will lead you to where you want to go. The relationship you desire will manifest as you become more in tune with you. It is there...waiting for you....WAITING for you to receive it. When you are ready, it will be.

What role does he have in regards to Jacob and myself? (I began to ask my own questions.)
He will be a part of this process. It will unfold. You will join together for humanity....for this life experience....for growth and expansion.

What exactly will be his role?
He will participate as much as he chooses. As he transitions to a new state of awareness in his life.....he will choose.
(At the time, I did not know this man very well. We were just beginning to connect. He has since become very present in my life, and has indeed played an extremely active role in my process.)

What can he do to get to the wonderful, happy place he desires?
Set yourself free of your demons (I sensed this was a specific term meant only for him in relationship to how he views things.).......

what you believe to have been holding you down.....holding you back. Release yourself. Those thoughts no longer serve you. You are coming to a transition point.....a new stage in your life. You are ready for more...... you crave more......you want more. It is here for you...waiting...and as you transition you will find yourself flowing very....freely....easily...smoothly. Flowing with others in this new vibration. Easy, smooth, gloriously free. It is all waiting for you. It is all waiting for you. (And yes, they said this twice.)

Is there anything else that will help him through this transition?
 Believe in yourself. Believe in who you are. Believe in what rings true for you from the very depth of your being. Follow your passion. Create the life that you want to create....know that you can and that it will be. Wield the power of the divine source that you are.

I feel like we're not done with this. Is there more you would like him to know?
 You are an incredible being on this path of greatness. Know this. Believe this. You ARE worthy. You ARE ready for this journey. Ready to move into the next vibration….you are shifting in consciousness. You feel awful right now because you are confused about who you are. You look to other things in a desperate attempt to feel better. We understand that you want to feel better and why you look for many ways to do so. You are source expressed. You cannot be anything other than divine. Everything you do and experience is simply another expression of source. This too is divine.

What would help him to feel better?
 Shifting your attention to who you are....connecting with the source that is you and allowing yourself to be expressed. That is the joy......and you will feel the love that you are in the expression of self. At those times when you look to other things to feel better, that is the moment to reclaim yourself....look within...connect with you.....and begin to express what you think and feel. Allow it to flow and become consciously aware of what those thoughts and feelings are for you. They will guide you to a greater awareness of self.
 End Session

The remainder of my email:
Well. This is it. Thank you so much for being a part of this. It is so helpful to me to have these questions as I explore what is going on with all of this. I feel like every question is taking me to a new level. Wow...this is really incredible.
I love you! I look forward to your thoughts on all of this.
Love, Kayite
This was his reply:
Amazing comes to mind, lovely, remarkable, brave..... (when you see dots.....this means that I am scanning for words too, or just want to indicate a pause in things). I am so honored to be near you in this most remarkable time, when you are opening to a whole new beginning, a whole new life, one that will surely have you traveling widely, interacting with people on a global scale.

Thank you for asking the questions I would ask. They did ring true, completely true. This was not so much like being nailed, as being discovered. Wow, these guys really know me, more than I seem to know myself. How cool is that?

My eyes grow tears of happiness and joy for the answers you give, from Jacob, and from you. I do not feel I am resisting, at least not on purpose. Resistance is there, no doubt, but only in knowing what the next step is, not in having the determination or courage to take it. My dear, sweet, laughing, wonderful beam of joy, there you are, I am in awe, in love with who you are, and totally in tune with where you are going. If it were not for where I am going, I would ask to come along. And perhaps I shall. (And indeed he did!)

9/23
What is going on with my love interest? Is he the one?

There is nothing "going on" with him. He is simply being who he is. There is no "one."... there is no one being that anyone is to be with. You are all here interacting with other beings as you choose. It is up to you to decide what it is that you want for your life experience. What the other person is doing is irrelevant. Love yourself.....feel the joy flow through you. If you choose him to be the one, he is only the one for this moment of now. And he is offering you an experience that you either consciously or unconsciously desire. There are many so called "ones."….. each offering a different experience based on where you are and what you desire at any moment…..this of course is ever-changing…….and why you may change partners as you grow and expand and your desires change. Many choices…..all leading to different paths....different directions... endless possibilities…growth and expansion. It is up to you to decide what you choose in this moment of now. What path? What do you want to experience. If you are not experiencing what you consciously desire….. then take a close look at what has already been created……acknowledge that you have created it on an unconscious level…..and ask yourself, what is the growth in this for me? What has this experience offered you? As you gain clarity about where you are and acknowledge your creation, you wield the power to create a conscious change.

Are you saying we are not to be together forever in this lifetime?

We are telling you that it is your choice. Choosing a lifetime to share the experience together is one of the many endless possibilities……… it is not your only choice…….and there is nothing that has to be. If it brings you joy…..embrace it. If you are desiring a different experience….. create change. The only question to ask yourself…..what do I want to experience?

When will this relationship be openly acknowledged by him and fulfilled?

"When" is not defined....as there is only the moment of now. There is not a question of "when" but "why." Why are you waiting? Why are you choosing to leave it to someone else? Why not choose to make a decision for yourself. What is it that you want? What is it that you would like to experience? Are you okay with where you are? Are you fine if this is never revealed? You want to feel good with the situation. In this moment of now this situation is not at ease with you…look to what you are feeling and allow it to guide you. This is about what you are creating together. What are you creating and what it is that you want? When you decide...it will change...one way or another. There is no "when" because your thoughts are ever changing and therefore the energy in motion is ever changing. The result is not always the same. There cannot be a clear concise answer because you are free to create your life ....and you are doing so.....now.

What should I do now to prepare for what's to come?
Find fulfillment within yourself. Live your life as you choose. Experience, express, expand. A partner is not necessary to experience the full bliss of life....the pure love....that you are. There is nothing to prepare for....allow yourself to be in this moment.....and choose what feels good to you right now. Thoughts of what is to come, is a distraction from your awareness of what is occurring in the moment. What do you choose for you in this moment? When you are living for you, joy is inevitable, as you are fully expressing yourself.

End Session

9/24
What is the purpose of work?
Growth and Expansion. How wonderful it is to try new jobs and do new things as you create experiences to grow and expand from. Not only creating it for yourself, but also for those who are co-creating with you. The possibilities are endless. Enjoy the variety of opportunities that await you.

Is it possible to create abundance through joy, fun and play?
It is not only possible but it is the easiest way to create because you are wide open to receive it. When you create with the feelings of joy, happiness, and fun......that energy carried along with your desires drives it to manifest much faster because you are less likely to have thoughts blocking the manifestation process when you feel good. It is a wonderful way....to experience life...in joy and play. It can be done and it makes for a more enjoyable experience.

What are some ways to get in touch with our options here on earth?
You have many options. Simply try new things and then see how you feel about it. Follow what you feel drawn to do. There are no limitations.

Just open yourself to a new experience, and then another, and then another. It is ever changing.......enjoy it. Enjoy observing what shows up for you. Enjoy the process of creation. Acknowledge every experience that shows up in your life. It is your divine creation and serves you well.

How can we live happily?

By becoming consciously aware of self. Know that there is nothing you need to do; there is no specific way you have to be or experience life. It is in the seeking to understand this that growth is offered. Know that you are a divine being who is worthy of all that you desire. Happiness is just a doorknob away. As you open the door to self-awareness, happiness is at your disposal.

How do we invite others, things and circumstances into our lives that we desire even when there is no evidence of those things?

You need not have evidence of anything. What is, is what has already been created and the only relevance it has is how you feel in your observation of it. Let us say that you have no money in your bank account. That is simply what is in this moment of now. It has nothing to do with creating your financial abundance to appear in the next moment except for the desire that is created in observation of the experience.

There may be no evidence that this abundance is possible. Everything you see tells you there is no money and you are not aware of any other financial avenues. Understand that that was the manifestation of your previous thought. You need only to choose what you wish to experience now...that which you desire. There will be no physical evidence until you choose it to be part of your experience.

Only then will the evidence appear as your creation is manifested. It is not about the evidence; it is about the enjoyment of the creation, the enjoyment of your journey. How you feel in the process. How you feel is the only proof you need. You will know when you connect with you. When you connect with the divine source that IS you. You will feel the love...the peace...the bliss. And you will trust and know that your desires will come to fruition.

9/25
What does it mean to fall in love?

Falling in love means falling in love with ones self. When you are interacting with other beings, you are falling in love with how you feel when you are with them. This is the love that you feel. You enjoy that part of you, the part they bring out in you, the part that rejoices in you. It is really falling in love with you.

And what does that mean?

Feeling pure joyous energy flowing through you......completely.... someone else reminding you of the magnificence that you are. That is the falling in love. You fall in love with another as they remind you of who you are. As they bring forth your awareness of source when you are with them.

What does it mean to love someone who does not reciprocate that love?

Loving someone who does not reciprocate that love indicates that you love who you are when you are with them but they do not love who they are when they are with you. For whatever reason....whatever place they are in. It has nothing to do with who you are, and everything to do with how they are feeling about themselves. Because falling in love is all about your self and if they are unable to reciprocate, then they are clearly stating where they are in their life experience. There are many reasons why this would be. All of them lead back to how they feel about themselves.

How do you get over heartache?

Heartache is something that is felt because you feel like something is missing....a hole...a place where you feel something needs to be filled. You get over heartache when you realize that there is no hole. There is nothing missing, that you are complete. And there is nothing else required. Whatever pain you are feeling from an experience....a circumstance....it creates this heartache. When you can look, take a closer look at what you have experienced.....what have you gained from this situation? What do you understand now that you did not before? Are you able to look from another perspective? Are you able say, I see now....I see why this occurred. Because now I can look back and know that I am in this place of now and this was a part of it. It was all a part of it. As you move forward in you life.....forward in the sense of releasing old vibrations and creating new ones, you will be able to release that heartache vibration. Welcome experiences that will help you create this shift. The heartache will go away as you are adding new vibrations in with love....love for all there is...love for who you are. When you are complete within yourself...heartache will no longer serve you and it will dissipate.

What can those of us who are choosing to live consciously do to create greater peace, love, and joy on the planet?

Be who you are....be aware....be awakened. Live your life openly. Express who you are and share this with others. That is the greatest gift you can give to another. Sharing you. Tremendous growth is offered to all who observe you. And in that experience of observation, an opportunity for change is created. If you desire peace, love, and joy, then express peace, love and joy. Those observing will be offered an opportunity to choose how they feel about it and if they want to bring it into their own life experience. Enjoy this process. It is perfection.

End Session

Notes

I was transcribing the conversation from the tape to the computer when I discovered the tape had ended. I had asked more questions but I realized all of the glorious responses I received did not get recorded. I must have been so zoned in that I never heard the recorder go off. I guess I will have to ask again. Perhaps there will be something more to share. I am open to all that will be revealed. I understand there is tremendous growth in this process not only for the one who is asking but for me as well. I am enjoying every moment.

Love

After the questions of what does it mean to "fall in love" as we call it, I decided to ask them what IS love, which was an entirely different question.

What is Love?
Love is who you are. Joy is love expressed. Love is all there is.

In knowing that love is who we are, the expression of ourselves is the joy we feel. Therefore, reciprocation of love is not necessary to experience joy. The joy comes from within as we express love, which is simply expressing ourselves. No wonder I feel so much joy in loving others, many of whom are not able to fully receive it or express it in return. Their participation is not required. How great is that! I'm feeling the joy. Yes!

9/26
Is my current profession the path for me for the next five years?
You can do whatever you choose. Does it bring you joy? Is this what you want to experience? It is up to you. There is no set path…..only that which you choose it to be….for as long as you choose the experience. Follow what you feel. Allow it to guide you.

If not, what should I be doing that can help me with that alignment and also with the path to follow?
Focus on what you want….what you desire. Open yourself…..be aware of what you are feeling….follow that…follow your passion. This will guide you. This will always guide you where you want to go. The answers are within you. Trust in that.

Are there specific modalities I can learn that will help me?
Any modality can be helpful if this is what you wish to experience. It is up to you. You are the creator of your life experience. It is in the seeking, the asking, the search for your passion, that growth is offered and direction revealed. Embrace the uncertainty that you feel, as it inspires you to continue to ask to know more. In the asking, clarity will come.

Some time ago I had several aha moments. Are these my new path?
Your aha moments are moments of inspiration…….divine alignment….. attunement to who you are. It can be your path if you choose it to be so. These are more…..guidelines of what can be….possibilities. And then it

is up to you to choose. Remember, there are endless possibilities. You are picking and choosing from only a few options that are now in your conscious awareness. As your awareness expands to include other possibilities, many more paths will become available to you. A path is nothing more than an experience that offers growth. All experiences offer this. There is no wrong turn here.

I also had a vision of a School of Studies. What is the next step toward realizing this vision? To whom should I be talking?

Your School of Studies is a grand vision. Continue to focus upon it. What do you want it to be? How do you envision it unfolding? Continue to focus on the entire process and that which you want will come to you. Those that can help you will appear in your life. It is for you to recognize them when they do. As you hold the vision for what you desire, energy is in motion for the creation. Get excited about the process and choose to consciously observe what shows up for you. These experiences will guide you.

How do I find the energy to keep my job, balance the time with my children, and work toward all of these goals?

If you are feeling you are lacking energy then you are out of alignment with you. You are either doing something you do not want to do or feeling resistant to what you feel.

Ask yourself – Is there something I am doing that does not feel good to me? Is there a thought I hold about this situation that feels draining to me? Am I allowing my self to feel all that I am feeling or do I have resistance to what is surfacing for me? Making adjustments in your life by choosing what feels good to you will bring you into alignment. In doing so, you will have the energy for all of your creations. You cannot feel drained when you are feeling good.

What priority should I place on the school idea? What priority should I place on the AHA moments?

Ask yourself – How do I feel about this? That which you have the greatest desire for will be your priority. There is no "right" answer, only that which you choose to experience.

Is there an entity/collective consciousness that can communicate directly with me, like "Jacob" does with Kayite? How does this communication begin?

There are many that can communicate directly with you. Simply relax....open yourself up.....be receptive for the information to flow. Focus....concentrate and let it be your greatest desire. If this is truly what you desire and wish to experience, then it can be. A time of meditation.... relaxation.....quiet... focus.....request and ask. State what you desire. State that you wish to communicate. Welcome them to join you.....welcome them to integrate with you. This is what Kayite has done. This has been her process. You can adjust your requests for what suits your desires.

Back in either 1972 or 1975 I had an overwhelming déjà vu experience in Georgia. I have no recollection, then or now, of some amount of time before awakening to that – could have been seconds, minutes, hours, or days. Can you explain what happened at that time?

These are "déjà vu" so to speak as you have experienced them before. A simple recall of what has been. A moment of lapse between this realm and the last and the one before that......all coming together at the same time...causing confusion. Your mind cannot process it and therefore creates a lapse to fill the void of that which you cannot process.

Prophecy speaks of Armageddon, or Heaven on Earth. Is this still a choice we as a world can make, or have we already chosen? Which one?

There is always a choice, always, although you have already chosen as well. Both occur. It is never ending....eternal. Even in "Armageddon" so to speak, new creations will still continue on. It is only the appearance of what the illusion is that changes. The creation will simply change form as you grow and expand. In new ways, different ways, lots of magnificent, glorious ways. It is all expansion, expansion for everyone. Eternal. Therefore, it does not matter. It is wonderful to move toward peace and love, heaven on earth so to speak but it is a growth process for experience, expression, expansion, and this will occur. It is never ending. It will continue always. Eternal.

Introducing Gym Jacob

I recently joined a local gym that is near my son's school. As part of the membership, I got a free evaluation with a trainer who would help set me up on a program. We had decided I would do the treadmill and also start off with the circuit weights. I always liked those. Well, I was on a treadmill on the upstairs balcony today when across the room I saw a young guy with a light around him. He was beaming. I could tell from his attire that he was an employee. He was working in the circuit weights area adjusting the settings for those who wished to use them. His light was so bright that I couldn't help but notice. It definitely got my attention.

After I was done, I headed downstairs to do the circuit weights for the first time. Another man adjusted my weights for me. There were eight machines in a row that I was to cycle through. I had gone through several when all of the sudden I looked up and there in front of me was this beam of light guy. He was talking to an older woman about her workout. He was very friendly. I was trying not to stare. Just then, he turned to walk away as his shift there had ended. In that moment, I got a glimpse of his nametag. And what did it say? Jacob! That's right. I about fell on the floor. My mouth just fell wide open. Jaw dropped. I was trying not to look too shocked but I couldn't believe it.

Was this just a sign from my Jacob? Was it their way of telling me they are here? I wasn't sure what it was but I definitely took notice. The fact that his light was shining from across the room and now the name, I am intrigued. It especially stood out because I have never known anyone by that name. I will definitely be exploring this more. Perhaps I will get a chance to speak with him next time. I decided to refer to him as Gym Jacob as to eliminate any confusion between the two.

Balance

Today I am thinking about balance in my life. How do I balance all of this? And should I stop asking how? I want to just let everything flow but I feel a need for some sort of balance between time with my son and the work with Jacob that I am participating in. It is interesting because even though I have this incredible communication happening in my life, I am still just this everyday person trying to make her way through life. I have come a long way from where I was. I live in the moment now most of the time but there are moments I get caught up. I can usually re-connect with myself and come into alignment pretty quickly these days but I am finding it harder to do as everything is moving faster and faster.

I feel like I'm on a roller coaster but not in the seat. I am hanging onto the side just trying to keep up. I want to be in the seat but then what? Is hanging on to the side so bad? At least I'm still flowing along. I didn't fall off somewhere. I didn't forget where I was going. I just bounced off a bit. Is that so bad? I ask myself these questions to help me clarify what it is I am doing here.

What do I want? I want to enjoy the time with my son. I love to play games, read books and teach him new things. We have the best time together. He loves to go to the park and walk on the nature trails. We talk to nature all the time and it is so great. He lights up my life and it is incredible to watch him grow. I can't believe he is almost four. Where did the time go?

He just started school this year and is attending for half days from 8 a.m. to noon. I have missed being with him but it is all divine timing and Jacob arrived at a time when I was ready to focus upon them. I choose to be consciously aware of all that I create in my life. No matter what appears, I acknowledge the creation of it. I rejoice in that. And I choose to enjoy every moment.

9/27

The following is an email I received from a friend along with her questions to follow:
Hi Kayite,

I am still so overwhelmed by what is happening to you. I guess you must be as well. You are the perfect person to be receiving this information. You are so open and clear that I am sure that Jacob finds it easy to come through you. I'm not so sure my ego would be happy about getting out of the way and not interfering with the reception of the material. You are doing wonderful work. You truly are making a difference for all of us. I just hope to be able to be as sure of everything as you are. I am grateful to have you as a wonderful example of what is possible.

These are some things that I would like to ask about.

How do I move beyond the sadness and negativity that has always been my nature. I think I am out of it and it comes right back.

It is what you have come to know and believe is your nature. This can shift as you choose for it to. As you open up to greater possibilities, you can then bring it forth into your life experience. State your desires and welcome the experiences in your life that will help you to create this shift in awareness. It is for you to recognize them when they show up. This is your conscious awareness at work. You can shift into a new vibration leaving the old vibration behind. That energy will dissipate. When you feel as though you have moved forward and it comes back it is because that old vibration is still there. You did not fully shift into the new vibration....you simply had a taste of the new one. You can fully release the congested energy. Focus on what you want.. Focus on all the wonderful things you wish to experience....all that you want to enjoy. In those moments of sadness ask yourself – What is this experience offering me? Is my current response a part of my previous pattern? How do I choose to experience it now? In this moment....I can experience it in any way I choose. This is a powerful moment that you can create change.

Do you choose the sadness or do you choose the joy? You are in this moment of now. One choice....sadness or joy, sadness or joy, sadness or joy...what do you choose? Every moment you have a choice. The more that you choose the joy, choose the joy, choose the joy....every time you choose the joy…… you release a little bit of the sadness, the energy that you have confined and held onto. You release it....release it...until finally there is nothing more to release because your joy has fully encompassed you.

There is tremendous growth in this process for you. And this joy, it is you, fully expressed. Embrace the sadness that surfaces for you and allow yourself to feel all of it. Identify the source of these feelings and consciously observe what you feel about those feelings. As you ask and seek to understand, experiences will show up to help you create the shift that you desire. And in those moments are when you can make a choice from a place of love, the very essence of you, fully expressed. And it is in that expression that joy will be experienced.

Are there talents and abilities that I have that I am unaware of or have been reluctant to acknowledge?

There are many talents and abilities that you have but that is for you to discover – to come to your own awareness. Ask yourself – What do I feel I am good at? Many things...we know you are good at so many things. Your abilities....beyond your own expectations. You are capable of anything. But what would you enjoy? What is your passion? Allow yourself to guide you. You will know. Try new things. See how you feel. You are capable of anything. It is for you to believe an idea is possible, and only then can you invite it into your life experience.

Why do humans (myself included) always think that they are less deserving of the "good stuff" than everyone else is? How to move beyond this?

Because that is the greatest contrast. What a wonderful world to come into and experience something so different than who you are. You are not only deserving of everything...of creating everything....but the feeling of being less deserving is actually a great gift. To feel the unworthiness... to feel the pain....to feel it all of serves great purpose. And when you can recognize the experience for the gift that it is, when you can embrace these feelings and look to what they are offering you, you can move beyond it.

As you create change in your experience, you can shift the congested energy. There is much growth in this process. The word deserving is not quite suitable as you are all creating. It is not whether someone is deserving or not but rather....it is.....their creation. That which one receives is that which one creates. It has nothing to do with deserving. Even just ridding yourself of that term will set you free. It is about saying – What am I choosing for my life? Am I choosing something really wonderful because I want to experience something wonderful? Not whether or not you deserve something wonderful. Because of course you do....but you must choose it. You must stand up and say – I want more...I choose more for me….I am worthy –...and know that you are magnificent in doing so.

What would be helpful for me to find balance in my life?
The balance you seek is nothing more than being centered and in tune with you. When you are connected with you, you feel joy….in just being, in expressing you….feeling good about where you are. This creates the balance because when you feel good, you feel the harmony of life. Look within. Ask your inner being for guidance. You will create the balance that you seek.

My husband passed away and I want to know if he is okay? And is he okay with me?
He is always well and always well with you. Life is eternal...never ending. There is no loss...just more of a pause, a pause in the moment of now. And in the next moment...you will be together again....this is his perspective. From where he is...this is how it will be. A pause...a moment... simply a few seconds...not even the turn of a hand. We understand from your perspective that it is hard for you. That this process seems long....a long time for you...and that it is your life and how do you move on. By understanding that it really is just a moment in time....a split moment.... ever so recent and just a pause.....and that there is no loss, just a moment of separation. And you are never really separated because he is always with you…connected….part of the whole…..all that is. But from your perspective, you feel the physical separation....you feel some sense of loss and we tell you this idea of loss is only your thought about it which affects how you are experiencing it. Life is eternal. This is just part of the process......feeling the loss and then deciding where you are in it. All of this has brought you to where you are…..where do you choose to go from here?

Will I ever be ready for another love?
It will begin with love of self first. It is always possible and waiting for you. It is waiting for you when you choose and decide that you are ready.

Moving on in your life....to the moment of now.....this is the living......live your life as you desire. He would very much want this for you.....he.....he does want this for you. He wants for you to experience great expansion, to experience love and joy as he is experiencing now........the sheer joy of being in pure energy form is wonderful.

Remember a pause....a moment...that is all. He simply hit the pause button, and in a moment you will appear again with him.....with everyone....and you will choose again.....another life....another experience. While you are still here now....before that pause button ends....why not go ahead and live the life that you state you desire? Go for it. Finish out the rest of the story. Fill it in. How do you want it to continue? Since you have this period of time that you can do whatever you choose, say – This is my story, I'm filling it in ...and what do I want to fill it with? Do I want to be sad...lonely....depressed. Do I want to end my story with this? Or do I choose the joy and happiness? I can fill it however I choose and it does not make any difference, except in the way that I feel. I choose to feel good. The choice is up to you. What is it that you wish to experience and this is what will be.

The following is an email I received from my friend regarding the previous responses:

Kayite,

I'm at a loss for words. I've read everything through about three times so far. The first two were through tears. It all rang so true for me. I cannot begin to express how precious this is to me. I have begun to realize I have needed permission to release the grief and pain not only from the loss of my husband but from all the hurts in my life. The truth is that I do not need anyone's permission. I can simply choose joy. Again, and again, and again until it becomes second nature for me. The sense of freedom all of this gives me is almost overwhelming.

It's like stories I heard of when immigrants came to this country from the former Soviet Union and were so overwhelmed by all of the choices that some of them couldn't cope and went back. I AM NOT GOING TO GO BACK! I am sure I will manage to adjust.

9/28

A friend of mine asked the following questions that really got me thinking:

We all have stuff we want. Some of us want a lot. Money, comfort, relationships, the perfect job, love, accomplishment, joy, peace, health, house, car, forgiveness, angel food cake, affection, an iPhone . . . the list goes on. Imagine you had everything you wanted. How would you feel? Seriously, how would you feel?

Pretend. You have everything. Now. You want for nothing. And imagine that tomorrow will be the same. No need to fear it will all go away. You have it all. Close your eyes. (Well, finish reading this first...) Close your eyes and imagine you have all the money you need.

Certainly there is nothing in the moment about a financial condition that prevents you from imagining you have enough. So, imagine it. Nothing at all in the moment that prevents you from experiencing the feeling of having it all. Same thing for relationships. Pretend you have the most incredible relationship….. He/she just happens to be out shopping at the moment. Health, you're an Olympian. Job, you get paid for doing what you would do for free. Good looks, well, you look like me (smiling). Imagine it. For a moment. Pretend.

Now, in that moment, when you have all you need and you have no fears, how would you answer the phone? How would you greet a stranger? What would you think to yourself as you passed a mirror and caught your reflection? Remember, when they come home from shopping they're going to want you in a big way. What would you think about tomorrow? What would people notice when they look at you? What would you say to the gnarly store clerk? What would you think about the fact that the lawn really needs to be cut soon? What would you say to a friend who asks "How are you?"

I ask these questions because it dawned on me tonight as I was at work, late, all by myself, reflecting on all of the good stuff I have going on, and understanding my gratitude journal needs large sheets of paper, that if I did actually have everything I wanted, I probably would not know how to respond.

Why don't I live my life as a succession of now moments in which I have everything I need and want for nothing? Do I really need to keep something in my back pocket to lament about? What's up with that? So, here's the million dollar question. What if everything I can imagine and want is actually out there waiting for me, but it's not going to show up until I learn how to behave when it does show up? What good is a new car if you don't know how to drive? What good is all of the stuff you want if you don't know what to do with it, or how to live with it, or how to be with it? Shouldn't we be practicing now? I'm just saying...........

My response: Many people often feel that if they could just right now have everything they could possibly want and need, it would somehow make them happy. That if they could just work really hard for many years to achieve it, they could – in retirement – kick back and finally enjoy life. Or they hope to win the lottery as a quick resolution. I asked myself how I would feel if I had everything I wanted and the answer may be quite surprising to you.

What a great thing to think about. I am aware that I already have everything I "need" which is my awareness of who I am and that I need for nothing. Wants and desires are entirely different. Honestly, the thought of already having, in this moment, every single thing I could possibly want and desire is an extremely depressing thought to me. The joy of life is continually creating and manifesting my desires and enjoying the experience along the way. If there were nothing to manifest, if it were already here, then there would be no purpose. So I rejoice there is always more to want for. Isn't that great?

I love living in a succession of moments where we know we have everything we need. Can we not also want and desire more while at the same time we are grateful for where we are? How would I treat others? With love. All the love that flows through me and will continue to flow no matter what I have, what I own, or what I do. I have seen motivational posters that say, "Life is a journey, not a destination." For the first time, I really get this. I get it. Life is about experiencing the moment and not about what is occurring in that moment. I just love to get up in the morning and ask myself, what do I want to create today?

A Book?

As I am writing all of my thoughts as well as transcribing the Jacob conversations for the asker, it comes to my awareness I might possibly be doing something with all of this material. Perhaps this will be a book? That feels really good to me. It was not my conscious intention but it just sort of unfolded. Although as a child, I always thought I would write books one day. I didn't know when or what they would be about, but I always felt sure of it. I guess I am finally ready to receive the manifestation of those intentions set forth long ago. Out of curiosity, I asked Jacob about this book idea.

Will we write books together?

We will be doing whatever you choose. We are here to communicate with you and to share with others as you choose. We bring our wisdom and knowledge of where we are in relationship to you. We are here in observance of you. Here for guidance, yes, but mainly observance. To interact, communicate with one another so that we may experience part of your journey, your expansion. We are all part of this grand experience.

Death

An old friend of mine just called me out of the blue. I had not spoken with her in over a year. She told me her dad died. I didn't know how to respond. I was in such a joyous space. I just felt love for him and joy for where he had gone. He had returned back to the bliss of pure energy form. (I now understand that nothing exists that is not pure energy. It just vibrates at different frequencies, which creates expressions of this energy in different forms.)

But how do I connect with her? Her father just died. I knew it was a difficult time for her. She was just so angry. And then became angry at me for not being angry and sad with her. I told her the love I have for him was not dependant upon the sadness I expressed. I knew this was a tough time and I wanted to support her. I didn't know what to say and I told her this. I just could not go to a place of sadness.

Death is not an awful thing to me. It is a beautiful moment of transition. We simply change form. And, of course, I will miss the people in my own life experience, but I choose to rejoice in the experiences I did have. I honor the journey they have chosen for themselves. I know they have not been separated from me but only appear to be in this life experience. This too is an illusion I now see beyond. I wanted to connect with my friend but she did not want anything to do with me if I were not going to be sad with her. I did understand where she was coming from. No one wants to hear joyful things at a time when they are feeling deep sadness and pain.

Of course, I was not sharing anything joyful at this time; it was more that I did not know what to say if it did not come from that place. I was calm and loving, just not distraught and emotional. This is all such a new transition for me. Perhaps I will come to know how to connect with others in situations like this – to know how to meet them from where I am to where they are. In the moment, I did the best I could with where I was.

My experience with my grandparents' passing was something quite wonderful. My grandfather transitioned in December 2000. He had been sick for a while on and off. He always seemed to bounce back so I thought he would do that this time as well. I went to visit him in the hospital. He had a picture of my grandmother, when she was very young, on the window sill where he could easily view it. He said he still saw her this way.

Even though he was physically tired from his illness, he was still making jokes with the doctors and nurses, which was how he always was. He loved to share the latest jokes he had heard. When he was in the hospital, he saw a vortex of light in the corner of the room and wondered if he was hallucinating. He said he felt peaceful and that the light was beautiful and that there were others in the room with him. The doctors had said he wouldn't make it through the night but he stayed around for quite a few days longer until everyone could come to see him in order to say good-bye. Then he waited until everyone left the room to go.

Some might view it that he died alone in that room. I know he was not alone, that being alone is not even possible. I did cry a lot because I missed him in my life and this was my first experience with death with someone with whom I had a very close relationship.

My grandmother transitioned in August 2001. There are those of us who believe she only stayed around long enough to get things in order and to see her first great grandchild be born. She had spent 55 years with my grandfather and it was clear she wanted to be with him. Eventually her heart gave out – her heart broken from missing him.

All of her children and grandchildren surrounded her bed in the hospital room. She shared with us about what a long and full life she experienced. She said she loved us all but she missed my grandfather and was ready to go. We all just naturally let go of her hands and gave her the space to leave. I said silently to her, "Go and be with Grandpa; we will be okay."

I was extremely close to my grandmother. I remember thinking as a child that if anything happened to her, I would want to die too. I asked for peace in the moment. The very moment she took her last breath, I could feel her energy release and I immediately saw an empty shell in the body I was viewing. I also immediately felt an overwhelming sense of peace envelop me. I could feel she was hugging me. Surrounding me. She was letting me know she was fine and all was well. I can honestly tell you the experience of being present during her transition was one of the most beautiful, amazing, incredible experiences of my life.

Both of these experiences created a shift for me in how I viewed death. I always knew there was more but I had not had the opportunity to experience it. I had seen and felt energy and had other types of "beyond physical" experiences but it was not the same as directly experiencing someone close to me transition.

I had observed in this world that death was supposed to be awful, that we were supposed to be sad and unhappy. Every movie I had seen confirmed this. Every interaction I had with others who had experienced a loss confirmed this.

The very first experience I remember was when my Great Aunt Tina died. I think I was about six years old. I just remember my mother coming in to tell my sister and I about it. It wasn't what she was saying but how she was feeling that stuck with me.

She was crying and so very sad. I could feel her pain. It was in that moment that I learned that death was awful and a deeply sad thing. But now I think, could it be possible for us to rejoice in another's transitioning? The experience with my grandmother was so beautiful to me. How could I not feel joy in that? Is it really such a sad thing or have we just been conditioned and taught that it is sad?

I chose to believe it. Had my Aunt Tina died and everyone said let's have a party to celebrate her journey and participation in our life experience, would it have been joyful to me? I do believe it would have. It was only my thought about death that created the sadness, not the actual death itself. As I shifted my perspective, it became joyful.

It is not my intention to be insensitive to those who have experienced tremendous grief and loss. If anything, I would hope it might be uplifting in offering another possibility of what can be. I understand deep pain and sadness. I lived it most of my life. I don't choose to live it anymore. And if you are experiencing this now, you too can make another choice. Anything is possible.

Now when the moment arises for my own transitioning, I say have a big ole party for me! Please celebrate the joy in that. I want those who have enjoyed my presence to celebrate the growth we experienced together. To rejoice in my return to the light, where in a blip, we will meet again as one. It is so incredibly wonderful.

So laugh, share wonderful stories, and continue to rejoice in your own life experience. I will be laughing along with you. I am sure of it. Those of you who know me are smiling now, as you know this to be so.

Direct Communication
9/29

Today my sister Jennifer and I decided to come together and meditate and see what would happen. This was the first opportunity for Jacob to have direct communication with another through me.

I wasn't sure if I would be able to relax enough with another person present to be able to allow Jacob to flow through. However, if I could do it with anyone, I felt most comfortable and relaxed with her and I felt it would be a good start. It was Saturday afternoon and we closed the drapes, put some peaceful music in the CD player, and lay down side by side on the dual reclining sofa. Immediately Jacob was with me.

They were saying *we are here* in my head but I was resistant to let the words come out of my mouth. I was nervous. I thought, what if this is said and then she asks a question and I am not able to flow the response through. It seemed silly at the time but I was having a battle within myself about letting go. Jacob kept telling me to just relax and let it flow. They were here and they would take care of everything. I need not concern myself with any of it. So I told myself I could do it. This is what I was here for. And finally after who knows how long, out came: *We are here. What would you like to talk about?*

I am sure you are wondering what my sister asked Jacob. Well, she actually ended up having about an hour-long conversation; however, when we played the tape back, there was nothing there. It was completely blank. We did not know if the intense energy I felt somehow affected the tape recorder or what happened. Although I am unable to share the conversation, I can share what we both experienced during this first interaction.

When my sister asked her first question, I began to feel like I was blocking the flow. It is much harder for me to allow the flow with those I am very close with (including myself) because I am not as easily detached from the outcome. I did not want my own thoughts to get in the way. When I am in the flow, I feel as though I have no thoughts. My mind is clear. As soon as I start thinking or having any thoughts whatsoever, this is when the flow is blocked. I said (silently) "Jacob, I need you to take over. I need you to take over here. I don't know how to detach." My whole body began to tingle. I felt numbness as if my whole body fell asleep. It was a blissful feeling.

At this point I began to feel tightness, a pull almost, around my face, jaw and throat area. It was like an invisible band wrapped around the front portion of my face and was pulling back. It was not uncomfortable, more of an interesting sensation. It was something incredible that I had never experienced before. The vibration was moving toward my face as if I had a hairdryer aimed toward it but instead of heat, it was blowing intense energy like a g-force in an aircraft.

My cheeks were literally flapping back. It was just the most incredibly intense vibration I have ever felt. It was vibrating so fast. I was in awe. It went on for a while. Long enough for me to just enjoy it. I kept thinking, this is really happening. Wow, this is incredible. I was blown away. I do not know how else to describe it. There is no way for me to fully describe it. This was a most profound experience.

There was silence for a little bit in between questions. The vibration began to slow and came down to a light buzz. As I simmered back into me, I felt complete. My sister looked at me and I told her of the amazing experience I had and what all was going on with me in my little recliner. She was excited. We both were in awe.

Yet it felt very normal at the same time. She then proceeded to tell me of her experience. She felt very peaceful. She knew they were here. She connected with what they had told her. It all made sense. She felt a shift. Something was happening. She felt better. It was a wonderful experience for us both. She also told me she had no more questions and had decided she would just sit there until I came back. I realize now that Jacob must have known she was done and this is why it ended at the same time she felt complete.

My sister and I decided to go out to dinner afterwards and I was still buzzing the whole time. It felt almost as if I had had a few drinks, which of course, I had not. I commented that I was glad she drove. We both laughed.

As I reflected upon the experience, I wasn't sure if the strong vibration was Jacob integrating more fully because I had asked them to take over or if it was having the presence of my sister in the room that somehow made it more powerful. Whatever it was, I am thrilled it occurred. I do sense that the more I allow myself to let go, the more they can flow into every part of my being. This is just the beginning.

Jennifer's Perspective

The following is what my sister wrote about her first experience with Jacob:

I was not nervous for once because I let go of expectations and just intended to enjoy the meditation of peace I knew I would experience with my sister. I thought about feeling peace, about being pure positive energy, and feeling oh so good. It was quiet for what seemed to be about ten minutes and then Jacob said, "We are here. What would you like to talk about?"

To my surprise, I was not at all surprised, nor did this seem strange. I was very relaxed and no questions came to me at first. Then after many minutes, I said "Who is my spirit guide and is that even important?" Keep in mind here all of Jacob's responses profoundly resonated with me, but I do not remember the exact words so I will provide the gist. Jacob said that Source is my guide, that it is me, and that the name is not important. They told me that the name would come to me if I continued to ask. (And eventually it did.) They also said something about letting go and just being me because I am still focused on taking the right path or doing things the right way.

I continued to relax with this and then many minutes later I asked, "Are you still there, Jacob?" They were. I said that I was very interested to know about Jacob's thoughts about mediums that I believed were speaking their truth, but so many talk about demons and crossing over while Abraham says as soon as you die you are Source, so I am just wondering about this. Jacob said that it is true only on this side of things as we have created it to be and I asked if they meant in the physical and they said yes. There is none of that in the nonphysical that is source energy. Only love. Love is all there is.

The next question was the first time I felt any discord. After many more minutes, a question came to mind and I began to feel anxiety about bothering Jacob and whether they were still there.

Finally, I said "Jacob, are you still there? Is it okay if I ask another question?" Jacob said that I could ask as many questions as I wished. I remembered reading Kayite's email to her group where Jacob said they are delighted to participate in the interaction with us. So, I was deeply in an altered state, but I said something to the effect of, "I have been really enjoying my time to myself and it feels good to me. I am curious if you sense that I am being resistant to intimacy in some way or if I am worried about this and that is being resistant to the time alone I know feels so good. I just feel confusion here."

Jacob said some brilliant things. Here is what I remember. It was said slowly and with pauses and a wonderful intensity. My smile got bigger and bigger as I heard my truth in their words and felt such peace. They said it is perfection for me to be where I am, that I am in my process and that I do not yet know who I am but I will. That I am shifting to a new vibration. Being around others reflects back to me where I am. I resist accepting and acknowledging where I am in this moment of now. That if I choose to embrace it, I open the door for a shift in consciousness to occur. There was talk of expansion and a sense of connection to Jacob. I felt the power of the words and I felt great peace as they spoke with absolute certainty. I felt my worries and any sense of competition and not enough to go around disappear.

Kayite and I discussed how many books there are out in the world now and how silly it is that I may have some worries about not enough room for us all to offer our own. But I do a little. Mine have been particularly strong in the last month. Later I said to Kayite, "I did not even have to do anything and I am having one of the most amazing experiences of my life."

That is the whole point, isn't it? Kayite could not have shared this with me if I were not in a place to be receptive to it. I was able to come to the awareness that I drew Jacob and this experience to me. I created it. I had this amazing connection with nonphysical right in Kayite's living room and this is only the beginning for us both. I love the ride! I have been feeling so very good for the last few days. That is my focus. I intend to feel good in all aspects of my life and enjoy all that I am, in all that is, in this very moment of now.

Lunch with a Friend

I went to Unity Church today as I do every Sunday. This is a beautiful experience that I began in July, not long after returning home from the retreat. I meet up with a friend and we usually go to lunch afterwards and talk for several hours. This time we ate lunch and then we went back to her house to look up airline flights to Florida as we are planning a trip to meet up with two other friends there for a weekend in October. They are all open to Jacob. I am not sure what will transpire with that but I am eager to see what will be revealed.

We booked a flight. We will be arriving at 4:00 p.m. Thursday and our return flight is not until 5:15 p.m. Sunday so we will be able to go to the Unity Church there and have time for a nice lunch before we depart. I am so very excited! My friend mentioned we might go dancing and I just lit up. I love to dance and that is something I always wanted to experience. It was wonderful to be with others who desired this as well. I envision lots of laughter and joy that weekend. It's going to be fantastic!

While I was at her house, I sensed this was the perfect time to share with her about Jacob. She was so excited and then she said "Do you think you could do it now?" I hadn't even thought about it. I figured, why not? I could give it a go. We lay down on her bed and Jacob came as before.

This time I had a shorter conversation about allowing myself to let go because they assured me they would take care of everything as they did with my sister. I trusted in that and it all happened so much more quickly. I know the more I do this that I will come to the point where it is almost instantaneous, as there will be no hesitation on my part. This experience was different in that there was numbness of my whole body. I did not experience the intense vibration around my head and throat but rather a lighter vibration that was over my entire body. When it was done, I could hardly move from the numbness. I got up to go to the bathroom and kind of staggered in. It was so funny because I could hardly grasp the toilet paper. I couldn't get my hand to close.

I was laughing and enjoying the moment. I knew all was well. It also felt weird to speak as if I had just had a visit to the dentist. My mouth was so numb that my lips felt lopsided when I spoke. It was something. I did not have my tape recorder to know all that transpired. What I do know is that the conversation was long and my friend felt really good about the experience.

Flight of the Sardines

I am curious to know how my flight to Florida will be. I have been scared to fly since my very first flight to Arizona. I was 17 at the time and had just graduated high school. I was going to visit my aunt for a week as a graduation present.

When I got on the plane, I felt extremely claustrophobic. I felt like a sardine in a tin can, packed in, like I couldn't move and there was no way out. I began to feel trapped. I felt very uncomfortable the entire flight but was somehow able to get through to the landing.

But then when we stopped, everyone stood up to get his or her bags and now I was really beginning to panic. I was toward the back of the plane and thought I couldn't wait another moment. I started yelling in a scared voice, "I need to get off the plane. Please let me off. I need to get off now. Please help me." People moved out of the way and let me by and the flight attendant guided me to the exit. I was so grateful. I was so panicked that I couldn't even feel embarrassed, although I did feel it a little later on.

But in that moment, my fear took over and I just wanted to get out and breathe. So I made it there but just one problem, I still had to get back home. When I arrived at the airport for my return flight, I explained to the attendants what had occurred on the way there. I asked if they could switch my seat to the very front of the plane. They were able to work it out for me. I still felt discomfort, but knowing I could get off right away made me feel more at ease. I made it home but I did not fly again for many years. The fear only became magnified over time.

Since Jacob has arrived, I have felt a shift for me. I have experienced a deeper understanding of life and a sense of absolute peace in knowing all is well. But until I actually get on the airplane, I will not know for sure what I will feel and what my experience will be with this new awareness.

Notes

I went to bed early last night. I think I will get a routine down. I am still in the adjustment phase. I am enjoying all of the questions and I'm grateful they are flowing in. I am just as eager to hear the responses and I find it hard to wait or hold off on the asking. But I think that will subside as I get used to it.

9/30
Will I be able to clear out the nodule on my thyroid in the midst of the situations around me?

It is possible as you clear your vibration. Release the congested energy…..that has created a blockage…..and shift into a new vibration. You can do this and as you create change…….the things around you will shift as well. It will not be in the midst of the current situation, as the current situation will change as you shift into a new vibration.

This is……inevitable. As your vibration is changing, it affects everything in your life. And therefore, the shift in energy…..is for your well-being….it is not so much a question of can you do it a midst everything. It is more that a midst everything, you have the opportunity to create change. As you shift yourself into a new vibration through experience, it shifts what is around you, and clears out what is going on within you. It is all a cycle….it all works together…a divine process. Release resistance, align with you and you can create it to be.

What is the cause of the congested energy? Is it others around me? My job? Is it me at this point? Nothing is working. I require clarity as this has been going on for so long and I am not sure I am a good judge.

It is all you because everything in your life is about you…..how you perceive it….how you choose to experience it. It is all you. Instead of looking to change others……look within yourself…..what it is that you want. What do you want to experience? You believe you are stuck and you are not. You always have a choice. Why do you believe that this cannot change? The only person stopping you is you. You are the only one holding you back. If you really wanted to experience something different, you would. You would create it to be……..you will make all the choices you wish to make. You are angry with others because they are not being the way you want them to be. You are feeling angry, frustrated and upset…..but outside situations are not within your control……..although you are so desperately trying to control them. You are trying….but you need not resist.

You are fighting against all of your being. You need not fight it. Allow yourself to flow freely…..to be WHO YOU ARE…..rejoice that others are being who they are……rejoice in the moment of GLORIOUS light shining through you…….reminding you of the magnificence that you are. Let it flow…..let it just embrace you….allow yourself to be happy in the moment of now……just as everything is…..JUST AS EVERYTHING IS…..because it is all perfection. In this moment of now, it is all perfect, all divine……every part of it. Every part of it is showing you something. What is the growth in this for you?

Gym Jacob

I saw Gym Jacob while I was on the treadmill today. I have not actually spoken to him yet. I really want to look into his eyes. I have noticed I am sensing so much more lately just in my everyday interactions with people. I feel in tune with them. I have received many confirmations from others that they were indeed feeling what I was sensing. This feels wonderful to know.

Goals and Discipline

I had the most interesting conversation with a friend today. She said she admired others who were disciplined and wished she could be so disciplined as to stick to the goals she sets for herself. This brought about a discussion in which I felt a huge shift in consciousness.

Discipline to me is like putting on the shackles, chains that bind me and limits me in the moment of now. From my perspective, how can I live in the now if I have already set up an expectation of a "must-meet" goal for the future? It is impossible to know how I will feel tomorrow, next week, or next month. Our goals are based on how we feel in the moment and next week I will be making my choices in the moment, not trying to live up to what I already decided for myself.

So discipline with a must-meet goal is so very limiting to me. It limits my choice in the moment if I have already committed to something else. Now the reason I use the term "must-meet" goal is because I do think having goals is great. Having goals puts forth our desires for that moment and that's how we create the life we want for ourselves.

If we choose something different than our initial goal and can be okay with that, then our goals simply become guidance rather than a set up for failure, disappointment and frustration. We can rejoice that we are living in the moment rather than beating ourselves up over not "meeting" the goal.

It's like beating yourself up because you dared to feel differently today than you felt yesterday or last week when you set the goal. I understand the desire for the feeling of achievement and completion. You want that feeling so the question is, can you achieve that feeling in another way simply by changing your perspective?

I can tell you that every time I consciously make a choice in the moment of now, I rejoice in it. I feel successful. I feel achievement. What can be better than that? Knowing that in this very moment, I hold all the power to choose whatever I want for myself, even if it is different than what I chose for myself before. Or should I say especially if it is different. Because then I am consciously acknowledging that my life is magnificently ever changing. I allow myself the freedom to choose in the now.

10/01

This is an email I sent to my friend who asked the questions that follow:

After our call, I went upstairs to take a bath. Even though it was late, I felt something in your energy that made me want to ask your questions right then. And so I did. And it flowed. I knew they were really good. They went on and on. I was so excited that I wanted to play the tape back to hear it and type it up right then. But then I looked at the clock and it was 12:45 a.m. I knew I wanted to get my rest so I decided to go to bed and review it this morning. Here it is:

In my quest to find my biological father, am I searching in the correct place? Is he still living? Will he be receptive? And my sisters and other family...will they be receptive?

You are on a search to find what you feel is missing. Know that nothing is missing.....everything is within you. When you know who you are, you will not look outside of yourself to feel better. You seek your father out to feel better.....to complete that missing piece. It was never missing. If you wish to find him.....to experience this.....that is wonderful. This experience creates expansion.

Follow where you are guided to. You know what you feel inside.... what your inner self is telling you. Follow it. It will guide you where you want to go. This experience is for you to follow it and choose. You do not need to commit to anything. You can continue for as long as it feels good to you. As you feel that you would like to.

You cannot control whether they will be receptive or not. Whether they will be upset....angry.....or joyous. You have no idea how they will be and it is okay. Enter into this knowing that you are in this for you. You are going for your own growth experience. You are going for you, no one else. Others reactions are irrelevant. How you choose to experience this journey and respond to them is. The seeking, the asking, the desire to know how it will be for you is all part of your opportunity for growth. You are going to experience this process.

Know that there will be great joy from this because there is great opportunity for growth and expansion, however it unfolds. Enter into it with love for what you are creating. You wanted to experience tremendous growth. What better way than to go through an experience like this. Something so scary and so uneasy to your system, and at the same time you are pushing yourself beyond your discomfort because it is what you so greatly desire.

Your desire created this.....your desire is taking you there. This is going to launch you to a whole new place.....to a new awareness. That is what you seek. Expansion is what you seek. The expansion of the experience with your father is what you seek, not your actual father, not your family. We do understand that you wish to know them, but ultimately what you seek is the growth and expansion from this experience. This is your soul's purpose in the physical life experience.

What more do I need to know regarding my biological father and family?

You need know nothing more about your biological father....your family. There is nothing you need know......only that which you seek. It is the experience that you seek. Go forth with the strength and power of knowing that THIS IS WHAT YOU WANTED. Not the end result, not the father, not the family, but the experience of this journey. Enjoy the experience. Embrace the experience. It is here for you now.

IT IS HERE FOR YOU NOW. Embrace it. EMBRACE IT WITH THE LOVE IN WHICH IT WAS GIVEN.......EMBRACE IT FOR

ALL THE GRAND GLORY THAT IT IS. Embrace it. It is here for you. It is here for you to explore. Take hold of it. Take hold of it and enjoy this process.

Will my trip provide a good opportunity to discover more about my father and his family?

Your trip will provide an opportunity for you to awaken to more of who you are. It is not about your father. This is one aspect and it is up to you how you wish to experience this. You always have a choice. Know this trip....the connection with these beings....is beneficial for growth.... expansion. This will be a joyous event if you choose it to be. (Indeed it was.)

How can I share with my mother, my desire to connect with my father's family?

(Oops! I must have missed this question during the session. I was going to ask again but before I had the chance, my friend had informed me that she had already spoken to her mother and it was just fine. She felt the absence of a response from Jacob was the perfect response as nothing was necessary. I found this very interesting. How perfect it all is indeed. That is, if we choose to see it. And I do. I really do.)

What is the value of "signs" as we travel through life?

Signs are simply you calling out to you. You are reminding yourself of what it is that you wanted. Where you wanted to go. You are guiding you....always.

What is a good way for those of us who do not channel as Kayite does to connect with our highest truths daily?

Connecting with your highest truth has nothing to do with channeling, with the connection with us. Kayite is no different than you. She must look within and connect with her inner being. This is for all of you. Connect with yourself. The part of you that knows its magnificence.... that is all knowing....that knows who they are. Everything.....all that is......is within you. You have all the answers. The answer is within you.

Look to yourself and ask that question. Ask that question. Say – I want to know who I am. I want to connect with myself. And ask yourself to guide you. That is all you need connect with to know your highest truth. Choose to consciously be aware of self.

What is the relevance of childhood experiences to adult experiences?

Your childhood experiences created a foundation for your growth and brought forth desires that have guided you to where you are now. There is no purpose for you to go back. No purpose for you to focus upon what has already been, unless you are making a comparison for your own growth and are utilizing it for your greatest benefit. In the experiences during your childhood, they created desire in you to choose what you wanted to experience next. Create....Experience....Grow....Expand...THIS IS THE PURPOSE OF THAT. This is the purpose of your entire life.

When you look at your childhood ask yourself – What did that cause me to desire....what did that cause me to create in my life? And then where did that take me in the next step, and where did that take me in the next step, and where did that take me in the next step, and where did that take me in the next step....until you are where you are. Utilize the observation of your childhood experiences to better understand your process of growth. In doing so, it allows you the opportunity to expand even further and create shifts in energy that you may have held around those experiences from not understanding their purpose in your life. Every experience has brought you to the place where you are now. You can rejoice in that. You can say – I rejoice in every experience that has brought me to this moment of now. And every experience I choose from this moment is going to take me to the next moment of now. The only question is what do you choose to fill this moment with? It is up to you.

What new opportunities should I be aware of regarding my livelihood?

There are always new opportunities. They are waiting at every corner, they are with you now, always. Always there, always there.... waiting....waiting for you. You decide what you want to experience. Choose the experience and the opportunities will present themselves. There are endless possibilities and you have access to all that is.

What is the significance of the use of this name Jacob in this experience?

The name Jacob was chosen by us because many will relate........ many relate to this name. What we speak will ring true for them....it will resonate and then they will know. We are here for the next phase.......the next evolution. As more and more are awakened......as more and more evolve to this state of being........we will guide them. We are here for all who seek us. We have been called forth by you....by all of you. Kayite has called us forth but it is at the request of many.....the request of many that joined with her.....the request of many that wanted this to be......as she was ready to receive us. It is not just Kayite that called us forth, but all of you who have been asking the questions, all of you who want to know more, all of you who want to be awakened. We are all joining together to create this magnificent collective awakening.....a conscious awareness of self. THIS is the awakening.

Gym Jacob

I finally communicated with Gym Jacob. He looked right at me – into my eyes – when we spoke. He appeared to be very sure of himself. What a bright light he is. I could feel his intense energy. I was still not sure of the purpose of his appearance in my life. I was enjoying the experience and was open to what would be revealed.

10/04

This is an email I sent to the asker of the following questions:

These are the longest responses I have gotten to any questions thus far (which is a fantastic, wonderful, joyous experience for me). I wasn't sure if they were ever going to stop yapping (just kidding). I just finally finished transcribing and I am off to bed.

How come I have such a challenge letting go of relationships with men in particular? I feel OCD at times.

You have a hard time letting go because you want to fix it. You want to fix everything. You believe there is something you can do to resolve it. You do not want to let go because you are trying to make everything right. There is no right. There simply is what is. If you are not connecting, if you are not flowing in the same direction, this is wonderful to know. Why not say – Thank you....thank you for this awareness and I am grateful......I am grateful to gain clarity on where I am. This is about growth and what growth is in this for you. There is great variety and you all desire many different experiences. You are all choosing and others show up to provide these experiences for you. You can release them.... by embracing the growth and recognizing what is being offered to you. Open yourself to what these experiences have been offering you. As you choose to respond differently, you can release congested energy and create change in which these experiences will no longer serve purpose to show up for you.

I seem to attract these relationships, jobs, experiences where I get to have no closure, it appears to me it is always something I do wrong, and I am relentless in blaming myself and can't seem to get past them or over them...or this pattern is so imbedded in my psyche that I feel I will never attract anything any different. Is there a way for me to shift this, to not play victim, or blame myself? Is there a way to not feel so much pain? How come most people in my life continue to leave? I know about shifts, changes in consciousness, vibrations...but I can't and don't want to go it alone.

The closure you are seeking is not available because you seek to fulfill it outside of yourself. Everything is within you....everything. When you align with who you are....connect with your inner self....know this..... you will feel the joy. YOU WILL FEEL THE JOY. When you know the magnificent being that YOU ARE, when you understand how brilliant YOU ARE, then you will not look to someone else to tell you the value of who YOU ARE.

The cycle continues as you continue to attract these people into your life that are giving you exactly what you are feeling and asking for. You are feeling so unworthy, that you feel you do not even deserve the closure and bring forth that experience in your life. What a powerful creator you are. Others simply up and leave, up and leave, up and leave. And because you fear this.....because you fear this happening it continues to occur.... because that is your main focus. You continue to bring it upon yourself the more it happens the more you focus on it, the more it happens the more you focus on it, the more it happens the more you focus on it....... you see where we're going here?

All the pain you feel.......ALL THE PAIN YOU FEEL......is from all the blame and all the beating up of yourself that you are doing. This pain is there because you are beating yourself up, beating yourself up, beating yourself up, and your soul knows this is not necessary. Your soul knows how glorious it is. What you are doing is fighting yourself. You are constantly fighting yourself. Resistance, resistance, resistance to the divine being that is you. YOU can embrace YOU.

There is no need to beat yourself up over being where you are......over helping show others where they are. Whether or not they wish to see it, allow them to be where they are. If they feel the need to run, allow them to run. It is in how you choose to experience them running that growth is offered. Stand strong and say – This is who I am and I am excited because when I love who I am, when I rejoice in who I am, I will then draw to me and attract those who love who I am and are loving themselves as they are and are ready to connect with me. They are going to embrace that as I embrace that in myself. How can I expect them not to run when I want to run away from me?

Embrace where you are. When you love and embrace yourself, they will love and embrace you. But look to you....look to you to love and embrace yourself. What are you doing wrong? Nothing. Nothing is wrong. You can do no wrong and focusing on beating yourself up is not getting you where you want to go. It is not wrong, it is just not what you wish to consciously experience anymore.

This is something that you want to change but you are not sure how to get there. You want to get to a place that you can feel good about where you are. Just knowing and understanding that you are a magnificent being just as you are can create a shift. Regardless of what you do, it does not matter because you being you Is magnificent and you are here experiencing life.....creation....expansion...all of it...right here...now. It is expansion and this is the purpose of life.

Every experience is an opportunity for growth and expansion. Every experience. Look to yourself within. Can you awaken to the beauty that is you? It is there for you. It is right there waiting for you....just waiting for you to see the magnificence. Waiting for you to say – I embrace you, I love you, and I welcome others into my life that will see this too. You are not alone. There are many waiting for you.

You are transitioning into a new vibration while still holding onto congested energy with thoughts that keep you where you are. As you are working your way to shifting into this new vibration, you go through these moments where you fear aloneness....you fear what is going to be on the other side when you come through it. We can assure you that many are waiting for you, and it is up to you to open yourself to receiving them.

I am so afraid, in great fear of never living out my purpose, or being able to be the free spirit, playful spirit I know I am.

Your only purpose is growth and expansion and you are already living it. Expansion is occurring. It is just whether or not you are conscious of it.

Am I crazy for not wanting, at times, to be on this planet anymore?

We understand...we understand when you have completely forgotten who you are....when you are enveloped in a pattern of this constant beating down...beating yourself down about your life and struggling because you do not understand what is showing up for you. You are unable to express and feel the joy. You are unable to feel deserving of this joy from your current perspective. Joy is expression of self. You are resisting self. As you begin to embrace yourself as you are, expression of self and joy will follow.

When the joy is full expression of self, when the joy is the exuberance of life...... how could one not feel they would not want to be a part of this world when they have cut themselves off from the joy? From where you are, we understand why you would feel this way. Envision yourself at a fork in the road – one road leading to a path of sadness and another to a path of joy.

If the only thing you had to do was push a button to decide which path to take......if nothing else was required....if all you had to do was push a button and choose which path.... not one is harder to get to than the other.......not one requires more hard work than the other......not one requires any special deserving of it.........if you simply just pushed the button, what would you choose? What would you choose? And if you are feeling unworthy, and if you are thinking for even a moment that you would choose the struggle, depression, sadness button – the only way you would be choosing this is because you would be feeling unworthy to go to the joyous path. Let us talk about this for a moment. You are part of all that is.

YOU ARE part of all that is...this magnificent, powerful, flowing source energy that has come forth into this life for the grand experience here in the physical form. We are all part of this magnificent source. How could you not be worthy? You are worthy just by being. There is no reason for you not to push that joy button and take off. There is no reason, except that of your choosing. Whatever has occurred in your life....every experience has brought you to this moment of now. It is a very exciting moment.

It is a very exciting moment as you are at this fork in the road. Which button do you choose? It is that simple. It is that simple. You either choose to live your joy, or you choose not to. But you do not need to beat yourself up over it anymore. Because you are worthy....you are deserving. What others feel about you is not about you. What others feel about you is about them. It is about how they feel in relationship to them self and what they see in you reflects that. You need not look outside of yourself. Choose to be who you are, know who you are. Ask to connect with your inner being. Ask for guidance.

Your inner self will guide you to where you want to go. Your inner self will lead the way. Allow yourself to flow freely and allow yourself to listen. And whenever those thoughts of doubt, those thoughts of unworthiness, those thoughts of beating myself up...what did I do wrong, why can't I get it right.....whenever those thoughts come into play....push the button. Push the button for joy. It is never too late to push the button. There is always an opening to the path of joy.

Am I too sensitive?

You are feeling sensitive because you are caring so much about what others think of you. You care so much because you are kind and loving and compassionate and you so want to be in that loving space and you so want to get it right. And...there is no right. You are love, you are kindness, you are compassion. It is a beautiful thing. But you must love yourself.

You have so much love for others, yet you are not loving of yourself. Embrace who you are, love who you are, and you will no longer feel this sensitivity in your life. You will be clear on what is occurring. You will be absolutely clear that when another turns from you....leaves you....or runs away....you will be clear that they are running away from who they are..... that they are not running away from you. When you have this clarity..... the feeling of sensitivity will be irrelevant.

We understand when we say embrace who you are, that you desire to but do not know how. Tell yourself – I am magnificent source and I have come here to experience the joy of this life and I AM DOING IT. And all of the stuff that is showing up in my life is an opportunity for me to grow and expand. State that you are open to change and welcome experiences into your life that will help you create the shift to embracing yourself and raising your consciousness and current vibration. You do not need to know the "how." All is accessible to you. You just need to allow it in.

When I am beating myself up....when I am feeling bad...it is because I am not seeing the opportunity for growth in the experience. I am beating myself up about what I did wrong rather than seeing that this is a glorious opportunity for me to respond differently to create change, from which I will grow. I'm feeling bad because I am not seeing the experience for what it is. I am thinking that there is something wrong with me and that I am doing something wrong. But instead I can say, hold up.....this is the contrast....this is the contrast showing me that which I do not want and providing me the opportunity to create a shift for the changes I desire. It can shift you in the direction you wish to go. Acknowledge it. Embrace it. Awaken to it.

I am afraid of my financial situation. Do you sense that shifting for me?

As long as you are afraid of your financial situation, it cannot shift. It cannot shift from a place of fear. It is in moving beyond the fear that you will create change. We understand that you are fearful. And you can....take it slowly, a little bit at a time. If you look at it and say – There is a lot of growth in this for me. What is being offered to me? How can I choose to see this experience differently? Continue to ask and clarity will come.

You can say – I am clear about what I want and I am beginning to create that. I am on this path that I feel drawn to. It feels good to me. I am beginning to do more and more of what I enjoy and am passionate about. The work that I am doing is really moving and.......I know that when I do things that I am passionate about, do things that I love, that abundance flows. There is great abundance here for you. And as you work your way through this process you will see there is much to be excited about. There is great abundance awaiting you. It is waiting for you to open up to receive it. And as you feel that sense of peace in where you are, experiences will arrive in your life to create change for it to manifest.

I am such a free spirit, and most things I do, especially to survive, seem so mundane, or bog me down, or simply are not fun or adventurous, or creative or playful. Maybe my question is...how come everything seems like such a struggle?

The only thing stopping you from your free spirit, your playfulness, your fun.....is you. You are the only one that is holding you back. It is only you that creates your limitations. It is only you that places yourself in a box and determines its size. When you can come to this awareness and set yourself free, you will fly....you will fly.....soaring high indeed. Everything seems like a struggle because of the framework through which you are viewing it from. You can shift and expand your perspective..... and you will begin to see the endless possibilities that are available to you, ENDLESS POSSIBILITIES.

Whatever you choose. If you are doing things that seem mundane to you...that bog you down......then look to what you are feeling in that and what does that cause you to desire? Is it causing you to desire fun and adventurous experiences..... if you want the creative and playful experiences then put those desires out there. Create it for your life. You are beginning to manifest those desires but you must feel like you are worthy of them....that they can be and that you can embrace them in order for them to show up in your life. You want the fun, you want all of these things yet....it is hard for you to believe that they can be.

You are not sure how to receive it. We tell you, YOU CAN LIVE YOUR JOY.........it is RIGHT THERE WAITING FOR YOU.....it is coming into your life experience through you...allow it in......it's knocking at the door...it's knocking at the door.....this playful, joyous, adventurous life that you so desire..........it is knocking at the door for you....but you are refusing to open it.

You are refusing to open it for fear of – what do I do with this joy, what do I do, what do I do?.....Embrace It, embrace it. This is the life that you can live. It is knocking at your door so that you can experience it. It is knocking at your door because you called it forth with your desire and have created the energy in motion, which has brought it to you.

You are just not aware that it is already here. You have been afraid to open the door. Your inner being knows you are worthy, your inner being brought this to you......it's knocking at your door...we know you want this, we know you deserve it, we know you are worthy of it, we know you can enjoy this, we know you want to let it in, we know you want to experience this......knock, knock, knock......the only question is – are you willing to open the door? Are you willing to face your fear? Are you ready to move beyond it to the joy that is there and has been there all along?

When you feel you are ready............the door is waiting. The door IS waiting. Open the door divine one. Open the door.

I would like to be a fairy! Is that possible? (kind of a joke)

A fairy is wonderful and we can assure you that when you align with who you are......when you allow the full joy of who you are to be expressed....you will feel like a fairy flying....happily playing.....and in your joyful expression of self, YOU WILL FEEL THIS. It is waiting for you.

I would like to dance, play and be in nature, and share the connection in our ever-evolving place in the universe...but how?

Open the door.....allow it to flow in. Welcome experiences that will help you to shift beyond your fears. It is for you to recognize these experiences when they show up and choose to respond differently to create change.

I feel so lost and alone...how come?

You feel so lonely because you are separated from yourself. Not because you require another in your life. You feel that hanging on to others will somehow fulfill this need....that it will fill a void that is missing. It cannot be filled from outside of yourself. The only person that can fulfill this is you connecting with you.

When you connect with yourself, the source that is you, the beautiful, magnificent, being that you are, it is impossible for you to feel lonely. For you will know exactly who you are and you will feel the connection to all that is. This is what you seek. Open the door. Allow yourself to know.........the magnificent being that you are. You are source, all that is.

End Session

The following is an email I sent the asker of the previous questions:

All I can say is wow, wow, wow. I felt the pure love of Jacob flow through me and it was incredible. What a joy it is for me to experience this. And I feel so connected to you. I am in awe. This one really blew me away.

I wish you could have heard them speak. They spoke with great passion. It is not the same as the words on the paper. There is so much more that I experienced. But perhaps you did feel them. Perhaps they connect with you wherever you are. I look forward to hearing your thoughts on all of this.

The response I received:
My Dear Kayite,

Wow! I wish I could talk to you now, but I am crying, or have been, and there is probably more but it is the get ready to get to work thing right now. This was truly awesome.

I know it to be true, as this has been my message, SELF LOVE. I love the way they repeat a phrase, and it is in that phrase I see myself and stuck patterns, and can find some humor in them when I read them.

Thank you, dear one. I will read it again later, and later, and later...this was truly awesome. Okay, I could probably go on...just want to say again, thank you, thank you for allowing yourself to open to this wonderful opportunity, and you, with Jacob, definitely have a great deal to offer.

I know, and can see you beaming.

A Smile

My arms went numb after this session. I had to close and open my hands trying to get the feeling back in order to type this. The experience is always different. Perhaps it has to do with the individual interacting with them?

I also had the funniest experience. I was thinking about when this all started a couple of weeks ago and the words were coming at a very slow pace with many pauses and now they seem to yap, yap, yap on and on from one question. As I thought this there was a huge grin on my face but it wasn't me. It felt so odd. I was like – Jacob, is that you smiling? Is that humorous to you? It was indeed. How funny!

Butterflies, Butterflies Everywhere

I took Xander to the park today to play with his cousins. As we were waiting for them to arrive, I saw a swarm of butterflies. There were at least 15 or 20 hovering around these beautiful purple flowered plants. I thought, wow, I have never seen so many butterflies together in my life. They must really love this type of plant.

As I was talking with my sister and mentioned how awesome all the butterflies were, she said, "Really, I hadn't noticed any." Ah, I see. They were there just for me. Sharing their beauty as I was sure to take notice of them. Thank you butterflies!

Right after that, my sister and I went to sit on a park bench to watch the kids play on the playground. We were chatting away when I felt something on my foot. I was wearing sandals. I looked down and it was some sort of odd, yes odd-looking, caterpillar.

I yelped and was squealing to my sister, "Get it off me, get it off me." Now please know I love these beautiful creatures; it just didn't feel all that comfortable to find one crawling on me. There were two ladies sitting on a bench nearby who got a good giggle. We were all laughing.

My sister gently picked the caterpillar up and placed it in the grass several feet in front of us. The moment she put it down, it turned around and began making its way back toward me. I thought to myself, this is interesting. Am I putting off an energy that is drawing this creature? Maybe it's just wandering around but the closer it got, it was definitely heading straight for me and yes, it eventually made its way right back to my foot. My sister was kind enough to pick it up once again and take it to the grass area behind where we were sitting which was much, much further away.

We were talking again for quite a while and getting lost in our conversation when all of the sudden I felt something on my foot. I yelped, look down and you guessed it, once again that little caterpillar had made its way to me. Okay I thought, I am paying attention now. You got my attention. I get it. This is a significant experience. What was it telling me? I am not sure exactly but something was occurring.

I shared this experience with a few close friends and I was delighted at the responses they gave me. Although I didn't know what my experience was signifying, they seemed to have some ideas about its purpose. This is what two of them shared with me:

What wonderful experiences! Perhaps that determined little caterpillar was looking to you for inspiration on just how to turn from an interesting caterpillar into a beautiful butterfly. You have experience at that. I know. I was there to witness it.

Well, yes these are wonderful, beautiful experiences whose tale is yet to be told. I see those butterflies you saw, 15 or more as those whose lives you have transformed, transpired, inspired, and the caterpillar as one who is saying, show me the way, for look at all the others who have changed, become aware of their beauty and birthright.

Gym Jacob

I was at the gym today and when it was time for my circuit weight training I headed over to the area and I was delighted to see Gym Jacob once again. He was shining to me as he spoke with one of the elderly men there. As he was adjusting my weights I just blurted out, "It's really great how you interact with others. It is so beautiful to witness."

"Oh" (surprised), "thank you," he said. "When you're in a job like this of service, it is important to connect with people."

"You definitely do," I said. "I see the way they light up when they talk with you. You have great energy and you are shining." He says he enjoys the interaction but also is aware some people just like to be to themselves and gives them the space to do so. I don't know if he thought I was a total oddball for saying it but he really is a beacon of light and I wanted him to know. I wanted him to know he was making a difference. That people did notice. That it was appreciated. It felt wonderful to share this.

Even better was a beautiful man who came along who must have been in his eighties. He had overheard the conversation and said he liked to talk too. He began to tell me jokes and was absolutely delightful. His name was Andy and he was an absolute joy. It was just pure joy shining through him. I had seen him there before and I was so glad I got to connect with him. I was beaming from this interaction. He just brought a huge smile to my face and I flowed with joy. Overflowed. It was fantastic.

10/05
When will I feel some sense of balance in my life? I feel like I am one big ball of energy right now and I am feeling very out of sync.

There is always balance as you are where you are. Sometimes you feel turned upside down but we can assure you that all is perfection. This is your process. The balance you are seeking is connection with you and awareness of self. This is what you seek.

As you are asking these questions you are shifting into a new vibration. The seeking of it is guiding you there. Only harmony exists. All else is your creation and how you choose to experience it. As you raise your consciousness and expand your awareness of self, balance will be experienced, as you will feel the vibrational harmony of the source that you are.

Look within yourself for you hold the key. No one else does. Only you can choose what you desire. What you wish to experience. All is always in balance. But if you are not viewing it from this perspective, we tell you to look within and ask yourself why. Why does it feel so chaotic to you? And that which does is the congested energy patterns that you wish to release from your vibration. As you shift into a new vibration, more will be revealed as you grow and expand.

(This was a very beneficial response for me because I was just talking with a friend about wanting to create balance in my own life between my son, Jacob, and all the rest. It has been a whirlwind of stuff floating around in my life but I am feeling good in knowing that it is all in balance and all is flowing to perfection. This is joyous to me.)

Is there anyone I need to forgive that I have not already forgiven?

There is no need for forgiveness. What is there to forgive? Forgive them for being where they are? There is no forgiveness necessary. There is only understanding and acknowledging where one is. Acknowledging that they are just where they are in their life experience and doing the best they can in the framework of their world. They are living their life where they are just as you are living your life where you are in this moment. Instead of asking who to forgive, why not ask – Have I embraced everyone that I can embrace? Embrace and love them for the divine beings that they are, for they are you. Source manifested in a different form to offer you growth.

This does not mean that they have to be an everyday part of your life. It simply means that for whatever hurt or pain you are feeling that has caused you to think that there must be forgiveness involved, you can look at them and say – I embrace you for who you are. I know that you are doing the best that you can in this moment of now. This is also a moment to ask your self – what is the growth in this for me? Every experience is a co-creative process.

Situations that have caused you pain were all created by you on an unconscious level. If you choose to acknowledge the creation and can see the opportunity for growth in the experience, you will then benefit tremendously from the growth and expansion of the experience. This is what you seek. This allows you to release the congested energy that keeps you stuck, keeps you where you are. Others in your life offer you many gifts. Many gifts that offer experiences for you to expand your perspective and create change in order to shift your consciousness. Embrace them all for they are here to facilitate your growth.

Will I be in a loving relationship with my soul mate soon?

Imagine you are at a fork in the road. Which path will you take? The path to love or the path to where you are now? You can stay in your current vibration or you can take the path to the love and joy you seek. You can do it all with the push of a button. If nothing else was required of you? If no path has harder to reach than the other? If all you had to do was push a button to choose which path you would take, what would you choose?

If deep love is what you truly desire, then we say push the button for the path of love. Imagine the path opening up for you. Every time you have doubt, that you ask – will I find this person in my life, that you question can it really be, PUSH the button. Push the button in your mind and imagine yourself going down that path of love and it will be. Experiences will show up in your life to make it so. It is right there waiting for you. RIGHT THERE waiting for you. Waiting for you to push the button. Waiting for you to choose more for you.

You haven't pushed the button. You haven't even acknowledged that the path of love is there. You know your current path is there and you know your current vibration that you experience. It is so easy to keep going down that same path. Easy to stay there because that is what you know and it fits the framework of where you are. We understand that shifting into a new vibration is not always so easy because it can feel much easier from where you are to maintain a familiar vibration even if it does not feel good to you. It is familiar and there is comfort in the familiar so you stay there. Make your choice. What is it that you really wish to experience? As you push that button, it calls forth desire, which calls forth the creation of energy in motion, which draws in a life experience, which can create the manifestation. Focus on that and you will begin to create change.

Will my business pick up enough in this quarter so I can end the year on a positive note?

Why is it that you feel your business must pick up in order for the year to end on a positive note? And how do you define what is positive? The year itself is not important. The only thing that is relevant is this moment of now. Living in the moment of now. This is the moment. This moment right here. RIGHT NOW in THIS MOMENT what are you choosing?

And if your year did not end on a so-called positive note, would this affect your thought on the entire year? The year is irrelevant. It is the moment of now that you are experiencing. It is the moment of now that is taking you where you want to go next. This moment is forever taking you to the next moment of now. So choose now what you wish to experience. If the work you are doing is what you are enjoying and you wish it to be abundant and successful, then believe it can be so and allow experiences into your life that will help facilitate this change. Know that all will unfold perfectly for you. Enjoy the process along the way. This is what you seek. ENJOY THE PROCESS ALONG THE WAY.

It is not about the end of the year. It is not about ending on a positive note. It is about the journey. You are not here to cross the finish line. You already have the gold medal. You are here to run the race. Enjoy the run, the experience, and the growth that is offered along the way. Release any focus on whether or not it will end on a positive note. If you choose to enjoy where you are right now, things will always end on a positive note because you are enjoying the journey. Enjoy it, embrace it, love it, and BE present in the moment.

When is the ideal time to start a business?

In this moment. The moment of now is the ideal time to create anything you wish. The moment of now is all there is. The moment *of now IS all there is. The moment of now IS ALL THERE IS. Are we coming through loud and clear? If you wish to create this then you choose when you want to experience it. The moment of now is all there is. We cannot say it enough. This is the place of your power. Take hold of this moment of now and consciously choose your creation. CONSCIOUSLY choose your creation, and begin to wield the divine power that is you.*

I have felt like I have been in a little of a holding pattern regarding starting my new business because it seems that my soul has been working on things within me on a personal level. Have most of the things been resolved?

You are still seeking outside of yourself and the answers are within you. The answers are within. Until you come to the full awareness that the answers are within you, that YOU are guiding YOU, there is no resolution. And when you understand that you are guiding you, you will understand that there is nothing to resolve. And with the understanding that there is nothing to resolve, then this is the so-called resolution because it is simply the awareness that you are creating and experiencing and will continually be growing. For all is perfect in every moment.

Is the person I know of a good person to get spiritual healing and advice from?

If you are drawn to this person, then follow what you are feeling. But listen to yourself as you receive this advice. And you choose if it is healing. You decide if it is healing for you. Follow what you feel. It has brought you to us. So here you are, here with us, yet we are guiding you... back to you. Do you find that interesting? Doesn't that feel wonderful?

Doesn't it feel wonderful to know that all of the power for the creation of your life is within you. That you need not look outside of yourself, to anyone. You need not look there for answers, but if in this moment you are feeling drawn to go to experience a process with this person, then there is growth in this for you. This is your choice to experience what you will.

We understand that you will still be looking outside of yourself until you fully awaken to you. Until you say – I think I see the light over the horizon. I understand now who I am. I understand that I am guiding me.

I understand that I am never alone. I am this magnificent source and I am guiding me. All-knowing glorious light source is guiding me. I embrace where I am now because embracing where I am now will allow me to easily shift and create the experiences that I desire. I must be consciously aware of myself, and love where I am now in order for this to occur.

So love who you are and embrace where you are and say – I have been seeking advice, and I may seek a bit more because it helps me to feel a little better to get that reassurance, that confirmation that the answers are within me. And...it might take me hearing it a little bit more, and a few more times, and maybe a few more times. But I know that the more I hear it, the more it is confirmed for me, that the more I will start to believe it. And so I ask a few more questions…...and then a few more.

With the continued confirmation that the answers are within me, I really start to believe it. I continue and I ask and ask again until the belief turns into knowing. An experience will show up in my life and help me to create a shift, and in that moment, I will awaken to the awareness of who I am and that all of the power is within me. And I feel so good, so wonderful, and so joyous that I am awake, aware, and knowing that I can experience anything I wish. I am the creator of my life experience and I can do anything I choose. Isn't it glorious? We always welcome you to ask as many questions as you desire. This is your process. Enjoy the process. Run the race.

Expressing Me

Today is the first day I have not had any questions for Jacob. It is Saturday and my son is with his father. I decided that today would be a great day to work on creating this book. I have all the questions and responses, emails sent to friends, and many notes of my thoughts and feelings along the way. All I have to do is put them together somehow. However, I am not a professional writer and have no idea what I am doing. I am just me. I am a being in this world and I am sharing my own life experience in the only way I know how. I know it is not about being good enough. I know I cannot possibly please everyone. And I am not here to do so. I am here to express me. I hope you enjoy what I share and the way I share it. But if not, I can only be me. And I will love you for feeling however you do.

Restaurant Delight

After spending all day working on the book, I was hungry and it was time for dinner. I decided to go out to eat. I chose one of my favorite restaurants and relaxed into a nice, comfortable booth. I had printed out a copy of what I had put together thus far and took it with me to review. I encountered one of the most delightful waiters I have ever experienced. It was the best service filled with love and kindness and it was beautiful! I read through the many pages, I enjoyed a good meal, and I enjoyed the interaction with this beautiful being. I took notice that as I entered with joy and was feeling wonderful that I had drawn to me a waiter who was also nothing but joyful and pleasant.

Television

After writing my notes, I am off to watch an episode of *Beauty and the Geek*. I enjoy this show because it is about personal growth. It is wonderful to witness the growth of another. I am just realizing I haven't been drawn to watch any television since this new transition in my life occurred. My life has been so incredibly fulfilling that I hadn't even noticed the television had not been turned on until now.

TV used to be a big part of my day. For hours every evening I would get lost in shows so that I wouldn't have to think about my life or my unhappiness. I could just focus on something else. I am rejoicing in how wonderful it is that this has shifted for me and how incredible it is that I didn't even notice. I have been so completely flowing with joy that it was not even in my awareness. It was as if I forgot the television even existed. It was just no longer relevant in my life. But on an occasion like this where I am feeling like I just want to sit down, relax and rest, I enjoy shows like this that I find to be uplifting. I may still watch something here or there. It is just no longer a focal point in my life.

Custody and Interaction

I just informed an old friend of mine about my separation. She asked me if my former husband and I still interact other than just with the shared custody? Absolutely. We don't even consider it custody. It's just not like that with us. We don't spend a lot of time together as we are both busy living the life experience we desire. Since we choose a different life experience and this is the reason we are choosing not to live together now, it would not serve our growth to spend a great deal of time together. We do still love and support one another.

And I gladly welcome a new lady in his life and into our family and I know he will do the same for me. It is just more people to love and to be a part of Xander's life. How great is that? And we do still get together for family dinners or a fun time with Xander and things like that. But overall, our lives are vastly different. And that is wonderful.

10/07

I attended Unity Church today and I continue to enjoy this experience in my life. This is part of the new me – the me who is getting out and connecting with others, spreading the love and joy, and living fully, completely. Today was an extra special day at Unity. It is the one-year anniversary of the new sanctuary that was created by the community. Rev. Richard Rogers, former senior minister of 4,500-member Unity of Phoenix, was the special guest speaker of the day. He was also holding a three-hour workshop after service on setting the soul free and knowing your self for the first time.

My initial thoughts were that I already know who I am and I am free. Living joy. I wasn't quite feeling drawn to go but a friend of mine wanted to attend the workshop and so I decided to join her in this process. I do love to connect with others and I did enjoy Reverend Rogers during the service. The whole time I could see a glow of energy around him. I began to see people's energy a few years ago but it was very faint. The more I have participated in this process with Jacob, the more others' light beams out at me so clearly. It was a very enjoyable experience. We were supposed to be doing a meditation but I had my eyes open and staring at the glowing energy. It was so beautiful that I did not want to take my eyes off of him.

The workshop began and I just felt pure love. As I sat there listening to others speak about wanting unconditional love and also wanting to give unconditional love, I realized what a gift this was for me. I knew I had transitioned to a new place but I had not yet experienced it. With every thing that was discussed and talked about, I knew I was already there, in that place of pure unconditional love. I just wanted to love and embrace everyone in that room. I was smiling the whole time because I felt great joy flowing through. It was beautiful.

It reminded me of the retreat. The only difference is that this time, I attended already knowing who I was and it really was magnificent. I felt deep love for each and every person in that room. I feel the deep love Jacob has for others and it has brought me to a whole new understanding of love. I am so glad my friend wanted to go and that I experienced the *Knowing* who I am.

After the workshop I felt compelled to give Reverend Rogers a hug and I told him what a Joy he is. I then went to several of the people who had spoken and shared their pain. They too received a big hug and I told them I had great love for them. It was so wonderful for me to share this. Especially when they were where I was just a few months ago. I could look at each of them and say, "That was me, that was me, that was me." I was able to relate to where they were and embrace them as others had embraced me. Months ago I would have been too shy to talk to anyone. And I definitely would not have felt I had anything to offer. Today, I rejoice in shining my light, loving all, and embracing everyone just as they are.

Tidbits from Xander

Xander often says the most glorious things. I cannot help but smile and feel the joy. I am delighted to share these tidbits with you. "I always wanted a mommy like you. Thank you for choosing to be my mommy." I thanked him for choosing to be my son. How wonderful!

Honeymoon Phase?

A friend of mine told me today she thought I was in a "Honeymoon Phase" – that phase where life is so wonderful and joyous and it is all so new and exciting. This was the second time she mentioned it, so I wanted to address it and clarify to her where I was. I told her I would agree with all but the phase part. A "phase" implies all of the joy and bliss will fade. I just replied, "Yes, except it's not a phase. It is my life. And it is here to stay because I choose it to be." Now could it fade?

Sure. Absolutely. Life is ever changing and that choice is there for me. Anything is possible. But in this moment, which is all there is, I choose the joy. She then basically told me to prepare myself for it all to to go to crap. I used to take things like this so personally but, for the first time, I could clearly see it for what it was. I knew this was only coming from where she is. She had once experienced what she considered to be great happiness in her life and has since been in a very unhappy space. She feels like it all fell apart for her and so she is warning me from the place of what she knows. From the experiences she has had. This statement says everything about where she is and really has nothing to do with me.

This is someone who has been struggling for a long time and instead of looking within to ask herself why she isn't living the joy, it is much easier for her to look outward to someone who is living the joy and state that it won't last. This helps her to feel better about where she is. If my life would be crappy soon, if the joy didn't last, then where she is in her life wouldn't feel so bad. She could just tell herself that everyone experiences this. That life is hard for everyone. I told myself the very same thing for quite a long time. I was unable to relate to the joy. I love and embrace my friend for where she is and I rejoice in her process. She is a beautiful being and I am grateful to her for the opportunity to declare where I am and what I choose for my life. Thank you for this gift.

She then began to share what she truly desired for her life. As she was talking I began to feel vibrations pulse through my body. It was Jacob and they were feeling excited for her process, for her growth. It was wonderful to feel and know this. I, too, was excited for her. We got into the discussion of the integration process and if Jacob were with me. Jacob is always with me.

Like a light switch, they are always connected and wired up to me, I simply have the on/off mode but they are always there. This is the best way I can describe it. The knowledge that they share has integrated with me and the more I continue the communication with them, the more I come to a greater understanding about the message they are bringing. I know I am different. I am different just being me as a result of the integration with them.

Even when I am not focused on the "channeling," they will be with me at times, sharing information or ideas pop up and I am clear it is them. Sometimes they smile or laugh through me. It sounds so odd to me as I am writing these things, yet it feels so very normal when they occur. Because I know they are nothing but love, it is easy for me to be comfortable with them and embrace them as part of my life.

Resistance Physically Manifested

I spoke with my sister this evening. She had planned to come over for a second session but she found herself not feeling well and just wanted to stay home. We talked about the fact that she was feeling some resistance and that this illness was a physical manifestation of that. She just wants to take it slow and maybe try again in three or four weeks. I honor her process and whatever she chooses to experience. I let her know I am always here for her. That Jacob is always available should she decide she would like to participate and communicate with them.

I do understand it is a lot to digest. A lot of changes can be a scary thing. It was a natural transition for me but I still had to walk through my fear in order to awaken to who I am. One can run and hide from where they are and create continual resistance. I did this for a very long time. Or one can face the fear and begin to create change. There is growth in either choice as both experiences have much to offer.

More Set in Place

I sent the following email to my Freedom Circle:

I am so grateful for each and every one of you. I am clear that this process would not have occurred without you. You are just as much a part of Jacob's creation in my life as I am. It was your support, excitement and embracement that have allowed it to flourish. I only told a few people directly about Jacob and already awareness of Jacob has spread through you and it is beautiful. I realized I didn't need to tell anyone else. Others are just naturally appearing in my life to participate in this process. One by one others are drawn to us and you created that. We all created it. I am rejoicing that we are all in this together. I was looking back at one of the first questions asked to Jacob:

What is the role of the Freedom Circle in regards to Jacob? Is there a common purpose among us?

Your freedom circle has come together because you all seek a deeper understanding of life, you seek more, you want more, you thrive for more. The combination together creates an opportunity for tremendous growth and expansion. Your vibrations draw one another. You will all work together....in creating great change.....for humanity.

When I first read this I thought – we are going to create great change for humanity? Wow. I knew it rang true but how was our little group going to do this? I see it so clearly that this is the launching pad for all that is to unfold with Jacob. The creation of a book is one of them. I am so glad you all decided to share with one another. The responses are indeed for everyone. This is part of the process. Sharing what is personal to you in order to help awaken others is a great service to humanity and it is a great joy for your soul to witness and experience. You can already see how reading each other's responses in our circle has been beneficial. Imagine many others reading about your process as it helps to create a shift in their consciousness. Doesn't that feel wonderful? Can you jump with joy for all of this? I sure want to. Thank you for choosing to be a part of my process. I love you.

I realized my Freedom Circle had been created and set in place for this very purpose, to launch me onward with Jacob and support me during the process. As a co-creative process, our group serves each of us involved in a different way. Offering each the growth experience they desire. For me, this is what it served as part of my life experience.

Simple Pleasures

On the way to school this morning, Xander and I were telling knock, knock jokes and laughing hysterically over nothing really. "Knock, Knock," said Xander. "Who's there?" I ask. My son says, "Tree." "Tree who?" I ask. He just laughs. He makes up anything and thinks it is the funniest thing. You cannot help but laugh right along with him as he clearly feels the joy in all of it.

Just then, he said, "Look at the beautiful sunrise, Mommy."

I looked over and saw a perfectly round blazing orange circle of a sun that was just above the misted mountains. It really was beautiful, incredible, a spectacular thing to witness. I just thought about how glad I was to have opened myself up to such beauty. These sunrises had always been there, but I never noticed them before. When I allowed all the love and joy to flow into my life, I also allowed all of the beautiful small details to appear in a grand manner in my life. I welcomed them. The more I welcomed them, the more they continued to flow in. The more I acknowledged them, the greater the beauty became. I am thoroughly enjoying this experience and I always get excited to see what will be revealed. I am aware, open and am sure to take notice. I don't know what you could say about noticing the sky for the very first time. The most magnificent beauty that had been there all along and then finally one day I awakened to its magic.

Butterfly Magic

I pulled into the parking lot at Xander's school. I saw four butterflies on the hillside. Two white ones flew by and then two brown ones. They were fluttering right by my car. When we got back home, there were two more white butterflies waiting for me in the driveway that fluttered around as we got out of the car. It was magical.

10/09
There is a woman at my place of work that I have a very hard time interacting with. She pushes my buttons. Is there any insight you can give me regarding this situation?

Love and embrace yourself and know that whatever this individual is doing, being, saying.......that it simply expresses everything about where they are. This is just where she is in her life experience but she is also offering an experience to you as well. You can choose to shine your light for her. Shine your light to remind her of who she is. Doesn't it feel better to be a shining light than to be another joining in....complaining about everything? Complaining solves nothing.

The more everyone complains about her, the more energy they are putting into creating an expansion of the situation. Show her how things can be different rather than giving her what she is creating for herself. You will find that by shining your light, your joy, that things will shift without you having to actually do anything else. Just by responding differently, great change can occur. Allow the divine being that you are to flow through. And allow her to be where she is. Rejoice in her freedom to express herself as you rejoice in your freedom to express yourself. Embrace the opportunities for growth in this experience. There are many gifts before you. It is for you to recognize them. Unwrap the packages and experience the growth.

Beacon of Light

I am currently witnessing one of my dear friends walking through her fear. She has felt nervous, scared, afraid to open her self up, afraid to feel, afraid of rejection. But today, she walks with strength and courage. She is choosing to face her fears, to walk through them. I feel nothing but joy for her because I know what is waiting on the other side. I felt so honored to be a part of her process. I never knew I could feel such love and joy for another. It just flows through me and it is glorious. As others are thanking Jacob and me for making a difference in their lives, I want to state what a difference they have all made in mine. Watching others awaken to who they are is the greatest joy and continues my expansion in a very deep and pleasurable way. It is incredible. Thank you all for your many gifts.

You are all shining lights. Sometimes you allow your light to dim, but your light is always there nonetheless. If you are struggling, just remember that the dimmer switch can be turned up. It may feel like you have a long way to go to get to the joy but just envision the switch. Turn the knob a little at a time as you are comfortable and before you know it you will have a bright beaming light for all to see. But how do you do this? How do you turn your dimmer into a beacon of light? Is this what you desire? Is this what you really want? Do you want to experience the pure love that is you? Begin by opening the door. Know that there is nothing to fear. Choose to let your light shine. Experiences will show up for you to create change.

Financial Peace

My former husband and I still share a bank account. We haven't quite sorted that out yet because there hasn't been anything left after paying the bills anyway. If you had looked at our income and bills, you would have said we would not have been able to separate and afford two households. I am glad that I was not looking at what was. I was looking to what I desired to create. I manifested the money for the move and even though it was only enough to last a few months, I had no concerns. I just trusted that all would unfold.

I am currently taking notice that I am in a situation where I don't know how I will pay my rent or mortgage next month. What I do know is that I created this experience and it is here to offer me growth. So I asked myself, what is this about for me? And then I asked Jacob. They told me everything would be fine, that I did not need to concern myself with it. I came to the awareness that this is an opportunity for me to experience total peace in the moment.

To know all is well in spite of what appears to be something entirely different on the surface. I KNOW all is well. I have no angst about it and I am clear the purpose of this was for me to experience the knowing of this. Now that I have, all will begin to flow into my life. I am clear there is nothing to "worry" about. This is huge for me. I used to really stress about things like this in my life. From the viewpoint of where I was just a few months ago, I would have thought my life was falling apart. How wonderful to experience the contrast. It feels so good to be at peace.

I am also clear that all will work itself out for me to be able to attend the Holiday New Year's Retreat with Neale Donald Walsch. (What a beautiful man he is!) I don't have the airfare or hotel booked yet but I know it is there for me. It will unfold at the perfect moment.

I didn't have the money to move out of our house to my apartment in September but I knew I had to go. I could no longer stay there. So I focused on just knowing it would work out. I didn't think about the "how." I just left it wide open for the universe to create it. We ended up selling a big job with the business and borrowed the money from that. It has lasted us this long and I just used the last of it.

But I know, just like with that manifestation, that something else will appear to carry me through. And if I had not taken that leap of faith and moved with no money, Jacob would not be here now. So it has to be perfect. Right? Yes, I say. Yes, I know. I also have a great desire to travel the world. So how will I go to Europe,

Africa or Thailand? I will create it in the same way. It is truly magnificent to see my conscious creations come to fruition. But the process is really what is most fantastic.

My Body

I am ready to create change in how I feel about my physical body. I have had issues with my weight since I was about twelve years old. My life was so chaotic that I began to express this physically with weight. This was something that continued throughout my adulthood. It was a continual up and down process.

I know that as I truly love and embrace every part of me, I will draw others who will do the same. I am absolutely delighted to know this. I am ready to experience it, as I know it will be manifested in my life. The knowing will not release it. It is the experience that will do so. I say bring on these lovely experiences. I choose to be free!

Butterfly in the Window

I was sitting in a booth at a restaurant having lunch. I was having a conversation when I noticed something in the window out of the corner of my eye. I looked over and a large butterfly had flown up to the window next to me. She was just hanging out, saying hello. Once again, I take notice.

Flying Fears to Joyful Tears
10/11

Today I am flying to Florida to visit my friends for a long weekend. It is the fourth time I will be traveling in an airplane. I am excited to see what transpires because of the fears I mentioned earlier. In fact, the last time I had to beg my doctor for some drugs in order to take a trip to Costa Rica. I was beginning to panic just at the thought of getting on a plane. I wasn't sure if I would be able to go without it.

My doctor agreed but only gave me two pills, just enough for the flight there and back home. I made it through just fine with that. But now, I am in a different space. Things have shifted so much for me that I feel nothing but peace at the thought of flying. However, thinking this is one thing, so let the experience begin. I am ready.

I boarded the plane along with my friend who was joining me. All I felt was excitement for the trip. My friend had the window seat and I was in the aisle seat. My friend and I began to play cards. The airplane took off and I felt peace, joy, knowing all was well. I looked out the window (which I was never able to do before) and the beauty of the sky just took my breath away. At some point, we flew right through these large puffs of bright white clouds that looked like you could just jump around on them. They were so magnificent that if I had to describe heaven, I thought that would be it. Tears of joy welled up in my eyes.

I just took it all in, all of the beauty in the moment. This experience let me know I was indeed free. I no longer carried that fearful energy. I knew there was nothing to fear. That nothing could "happen" to me and if I chose to go back home, back to source, it would be glorious. With that awareness, flying no longer triggered fear for me. My trigger point dissipated and would no longer activate fear since the congested energy had been released. This was yet another opportunity to experience peace in the moment.

First Group Experience

As we arrived in Tampa and headed for baggage claim, our friend Jan was there to greet us. We went back to his house and our other friend had driven in and was there waiting. It was a wonderful reunion. It was the first time I had seen anyone since the retreat. It was great to get together. It was evening time and Jan cooked dinner for all of us. He is an excellent cook. We talked and enjoyed the evening.

As we were talking, I could feel Jacob being drawn out by the others and what they were discussing. So I let go and allowed them to flow through. My friends spent several hours asking questions and communicating. I had not anticipated Jacob just showing up while we were all chatting on the sectional sofa, so I did not have my tape recorder ready.

Although we did not get the conversation recorded, I can tell you that it was a wonderful experience and very beneficial to all. I enjoyed my very first group experience. It was fantastic and it was really great to get feedback from my friends about their experience with Jacob and how they perceived it.

10/12

We were up late the night before and we all slept in. We had a lovely pancake breakfast and headed off to the beach for the afternoon. I was sitting on a towel and talking with a friend when all of the sudden she got very excited and asked, "Did you just see that?" "What?" I asked. She said a butterfly just flew right over my head. I said, "Oh yes, wasn't it beautiful." I told her I see them everyday. She said she was not surprised it found me on the beach too. How wonderful!

Let's Dance

There was a Swing Dancing event later that evening that we all wanted to attend. I was very excited about it. I had never done anything like this before and was thrilled about this new experience. They began with a lesson that taught the basic steps. This was enough so that we could all at least participate. It was a wonderful place. There were at least 100 people. Everyone was so friendly and I always had someone to dance with. I thought I did pretty well for my first go at it. I couldn't have done too badly at it or I think I would have run out of partners! We laughed and had a great time. We returned home at a late hour and went straight to bed.

10/13

We had a relaxing day and just enjoyed our time together. Later in the evening, there was a second encounter with Jacob, the only one that was taped and it cut off at some point. The following is what we got. When I played the tape I heard laughter and giggles and it was joyous. This communication came in the form of conversation. There was much conversation between the participants as they chimed in to speak with Jacob throughout. It was interesting and very different from any of the previous experiences I have had with just the questions and responses. Yet both are very enjoyable, just different.

Are you ready for us to speak with you? *Yes*

We were just talking about knowing in our hearts that we are here to have fun at the game of life in our physical form. We know we have chosen that. We have chosen it to be a part of our experience and we can choose it a hundred times over. And we can choose it in a different way. I know I can always work and get things done. We can know certain things but I get caught up in my desire for total perfection because someone has beeped that into my head.
Everything is always perfection.

Even though I may not find it perfect? *Yes. It is your perspective.*

You're right. Someone has instilled this lovely perspective that I can't quite ditch yet. *You have. Someone else does not have control over your experience. You are in the driver's seat. It is you that has chosen to believe what others have told you and created that as your current reality.*

I have allowed my parents' values to become my values without rhyme or reason. *You can change it today, this moment if you choose.*

I wonder if there is a certain safety net whether it is failure or not in keeping to somebody's values that were before you. *There are no failures.* **Well it sucks.** *Every experience creates an opportunity for growth and expansion. This is the purpose. And if you choose to accept this, then you will see that everything you have experienced has brought you to where you are. That you have grown….expanded…..and it is all successful. Failure only exists in your thought about what you* *are experiencing. You are defining your experience. As you shift your perspective, that definition will change.*

So the ditching of that thought becomes a powerful empowering experience? *It is very powerful. It completely changes the framework through which you experience your world.*

What am I to do about this person who irritates me? She is so needy and I tend to move needy people out of my life. *Are you afraid of being needy?* **Oh my goodness. Yes. Yes, I think I do have trouble with that.**

When others are showing you that which you are resistant to in yourself, you become distant. And when you embrace that part of yourself, you will easily embrace others where they are, because it will no longer bother you.

I have also had this issue with my car. I worried about it breaking down and loss of transportation to me means total dependence on a man. *The focus on loss is your creation. That fear, the worry, creates where you are. You are continually being offered experiences to create change in this in order to grow. You will continue to see this show up in your life experience until you choose to respond differently to create change. Your thought of dependence on a man is telling you much about your current thought pattern and reveals to you more about where you are. Utilize this information as a tool for growth.*

And the interesting thing is there is money here. And that money can be a protection device but it can also be the means to creating more.

All you need is yourself. **Oh. I see. Well, there is some wisdom out there that says if you have some money and you spend it, you are generating the cycle that begins the abundance cycle.**

It is your thought process of that cycle that creates it. Not the money itself. **Oh, I do have that money issue.** *You are doing just fine. Embrace where you are. You are creating many experiences for growth. This is all part of your process. Just because these creations do not always show up in the form you expect it to does not mean that they are not absolutely beautiful. Allow yourself to experience them with joy.*

I've learned a lot today. The process is good.

Jacob, talk to me about my father. I would like to know what is in his heart? *Love.*

It is great love for you that has been waiting for you to be ready. It has been there. And now you have come to meet with that vibration. You have come to this place where you are ready to receive it and are open to the tremendous growth and expansion of this experience.

We can't ask you predictions about the future because you always tell us to look inside. *There is no prediction offered because your life experience is always being created by you. We are here to guide you to this awareness. It is ever changing.* **But what about psychics?** *Others may read the energy you currently vibrate but it can still change based on your choosing. You always wield the power and there are endless possibilities.*

What about big events? *It is the collective consciousness that creates the larger events and this too is ever changing. Yet there is energy in motion that can be received and read by others.*

You can predict that you can't be right. Statistics tend to be true and are true. Is that close to what you are saying? *Statistics are irrelevant.* **Statistics are irrelevant?** *Yes, irrelevant.*

This is information being presented to you in a form that is telling you what is. It is for you to decide what is so for you. You can choose to believe it if you want to and that will become your reality. But it also creates limitations. Create your life with endless possibilities. Use what is being presented as an opportunity for you to clarify where you are and how you feel. Allow this to guide you.

I've heard it said that we create and that our next job is just to observe. *It is to create and experience because it is the experience that offers growth, which in turn creates the expansion and this is the purpose of life. Observe what is being offered in order to recognize the growth in the experience.*

This is the first time I have heard there is disconnect between statistical, mathematical models and what is spiritual or actual.

They serve purpose. They are part of the life experience that the collective has created.

In other words that is yet another illusion?

Yes. It is up to you to choose what you wish to embrace and bring into your life experience.

You always say that. *Because it is so.*

And I know many of those things have stopped me…stop me still. That kind of answer is perfection for me. *We have only love for you.* **I'm surrounded by it………I am moved to tears.**

I know for myself in the work that I've chosen that I am confronted with having sort of too many choices. Is there any wisdom that can be brought to bear on that problem? Are there choices that can help us move forward?

Choose the joy. If you are not feeling joy in your decision, if you are not feeling joy in what you are doing, then choose what brings you joy. Joy is the fullness of you expressed. When you are not resistant but express yourself freely, you will experience joy in everything you do. **Okay. That makes sense in a way but when I am doing a design for a house, does that work there as well?** *Yes.*

So what gives me the greatest joy is what is right for the client even if they have completely different choices?

What feels good for you is not dependant on the outcome. Having the client love it is not the joy. Loving what you are experiencing IS. We understand the work you are doing is for the client but when you work from a place of joy, all unfolds beautifully and the rest will take care of itself. The client is co-creating with you. All is perfection.

If I embrace this knowledge of joy, it may push people away. *Who would be pushed away?* **It was totally hypothetical. My family, my friends I guess. I have often, in the past, had people become born-again Christians and my immediate choice is to move away from that. I didn't understand it for one and because I didn't think it was real for another.** *You do not need to understand it.* **I have my issues with that.** *What are your issues?* **I don't know.**

You do not need to understand the religion. What is to understand is that they are giving you a gift. They are offering you an experience for you to decide how you feel about it. You feel disconnect because what is offered is not in alignment with what you know to be so. This is not about what is real, right, or accurate. There is no right choice. This is about an opportunity for growth, for you to declare where you are and how you feel. It is also an opportunity to embrace those who have offered you this experience and have chosen to participate in your process.

So he is moving away because he doesn't resonate with their message of being born again? *Yes.*

And he should rejoice that he's moving away because he is learning something about himself and he knows that in that learning he is drawing something different to himself?

He is declaring where he is and gaining clarity about what he wants to experience. This clarity will invite opportunities to create change.

So there should be no fear, disappointment, anger or negativity in dealing with people who show us who we are?

When you awaken to the value of the growth they are offering you, you will only feel gratitude for their appearance in your life.

What steps can he take to become more familiar with how these things affect or discourage him?

Is he asking?

I don't know. I'm asking about people in general. How about that? Is that a good way to put it?

Take notice of what appears in your life. Consciously observe your experiences. Ask yourself, what is the growth in this for me? It is always there and the more you consciously focus on it, it will be revealed to you. When you can see the divine beauty of this process, you will welcome it and release all resistance.

Exactly. I like the answer I heard because it didn't let me off the hook. It allowed me to continue to be who I was without feeling like I was failing or not being worthy or most of the things

wrapped up in that. I didn't have to teach them that they're wrong and I'm right. I just...I recognize that I don't agree with that. If you would like to talk about how I feel, that's different. I can go there. I can't always go there without getting angry but...

What are you so angry about?

It seems silly. Sometimes I just get angry at people that try to tell me that the Bible is 100 percent right and that there is only one way to God.

But what is it that you are angry about in this. What is the source of the anger?

It's not so much about me, it's that they are holding so many other people back.

Are they holding them back?

I feel that for people yes.

Everyone chooses the life experience they seek. Everyone. What may appear on the surface as one being held back is actually an opportunity for growth. You need not concern yourself with anyone else. You cannot know the growth of another. Focus on the life experience you desire to create for yourself and you will find it to be a much more pleasurable experience.

I'm getting that but I'm not there yet.

We understand. Know that these people that you disagree with would not be here if you and others were not asking for the experience. It may not be on a conscious level but everyone involved is always a part of the creation. The fact that they exist, the fact that they are here providing this information, is all part of the experience that others seek. We are all part of one divine source and have come forth to interact with one another to offer experiences for growth and expansion.

Okay, let's boil it down here.
1. We're all one.
2. We're all one.

Need I go on?
We appreciate your humor.

The more I learn about this the less there is to know anyway.
When you know that everyone is creating their reality and you fully understand this, there is a release because you understand they are all experiencing their own growth process. And when you can just let go and rejoice that you are all creating, growing and expanding, it is a beautiful thing. It is beautiful even if it appears from your perspective to be something awful. We assure you, it is not.

Intellectually I am getting it but sometimes I forget. In the spiritual realm scheme of things I am so getting it. It's not so much that I don't care anymore it's that….I don't have to care. I just feel like I can just be compassionate, I can just be real, I can just be me, express who I am and not worry about what other people think.
Be yourself. There is no need to worry about what other people think about your life because you are the one who is experiencing it. Others can make their judgments, but they are not experiencing the world as you are. They have a different framework through which they view life and their thoughts about your life will come from that space. You choose what you want for you from the framework of where you are. Allow it to guide you as you grow and expand your own framing.

I'm getting it but you know…sometimes I care.
We understand. Focus that energy on you. The more you care about yourself, desire to expand your perspective for growth, desire to expand your awareness of who you are, the more glorious it will be for you.

I'm getting it. Is there anything specific I can do to share that further? Besides be who I am.
That is the way.

I'm remembering. I'm remembering it all. It only took me all these years to remember it but…
But you are still struggling

Yes I know. I am struggling but...
Just be. Allow yourself to just BE.

I never heard that. Fabulous.

So do you want to talk to us a little bit about some of the things we do on the surface that stop us from getting what we deeply know we want. And some of it is the words we use saying things like "I can't do that, I'm not going to have what I want, I'm having a hard time, I can't let go." How are we affecting our choices with those types of phrases?
In every way.

Are words reality?
It is your thoughts and feelings as you speak these words that make it so.

I am not sure I understand what you are saying there.
Words are words. They have no meaning except what you place upon them. It is your thoughts and feelings about what you are expressing that creates the experience.

So if we are saying I can't stand something, I'm struggling, then we are creating more of that?
Adding power to those words? *Yes, because you are stating these words due to a belief that it is true for you. Therefore, you invite it into your experience as your reality.*

And if we're saying gosh, I'm not going to struggle anymore then we are giving more positive power to that?
We would not say I am not going to struggle anymore. Wouldn't it feel better to say everything is going smoothly in my life? Just stating you are not going to struggle is resistance. It keeps the focus on struggle rather than on what you wish to experience.

It has been said that the universe doesn't hear "not."
*It is your own self who does not hear it. If you focus on what you want, what you wish to experience....***So it's not the surface words...**

It is not the words because you make your jokes, you say things and it is irrelevant because it is what you are feeling at the moment that creates your experience. And if you feel good about what you are expressing, then it doesn't make a difference. And the reason you would feel good is because your thought about it would be good to you. Many times your words can sound positive but if you are still feeling unworthy inside, this is what translates and is created. And this is why people ask why they have not manifested their desires. It is because they were not feeling the words being stated. Their true thought is that it cannot really be for them. And even though they are saying the words, the words are irrelevant if you do not really believe it.

Is there something specific that we can teach to bring about a better world?

The world is already a beautiful place. It is a divine creation. It is for you to awaken to see this. It is not your job to teach others but to offer experiences for growth. You will naturally attract those that will co-create experiences where there is opportunity for growth in it for all participating. Take notice of the growth process and utilize it. In doing so, your view of your world will change.

When I look within and ask myself questions, how will I know that my answer is coming from a good space and not total confusion?

When you feel joy in the answer. When you feel no angst, when you feel the peace and stillness. Whatever the answer, there is purpose in it.

Feeling the joy is a great answer but I find it very difficult to understand. Knowing what and when that is and differentiating it from the self-doubt and all the other things that go on in most people's lives is the true difficulty in knowing sort of when you've arrived at a real answer.

Too many thoughts distract you and block your way. When you are still. When you are calm. When you connect, you will know. You are thinking yourself out of it. Roadblock, roadblock, roadblock. Just relax and allow it to flow in.

So you're telling us to shut up and just listen.

Listen to you.

Is it correct that everything is up to an individual's perspective. For example, someone could have an irritation with someone and those issues could have nothing to do with where I am.

It can only ever be from the framework of where they are. Always. If someone stands out to you in such a manner, this is the moment to ask yourself why. What trigger point is this setting off for me? It has nothing to do with the other person. It never does.

It never does?

It never does. They are simply offering you an experience to help surface your issues, which gives you the opportunity to respond differently and create change. It is an opportunity to release the congested energy pattern that you hold. An irritation will arise as they set off a trigger point for you. When you release the congested energy by choosing to respond differently, what another says or does regarding that specific issue will no longer be a trigger for you. There is growth offered in this shift of energy and change is created in your experience.

Do you think Jacob will grow with Kayite in a way that Kayite will grow with Jacob?

The growth of where we are cannot be compared to where you are. We are here to participate and co-create. Kayite's growth will unfold at her own pace and at her choosing. It is perfection.

Are you always there with Kayite and it is what she chooses? She may choose to tune you out.

If she did not wish for us to be here, we would not be. We are always here because she has embraced us to be an integrated part of her life experience. And she has embraced this process as her life. She is choosing what feels good for her. It is her great joy to participate in this process and to share the message of Jacob with those who seek it.

Is there anything you would like me to know?

We want you to know that it is okay to let go. Let go of concern and worry.

I am surprisingly not worried right now. I feel really good.

Enjoy the process. Embrace all the many experiences that appear in your life. They are tools. Utilize them for your greatest growth and be grateful for these gifts.

End. The tape had reached the end but everyone was so involved in the experience that they did not notice. The conversation continued for quite a while. It was an amazing evening.

10/14

It was a beautiful Sunday morning. We all got dressed up and headed off to the local Unity Church. As I sat in the pew, I could feel Jacob's presence and my whole body went numb. I just sat with them throughout the service enjoying the blissful feeling. The numbness felt very strange, though. Especially when it was time to go and I could barely stand and was stumbling out! Ha! Ha! You should have seen it. It was quite hilarious. But it did feel wonderful. We all laughed and got a kick out of it. We then went out to lunch to enjoy our final meal together before heading to the airport. It had been a delightful trip. I just took it all in. I was enjoying every moment. My return trip home was excellent.

Many Gifts

Many gifts arrive in our lives in the most unexpected ways. They are experiences that offer us the opportunity to grow. And when we consciously choose to look for these gifts, they always reveal themselves. These special packages are always before us. It is up to us to take notice of them, and as we acknowledge them, we are then able to unwrap their magnificence and welcome it into our lives. The following experience is one of many incredible moments that have brought much growth and expansion into my life.

School was closed today for a teacher workday. I was delighted about this because I just returned from my trip to Florida and I am glad to have the whole day to spend with my son. He wanted to go to the McDonald's Playland and so we did. We went at the very busy time during lunch because this is when there are usually a lot of other kids to play with. Xander went outside to play as I happily waited in a long line to order our food. I enjoyed looking at all of the beautiful souls around me.

When I got to the front of the line, I noticed a tall man in the line next to me. He had a daughter who was about my son's age. This man was just receiving his medium-sized cup for the meal he purchased and began to question the size. He stated it was suppose to be the large size Styrofoam cup that was included and not the medium one. The lovely lady behind the counter explained ever so nicely that the medium was indeed what came with the meal. This man began to raise his voice and called for the manager. She too explained the same thing to him.

He was so angry. In that moment, I just wanted to hug him. Love him. I wanted to ask him why he was so angry. What was it that was really occurring in his life that had caused him to lash out at others over a thirty-nine cents difference in price? I thought what could I do to make his world a better place? I wanted to do all of these things, yet I stood there staring like everyone else. This man began yelling that he wasn't about to get ripped off and he wanted his money back. The manager gladly gave him a refund. After he left, I could hear the other customers talking about what a jerk he was. I felt nothing but love for this man. He was angry because he was in pain and expressing it in the only way he knew how.

I wished I had said something. I asked myself why I had not. Perhaps it was because there was a large room full of people and I did not feel he would be receptive in that moment. He wanted to be angry and so he was. And that is okay. I wanted to love him and so I did, even if I was just doing so from standing in my place in line and sending the love his way. I could feel it flowing through. Perhaps he will feel it later. I do not know.

What I do know is that this experience was not about him. It was about me. I have been taking notice of all the things occurring in my life. I take notice that this incident occurred right in front of me. At the moment he was next to me in line. There was indeed purpose for this. It was an opportunity for me to experience growth in this process. In the past few weeks I have felt even more compelled to reach out to others. To love and embrace those I know and those I do not. Although those two have blended together, I am aware there is no one I do not know. Their soul is pouring out to me and I take notice. I see them for who they really are and I am compelled to say, "I love you."

Another wonderful experience was with the beautiful woman behind the counter. As this man walked away yelling, I saw her face of sadness and that this had clearly upset her. And then she turned and looked right at me. I was there with a big smile that was filled with love. She smiled back at me. I wanted to say something to her but it was so busy at the time. I went outside to the Playland for a while and reflected upon what had occurred.

When it was time to leave, there was no one in line. I went up to the counter and leaned in toward this woman. I spoke softly, looked into her eyes, and told her how wonderful she is. I put my hand out for hers and she grabbed hold of it tightly. In those moments, time stood still. We had a soul connection. I told her this man was in pain. She nodded in agreement. She said the Devil had gotten hold of him and that he needed to find God.

I smiled knowing that finding God meant connecting to the God within him. It was all the same. I don't remember exactly what else was said but I do remember how incredible it felt. We spoke a few more words and then I asked her name. Cindy, she said brightly. Then she leaned over the counter to give me a big hug. I told her to keep smiling and enjoy this beautiful day. As I walked out the door I heard her say, "I was blessed by an angel."

So what do I feel in this moment of now? What was the growth in this for me? I am grateful to this man who provided me with the gift of experiencing pure unconditional love. Who offered me the opportunity to see past the surface issues and embrace the divine being he is. I gained clarity about anger and pain, and how it can manifest in many forms.

He also provided me the opportunity to reach out to Cindy and experience the joy of connecting with her. The more I have reached out to others, the more I see how they delightfully and so willingly embrace a perfect stranger. For when they look into my eyes, I know they see me too. I know they know I am not a stranger. I am grateful to Cindy for her gift of allowing my love to flow through and sharing her love, herself, with me. I am ever so grateful as I have perfect clarity that this is the direction of my life. My heart is wide open. I am filled with so much love. I am here for all who seek me. It is joyous and I feel great peace in knowing this is so. I also rejoice in knowing there is an "angel" in all of us.

WTF?

During my trip to Florida, I made a deep connection with my friend Jan. Going into the trip, the thought of anything romantic with him never even crossed my mind. But something shifted for me after he had a conversation with Jacob. I saw him in a way that I had not seen him before, through Jacob's eyes. I felt connected to his soul. I sensed so strongly that there was tremendous opportunity for growth with him and I just knew there was something more for me to experience with him. I went with what I felt. We ended up making mad passionate love that weekend and it was incredible. We had both agreed that we desired only to experience the pleasure and joy in the moment and had no expectations of anything more. It was a spiritual connection and experience that was far beyond just sex. It was a sacred encounter. This felt great to me.

Well, I just recently received a letter from him that many women would have been extremely angry about and most likely walked away from him. In fact, several of my friends that I shared this with were so upset about it and recommended I tell him to go to hell. What had gotten them so upset?

He made the comment that when he first saw me at the airport, he felt great disappointment. Not exactly what you want to hear from the person you just had sex with. But his intention was to share with me his growth as he had always dated smaller-sized women and had the perspective that this is what was attractive and what America thinks is attractive. But after spending time with me, something shifted for him. He also said, "I don't care what America thinks of you, I think you are beautiful." I must admit my only thought in that moment was WTF? It caught me by surprise and threw me way out of alignment.

Although I knew he was trying to tell me how much this experience had changed him and that he was growing, it hit a trigger point for me. He was basically saying that America finds me unattractive. And how does one consider having sex again or any kind of relationship with someone who thought even for a moment that I was a great disappointment? Where do we go from here? I chose to look within, re-align myself and I came to a place of clarity about where he was, where I am, and what this was about.

I could have gotten angry. I could have said hurtful things in return. But what purpose would this have served? I am also aware that everything is a co-creative process so of course, I was a part of it. How could I be angry when I had created it? The only questions to ask myself are why did I create this experience and what is the growth in this for me? For so long I was told my physical body was not good enough. Even at a size four.

For so many years I have chosen to believe it and now it is time for me to let it go. I know how amazing I am inside, that I have much to offer. But when it comes to the outside, I have still held on to some of these beliefs. And so of course I have drawn to me those who will reflect how I have felt about me. I recognized this as an opportunity to create change. In fact, I recall stating earlier that I wished to create change about how I feel about my body and welcomed the experiences to do so. Well, here one is. Clear as day. So I shared all of my feelings about this with him. I shared that it was a trigger point for me. And he shared his. (This was the beginning of the most incredible relationship I have ever experienced.)

Once I was able to acknowledge my trigger point and talk it through, I was able to open myself to see his perspective with greater clarity. His comments weren't about me. It really had nothing at all to do with me. This was about him, where he was and his issues he has held onto. And I was able to feel joy for his process. I was able to see what a huge shift had occurred for him during his experience with me. If I was able to help him open up to see the beauty beyond the physical, I can only rejoice in that. What an incredible moment that was.

He talked things through with me; he was present, did not get angry or defensive, but just listened and was open. He too had desired to create change. We provided each other exactly the experiences we needed to create a shift. So many great things have been coming out of all this stuff that appeared on the surface to be very unpleasant. But it is absolutely beautiful, absolutely amazing. Absolute perfection. I have received many gifts. I am grateful.

Gym Jacob

I am feeling so incredibly joyous today. I saw Gym Jacob this morning. He always puts little pep in my step. His light is always beaming, even when he doesn't feel it, which I find so incredibly interesting. He is just delightful. We talked today and I shared that I was writing a book since I was working on putting it all together at the gym at their computer cafe. I was trying to fill in my childhood. Fill in my feelings about all of these amazing things occurring in my life.

It is a good time for me to do it while Xander is in school. The evenings are so busy with communication and transcribing that I barely have time for my own thoughts of reflections. However, I wasn't feeling a flow to write today so I did my circuit weights instead. I usually do them every other day and this was my off day. But for some reason, I felt drawn to it in that moment. I am glad I went with what I felt because I was so inspired as Gym Jacob and I began to chat about the joys of a workout and how he doesn't always feel like working out (and this is someone who is extremely fit).

I told him I do what I feel. I set no obligations. If I am feeling it, I do it and I enjoy it so much more having given myself the choice. He said he wished everything in life was that simple. I smiled as I said, "It is. It really is. I live my joy everyday. It really can be." I told him this was actually what my book was about. How interesting that he brought this up to discuss. I am fascinated. I knew it all might sound weird to him yet I chose to be me. This is just my life and where I am. If others choose to define it as weird, I embrace that.

I am still intrigued by the connection. What is it about this beautiful being that is drawing me? A beacon of light is the only way to describe him. I cannot say it enough. Well, I think I just answered my own question. Of course I am drawn to the light, but what about the name?

I am still in awe of how this has unfolded. I am looking forward to finding out more about him. I feel like the more I interact with him, the purpose will be revealed. I have not told him about my Jacob and the significance of his name. I am curious to know what he would think about that. I have not felt drawn to do so. I know all is well and I rejoice in allowing it to flow and unfold. I pay attention to what I feel in the moment and I know I will speak and express many things when it feels right to me, feels good to me.

The following day was my regular day to do circuit weights and I did them again to get back on schedule. Gym Jacob was there and I decided to ask him how old he is. "Twenty-five," he said. He just turned twenty-five the previous month. I have found I really don't notice the age of a person as I only see who they are, where they are, and how they choose to experience life. I really just asked out of curiosity. I was curious to know more about this person who draws me. I am most intrigued because ever since my Jacob arrived, it is others who have been drawn to me. Continually showing up in my life. But for some reason, I am feeling a pull from Gym Jacob and I find this interesting.

What is the experience about for me? I asked more about him. His goals? He said he just wants to make enough money to get married and have children. I just thought that was the sweetest thing. He said he is broke and wished he had gotten more of an education. I thought, he has all of these thoughts going on and is still beaming. Just beaming.

I finally shared with him that I have been working with others to help them gain clarity about where they are in their life experience and what it is they want for themselves. This is the only way I knew how to phrase it without freaking him out. I was definitely not feeling it was time to tell him about Jacob. Perhaps one day. Perhaps he is reading this now.

But I did tell him I felt some sort of connection to him and that I have been trying to figure out what it was about him that was standing out to me. Let me be clear there is no romantic interest here. It is nothing like that at all. This is about something deeper. I also stated I understood that what I was saying might sound weird to him. He said, "Just a little." I then explained I am a very open person – an open book – and I love to connect with people and the depth of who they are. He said, "That's cool." I am not sure if he was just trying to be polite or not. Perhaps he was thinking get me the hell out of here. I feel content at sharing what I did. I sense and know there is more to come.

Enjoy the Ride

As I am driving my son home from school he continually asks me when we are going to get home. Sometimes he gets impatient and just wants to be there. At three years old, I get that. I tell him we will get there when we get there. That the trip will take as long as it does and that getting upset about it will not change the time frame. So I say to him, why not enjoy the ride? You have a choice. You can choose to be upset and cranky the whole way home or you can choose to enjoy all that is present along the way. Either way, it will still take as long as it does. So how do you choose to experience it? We are driving through the mountains with gorgeous trees, beautiful clouds in the sky, so much beauty to take in. We talk about these things and I let him know that it is not about where we are going. It is about enjoying the moment of now. So enjoy the ride. Enjoy all of it. He said, "Okay, Mommy. I love this ride."

Notes

I have noticed that I have come to such a deep understanding of people. I cannot even begin to tell you the love I feel for all. This has truly been the most incredible experience of my life. It is as if I talk with someone and know his or her soul. It is so clear. All the other stuff in the way just dissipates and I only see who the person really is. It is beautiful.

Jacob Types

I am intrigued by this new experience I am having with Jacob flowing through as I just sit here at the computer. They joined me and we began typing the conversation directly. Wow, things are really progressing quickly with my own interaction with them. It is exciting. I was laughing at Jacob as I saw spelling errors. I told them jokingly they couldn't type. They laughed because they said that I was the one typing; they were just providing the dialogue. It was really funny. This is very surreal, yet normal. How can that be? Yet, so it is. This is my life.

10/16

In a conversation with a friend, he told me Jacob said there is so much love waiting for him. Do you think they have any GPS coordinates he asked jokingly?

My reply: The GPS coordinates all lead back to you. I am sure that isn't much help at the moment but it is true. Your intellectual side is beautiful and has served great purpose for you but it can create a blockage to the inner self because you want to define things rather than allow them to just be. Can you be still and envision a blank slate in your mind? It is really a non-focus. No thought. Just be. Be still. Allow yourself to zone in. Listen to the inner voice. It has always been there. Communicating. Calling you. It will guide you.

I have never been someone in my head. I have always made decisions based on my emotions and how I felt. People thought

I was crazy that I didn't require facts, only feelings. I began to doubt myself because I allowed others' perspectives of me to affect me. Now I am clear I knew what I was doing all along. I was guiding myself.

Divine Oneness

Today I witnessed the most beautiful blue sky I have ever seen. The clouds were so white that the contrast against the sky was amazing. The clouds swirled all across the sky. It was absolutely gorgeous. It brought tears to my eyes. If you have the desire to connect with you and the oneness with all, I recommend taking a look up. Just look up at the sky with new eyes, from the perspective that we are all one with everything. We are a part of this magnificence.

10/17

Before the retreat I only had my sister to discuss spirituality with. I longed to know others like me. Who would understand me? The friendships I had before felt very superficial to me because there was no depth. People would not let me in. They only showed me what they wanted me to see. And I felt like I couldn't fully be myself either. (Of course, I understand I created this and that this was only my perspective.) It was very hard for me. I am ever so grateful to have the most amazing friends in my life now who know all of me. I hold nothing back. I love to just be me. It is glorious.

My Mother

Here I am experiencing this incredible journey with Jacob and I have yet to share it with my own mother. My sister was one of the first people I shared this with. I finally felt it was the right moment to share Jacob with my mom. This was the email I sent her:

Hi Mom,

I wanted to fill you in on what has been going on in my life. I thought I would write this and give you time to digest it all. It is pretty incredible and it has been a whirlwind of things. Ever since I left my relationship and moved, I have just been fully living my joy. Feeling right on course with myself.

On the eve of my birthday I was in the tub doing a meditation as always, asking to communicate with those who seek enlightenment through my process. I had done this meditation for about three months, but on that evening, I had a two-hour conversation with a group of entities that go by the name of Jacob. They let me know that they were here to stay. There is much for us to experience together. I knew this was my path. What I had greatly desired. They had been waiting for me all along. Waiting for me to shift into a matching vibration that allowed them to flow through. It has only been a month but it feels like a lifetime that they have been with me.

My inner circle of friends are now all very used to Kayite/Jacob. They find it surprisingly normal. Clearly I am with the right group. It all unfolded so beautifully. I have pretty much spent almost every night doing sessions or typing them up. (I am looking into the voice recognition software.) I have been writing a lot about my experiences and along with all of the Jacob Material, I am putting together a wonderful book about my journey.

The book is transforming before me. I look forward to sharing it with all those who seek it. I am thrilled. I have had several one-on-one sessions with people where I felt the most incredible vibrations I cannot even describe. During my trip to Florida, Jacob flowed through while my three friends asked questions for hours. It didn't seem that long for me.

I love interaction with others and best of all, I now see others through Jacob's eyes. I have no judgments, only observations. I feel nothing but pure unconditional love for all. It is just incredible. We are blended now as much of their knowledge and deep understanding remains with me even when they are not directly coming through. I just finally stepped into the life that had been awaiting me. When I opened myself up, all of my desires flowed through. My whole life changed. Everything I have wanted has appeared in my life almost all at once. Much more is on its way. The title of my book is *Awakening to the Extraordinary YOU*.

I have experienced so much growth and expansion. The sheer joy and love that flows through me is the most amazing thing I have ever felt. It is all perfection. I see the beauty in everything. I look at the sky every day and take it in. I take notice of everything and every person I encounter. Butterflies follow me. I see them everyday now. Sometimes landing on me. Well, there is so much more but this is the gist of it. I am ecstatic to finally be living the life that I always knew on some level was there for me. It has been an incredible journey and this is just the beginning.

I look forward to talking with you more about this and to hear your thoughts.

Who's My Jerry?

People keep asking me who is my "Jerry." They are referring to Jerry Hicks, husband of Esther who communicates with Abraham. Jerry had many questions to ask Abraham so others want to know who will be the one to ask Jacob all the questions in this beginning stage for me? I have no idea but a "Jerry" sounds lovely at some point. Honestly, right now I am greatly enjoying my space. I am enjoying the experience of living on my own for the very first time. My desires are ever-changing; I know that should I come to a place where I desire a life mate to participate in this process, that I will create it to be. I know that he will arrive at the perfect moment.

So a life mate relationship, yes, just not marriage. Marriage is no longer relevant to my life experience as I choose to live in the now and allow my relationships to flow as they will. What is interesting is that I never felt so lonely as I did in all the years of my marriage, and now that I am living alone, I have never felt so connected to everyone and every thing. For now, I rejoice in the beautiful flow of my life experience. I am content to be a free spirit, expressing my love to whomever I choose. It has been very freeing. So who will ask the questions then? Perhaps it will be you!

Tidbits from Xander

We were having dinner at a restaurant and my son just looked up at me and said "Thank you." I asked him what it was he was thanking me for. He said "For all the love." What a joy he is.

Breaking the Dam

In this moment I am feeling in awe of my own life. It has just been so incredible. I feel I am settling into the comfort of Jacob. Just being used to the constant connection. I love them so much and I am ever so grateful they are here. I am grateful that we are on this journey together and that I am experiencing, growing and expanding. I am excited about what the future holds as I enjoy the moment of now.

As I am sitting here thinking loving thoughts of Jacob, I can feel their presence come through. Since they are here, I will ask if they have anything they would like to share.

When you release resistance and embrace what is, you will break the dam and allow the joy to flow through you. The energy you choose to hold onto from past experiences congests and blocks the flow of your natural well-being. Over many years you have built a dam. The congested energy then manifests into physical and mental dis-ease. As you choose to create change, experiences will appear in your life that will set off your trigger points. You can continue to allow them to activate your anger, resentment, pain, fear, or you can choose to acknowledge them as an opportunity to shift the energy. As you recognize and embrace these moments as a trigger point for you, a shift begins. And walking through the experience with another can completely shift your vibration and clear the congested energy. If an experience appears in your life that has you asking – why did this show up again? Know that this is a grand opportunity to break the dam. Embrace the experience for the gift that it is.

Soul Whisperer?

I took Xander to the Children's Museum today. He was playing with a train set when another little boy and his grandmother came over to join us. As the kids were happily playing together, this lovely woman sat down in the chair in next to me. She then began to share with me that her name is Doreen, she is 72 years old and watching her grandkids while her daughter is away for four days. She just started talking to me as if she had known me for years. She was sharing how stressed and overwhelmed she was and began to share her current life situation.

I had a moment where I thought – do I have a sign that says share your life story with me? I say this in the most joyous way as I thought it was delightful and I have noticed that more people are coming up to me in this manner. I felt like the Ghost Whisperer, only with living people. Like she somehow knew to come talk to me. Knew that I was someone who would embrace her. Knew that I was someone that would listen, someone that would be fully present with her. And of course, this was another opportunity for growth.

I had just sent my mother the email to tell her all about Jacob the night before. She had told me she looked forward to talking to me more about it but as of yet, nothing has transpired.

Doreen began to ask a lot of questions about my mother. I thought, oh, this is interesting. She wanted to know if my mother watches Xander while I am away. The answer is no. She doesn't watch him. We barely visit. We live two hours apart but I am willing to make the drive. I desire to know her and be a part of her life. My mother and I are just not connecting at this point in this moment. I hold the intention to create change in this and I am open to experiences that will help facilitate this process.

Doreen had a similar situation with her daughter, only she said that she is the open book and wants to be more of a part of her daughter's life. We talked for two hours and it was just amazing. She finally had to leave to pick up the other grandkids from school. She said she did not want to go as she so enjoyed our conversation.

I gave her a huge hug good-bye and told her what a joy she is and how delightful it was to speak with her. She had tears in her eyes. It had clearly been a long time since anyone told her this. She said she was leaving feeling total peace. I, too, was feeling great joy in this interaction and great peace with my own mother as well. Thank you for this gift, Doreen. What a great day this has been.

I did finally hear from my mother. She was happy for me and excited for my process. And although we did not talk much about Jacob, it was wonderful to share where I am and what is going on in my life. I would very much like to connect with her and I know it will all unfold in the perfect moment.

I love her and I honor where she is. Our relationship now is just what we are currently creating together. I am aware that we are not meeting up at a vibrational level and that as we grow, things can shift for us at any moment to connect. I am open. I know there is much growth to be offered in my experiences with her and I welcome it. I allow it all to flow with ease and unfold, as it will. I am enjoying the process.

Late Night Calls

Ever since "the incident" with Jan, as we like to call it, we have been experiencing the most wonderful conversations several nights a week. We talk and share for hours. I could still sense very strongly that there was more for us to experience together. How we handled the previous situation told me a lot about what might be possible for us. I am open to this experience with him. I choose to be in the moment as I jump along for the ride, moment-to-moment. We will see where it takes us.

Jacob at Red Lobster?

I met a friend for dinner at Red Lobster. I ordered a grilled cheese. Those who know me know that I love grilled cheese sandwiches. My grandmother used to make them when I was a kid and they hold a special memory for me. I get them pretty much everywhere I go. My friend and I were sitting in a booth and began a lovely conversation. She started sharing about where she was, her confusion, and began to ask many questions. Once again, I could feel Jacob coming through. I let go and just like that, my friend was having a conversation with Jacob right at the dinner table at Red Lobster. It was great! After dinner, we went to see a movie at Unity "10 Questions for the Dalai Lama." It was a fantastic evening.

10/20
I went Swing Dancing tonight with a friend of mine. After having so much fun in Florida, we decided to look for a local dance group here. It was a great time. Again, they offered a lesson beforehand so I could at least have some idea of what to do. At the dance in Florida we learned East Coast Swing but this time we were learning West Coast Swing, which I found a bit harder to grasp. I was only able to dance a little this time but my intention was to enjoy myself and meet some new people. And that I did!

Evolving with Jacob

My experience with Jacob coming through is always different. There is head nodding and many times a smile on my face as I feel the sheer bliss of them. If I am lying down on the bed I may feel vibrations all over. It has also varied depending on whom they are interacting with and whether I am sitting up, in the recliner or in bed. It is progressing. Right now I keep my eyes closed throughout because that enables me to really let go and allow them to flow. I have no doubt that I will get to the point where my eyes will be open and it will not affect the connection. That is my own limitation for me to shift beyond.

Chuck E. Cheese Party Time

Today I drove to Richmond to celebrate my son's fourth birthday at Chuck E. Cheese. My former husband was there along with my sister, brother-in-law, nephews and my mother and stepfather. The kids had the best time. It was such a joy to watch them play, laugh and be silly. I loved to see the many smiles that appeared on their cute little faces. We all sat at a large booth and had some really wonderful conversations. It was a great day!

10/21
I would like to have greater clarity about a situation in which a woman is overspending and it is greatly affecting the family. Doesn't she have a responsibility to the children involved? They are helpless. That doesn't seem right.

Every experience is a co-creative process. We understand that from the perspective of where you are, you think that these choices do not serve them. We can assure you that children are never without a choice for they have already chosen. The best interest of children is the same for all humans. Experiencing, growing and expanding. This is the purpose. They are making their choices as they experience and participate in that process even if it appears from your perspective that they are helpless. We tell you that they are not. They have indeed agreed to all of it and their soul welcomes the experience. They seek the experience. This woman is actually providing a wonderful gift to her children. These experiences offer a foundation for growth.

I can relate to this from my own childhood experience – the neglect and unworthiness I felt. Our chaotic family life would have looked pretty awful to outsiders. It was awful to me at the time. But now being where I am, knowing what I know, I am grateful for all of it. I am certain, absolutely clear that I chose it. Those experiences were so important to my growth process.

They have all brought me to this moment of now – the most extraordinary life I could ever imagine. And it is so much more glorious to experience where I am now having experienced the contrast of it. And if I could do it all over, I wouldn't change a thing. It is all perfection. It is beautiful. My mother has given me tremendous gifts and I thank her for choosing to be a part of my process. And my father, as angry as he was, perhaps gave me some of the greatest gifts and I thank him for choosing to be a part of my process.

The Communication Process

I was recently asked the following questions about the communication process:

How does Jacob speak through you? Is it a voice coming out of your mouth? Does it sound male or female like and is it different from your voice? Are you conscious of what Jacob is saying or only after you listen to the tape? This process fascinates me and this is why I am asking.

My reply: It is my voice that is speaking. I am almost in a trance-like state and information is being downloaded as I interpret and the words come out. I don't really know what is said until it is flowing out. I am aware of what is being said at the time but I don't always remember everything. I am present but in a very relaxed state. It is very blissful. I have found that when I play back the tape, I am always in amazement at what has flowed through. Many times during a session I might feel like I got some good stuff. But then I play the tape back and I think wow, this is really incredible stuff here. It is always way better than I remember.

They are using my vocabulary or I am using mine to decipher theirs? Of course, there are similarities in us as we are blended as one. I will use the words magnificent and tremendous and things like that because it is the only way I know how to interpret what they are saying when it is of great magnitude. Also, I have begun to speak more in terms that they have used as I am changing with them as well. It really is a blending, an integration. That's the only way I can describe it. We are one and so, of course, there will be similarities as we have come together. I know that as I do this over time, it will grow.

In just the past month, I have already come a long way. When they first spoke, there were many pauses, as they would scan for a word or two at a time. Now they just speak more freely and flowing but it still may be shorter in length. I have noticed that the length and flow of responses is increasing. I can only imagine where this will take me in another month or two, or a year.

It is a learning process for me as well and I am adjusting to them as I become more comfortable and come to a greater understanding of it all. As far as the sound of the voice, I am honestly not sure. I do believe the tone changes but it is hard for me to tell from where I am. There is definitely a distinctive difference between them and myself. No doubt about that. It may not be as much in the voice as it is in their presence and how they interact. I am still in awe of my own life. Really. And this is just the beginning. Where to next? I don't know, but I am going to enjoy the ride.

Question: If I understood you right you are not consciously translating a voiceless voice but instead Jacob is using your vocal cords to speak and it is as if you are listening to another voice and can hear it but don't remember it very well until you listen to the recording? Is that it? Does the voice sound masculine, feminine or androgynous? Is it is loud or soft?

My Reply: I am laughing now. It is not always so easy to explain how Jacob integrates. It is not like I imagined it would be. It is my voice. I am speaking but the information is coming through and I speak it right at that moment. The interpretation is occurring in that moment and out it is coming and it is happening so fast that I am hearing it then, even though I am also interpreting too. I am allowing the flow to occur. The information is there. It is almost like they are pushing it out of me. There have been times where I resisted saying something that I knew they wanted me to. Like when my Tuesday night conference group went around and asked everybody about their life purpose, Jacob wanted me to say that I am here to guide others to a higher consciousness. I was very resistant to that because it was so big that it was a bit overwhelming. It was just so soon and I was still adjusting to the magnitude of it all. Yet they were practically forcing it out of me and I knew it to be so. And so, out it came. And of course, my group embraced it.

I spoke to a friend today and decided to ask her about her experience with Jacob. What was it like from her perspective? She said there was a different tone in my voice. It is a tone of calmness and certainty when they speak. She said that she feels the difference in the energy between when they are present and when it is just me. The voice is a soft voice, most of the time.

I know that the voice is soft right now because I am adjusting to all that is occurring and a lot of times I feel heaviness and it can be hard to get the breathe out. At times they get very passionate and then they get loud. I feel it when it is happening and also hear it on the tape. I feel their tremendous passion for wanting us to know just how magnificent we really are. It is the most glorious feeling. So to sum it up, it is my voice and I am hearing my voice but I know that the intense energy presence and information flowing through me is not me. I don't know if this is any clearer. (Can we all just have a good laugh now?)

10/23
Why don't people handle negative replies well on these online dating sites? Some people just don't respond and I think that's rude.

No one wants to feel rejected. They handle it in this manner because they do not want to hurt another's feelings, as they know that they do not want to experience rejection themselves. Many take it all so personally. It is not a personal thing. Someone who appears to be rejecting you has nothing to do with you and everything to do with where they are in their life and it is not a match to you. If you all understand this, no one would feel rejection because they would know it is not about them. They would actually feel grateful to easily clear out what is not a match. As they feel this rejection, they feel something is wrong with them. They question themselves, have doubts, and it is unpleasant. And if they are the ones doing the rejection, they see it in the same manner. They do not wish another to feel badly as they know they would.

So instead, they take the route of silence that feels the least hurtful to them. Their silence is their way of showing compassion, their way of trying to handle it in the most polite and gentle manner. We understand where you are but not everyone has had your experiences that have led you to believe that it is courteous to respond. You are doing what feels best to you. They are doing what feels best to them. What you consider rudeness is really their way of trying to be kind. Can you see this? They are doing the best they can. Embrace them.

I have been attracting the type of women that I do not consciously seek. The last person was really boring. It was only that one time though. I am not aware of why I might be doing this but I can't be a good judge of that. Are there any past life issues?

You don't need to be the judge of that. Your life is the example of it. Those who have been manifested in your life are all your creation. Just look to those experiences and they will tell you exactly where you are. As you continue to draw these women into your life that are not a match to what you think you are wanting, this is the moment to ask yourself – why am I drawing this? It is clear it is always you. Always. Look within. This is part of the process. You wield the power. You need not worry about past life issues. They are irrelevant. The only moment is the moment of now.

What are you choosing for you in this moment? What are you choosing to experience? You attracted what you consider to be a boring person but you state it was only this one time. This one time is the most recent time and the best indicator of where you are now. Look within yourself to know why you are creating this. You have all of the answers. You need not seek it outside of yourself. Everything is within you. As you gain greater clarity about what these experiences are offering you, you can begin to respond differently to create a shift. It is you that is creating this and it is also you that can change it.

What can I do?

Begin with love of self. How do you feel about you?

Loving the self almost comes across as selfish. How do you explain that you are not in love with them but the feeling of love of self? How does one explain that?

It is not something that needs explaining. It is simply for you to know and understand as you are seeking this. There is nothing wrong with being selfish. Everything is about the self. Always. Everything. EVERYTHING. (yes, they are speaking loudly, passionately) ALWAYS about the self.

Kayite has great love for you. You know this. But do you know that when she speaks this it is because she has great love of herself. She loves how she feels when she is interacting with you. This is the sheer joy that she feels. This is that love but there is no need for her to tell you. There is no need to tell you because it is irrelevant. Her love for you is still expressed. When you are loving of yourself so much that you overflow with that love, it is then expanded to all in your presence. In essence, Kayite is indeed loving you and expanding the love of self to you, which you can indeed feel. Are you following us here? There is still a giving of love but the love always starts with the self first. And because you are love, the giving and receiving of love is simply the sharing of the essence of you.

Are there any messages from my mother or father?

Your mother and father want the same things for you as we do. For you to experience, grow and expand where you are. This is the purpose of life. We are here to guide you to the life that is awaiting you. The life you have been asking and seeking to experience.

Do we have specific themes or plans? What did I choose on the spiritual plane?

Yes, many choose paths in which they want to experience before they come into the physical form. But understand that you have both pre-choice and in the moment choice. That you are continually choosing in every moment. A path is simply a guideline. As you arrive here and begin to experience this world, your desires are ever changing based on your experiences. Your source will remind you of where you wanted to go, but you are always free to choose in the moment what you wish to experience. It is always your choice. It is not a set thing. Kayite chose this path before she came but she also has a choice in this moment of now. She can choose to continue with this process or not. She is choosing in this moment to continue because it feels so wonderful to her to do so. As she has lined up with what she has already chosen, she feels the pure elation of it. You are choosing in every moment, creating your life, creating, experiencing, expressing, growing, expanding, and this is what is occurring. You have a general theme of what you wish to experience but knowing it is......not so important because you are being led there by you. And we.......would not deny you the joy of the experience along the way by telling you your path. This is your journey. It is the experience that you seek to explore this and the growth and expansion that comes with the journey of it all. This IS what you are seeking. Enjoy the experience. Enjoy the journey.

I wasn't sure if this question was for Jacob or myself and so I will defer to them:

With me, you are singing to the choir. But the time will come when you will be talking to skeptics. How will this be handled? How will you prove yourself? Can you tell them something no one else knows like a psychic?

We are only here for those who seek us. We are here to observe and guide you back to you. We are not here to convince anyone of anything. We are here to offer guidance and everyone is always free to choose. Free to choose to accept the message we share or not. Free to choose to look within or not. But if we are interacting with them, on some level, they have indeed been asking. The proof is not in telling them something about themselves. The proof is in their awakening to their own life experience. As you awaken to the divine being that you are, you will know. You will feel it. It is absolute. There can be no substitute. And if one is requiring proof outside of their self, then they are not in a space to look within and awaken. It is not necessary for them to believe in Jacob. Only themselves. Kayite has asked many questions regarding this and the responsibility she has felt at times for it all. We have assured her that all is flowing to perfection and that no one being is responsible as we are all co-creating here.

Gym Jacob Revealed

Since travel was recently on my mind, when I talked to Gym Jacob today, I asked him if he would rather go to Europe or on an African safari. I have been thinking about these trips for myself and just curious what he would say. I had already decided I wanted to go to Africa. Well, he has already been to Europe and said an African safari would be a fun adventure. And then, like a lightning bolt, the thought popped into my head to ask him to go with me. And so I did. Is this crazy or what? What an adventure that would be! To take off to a place that just a few months ago, I never thought I would have ever seen. And to go with someone I barely know yet feel I know his soul and know I would have the absolute time of my life.

Well, the look on his face was priceless! He said, "Um, well, that would be nice but it doesn't quite fit in with my current life plan." It was so fantastic. I knew in that moment, the growth experience he was to offer me had been fulfilled. This wasn't about his response. This was about me going for it, doing something fun, exciting, and on a whim. It was wonderful to not just think about it, but experience the knowing that I could do this. So although he said no, I rejoice in the freedom I have allowed myself to just go for it and that is wonderful.

And had he said yes, I was indeed ready to go off on an adventure, just like that. This was something that I never even thought possible before. And now, I know I have expanded beyond those limitations and am open to many new possibilities. This was a huge gift for me. I know this all unfolded perfectly and that many adventures await me. I rejoice in knowing this is so. I felt the energy dissipate with him and knew that our interaction was complete. The purpose had been served. It is so interesting to feel it so clearly. I am really paying attention to that as I continue to develop a greater awareness of my energy connections with others. Thank you, Gym Jacob, for shining your light for me.

An Interesting Offer

We finally received an offer on our house. With everything the buyers were requesting, the offer was essentially $27,000 less than the asking price and they wanted to close the end of December. With our financial situation of not knowing how we were going to be able to pay our bills the following month of November, you would think we might have felt we had no choice but to accept it. Regardless of what the situation appeared to be, I still felt nothing but peace. Jacob had told me that all was perfection and that I did not need to concern myself. We made a counter offer which was full price with closing costs. They again came back very low. My former husband was nervous and stressed about it. He thought, what if they walk away and we end up unable to pay our bills? I asked him to please trust in me. We came up with a figure that felt good to us and told our agent to please let them know that it was our final offer. This was it and they could take it or leave it. I asked my former husband to go to a peaceful place, to just envision the contract being accepted and that all would go smoothly. We sent it off and I gave it no further thought, as we would wait for a response.

10/24
I am still really struggling with a woman at work. She wants things her way. I know this is all about me but I don't know why I am drawing this or how to go about changing it. What can I do?
You desire control, control of your life. Control of what is going on in your world. Let go of trying to control things outside of yourself. Your control is within you and how you choose to respond and experience this interaction. What is the growth in this experience for you? Embrace it as an opportunity to create change. Offering a different response can shift the energy. Utilize what is showing up for you to gain greater clarity about where you are.

Why is there so much drama?
The drama allows you to stay where you are. You get caught up in it. You stay in it and focus on it. And as long as you are focused on the drama, you do not have to focus on yourself. This may be hard at times to look within and really decide where it is you want to go with the joy. How do I really live the spiritual life that I've wanted? It is so easy to focus on the drama because then you do not have to pay attention to everything else that is going on in your life. You can forget...get lost in the moment.

And you can choose in this moment to let it go. Let it be. Open the door to the joy. Open it. Envision it. Open the door and step in and leave all the rest behind. You need not take it with you – all the drama, all the craziness, all the control. You have total control of your own life, your own experience, what you create in it. There is no control over another, over things, over work. This is all irrelevant. It only gives the illusion of some sort of security, some sort of comfort or safety in where you are. It is not the reality of who you are. If you choose to step into the joy, you will not be seeking to feel better by controlling outside circumstances. Instead of beating yourself up and feeling frustrated, can you open yourself to enjoying this experience for all that it has to offer you, all the growth and expansion? It IS that which you seek. Can you rejoice in knowing this is so?

I hear you but where exactly do I start? How do I open the so-called door? What do I do?

The focus on this person only creates more disharmony. If you were to take all the attention and focus off of her and place that focus onto you and consciously choose what you want to experience, you will have an entirely different outcome without actually having to "do" anything. This is opening the door. In those moments of frustration, ask yourself what you really wish to experience in that moment. When you look to the source of what this is about for you, you can create change in your experience. It is not about the other person. They are just showing up to participate and facilitate your process.

10/25
Why has a man from a previous relationship entered my life again? Will he continue to be a part of my spiritual evolution? Can I remain friends with him without compromising my integrity? Please provide clarity for me around my relationship with him as it relates to his marriage and family. What is this connection we have all about?

Every individual who enters your life is part of your evolution, a part of your growth and expansion. Each and every being who enters your life, even for a moment, is part of this process. In every moment it is up to you to decide whether they serve your growth or not, whether they are flowing with you or not. It is ever changing. It is a possibility and up to you to decide which avenue you wish to take for the desired experience you are choosing in the moment.

Whether your friendship remains without compromising your integrity is entirely up to your perspective. Your experience is a result of how you view the situation from the framework of where you currently are. Look within. How do you feel about this situation? There is nothing we can tell you because it is all about how YOU feel. It is important for you to feel good about what you are experiencing and feeling good is determined by you.

This is your experience. What is the growth in this for you? How do you choose to experience this? What you feel would fit the integrity outline for you is dependent upon how you choose to define this. That definition is different for everyone and is based on their current framing. As you come to know and understand more about where you are in your current frame, you can then begin to have a greater understanding of yourself and your world and begin to expand your framing while having a conscious awareness of it.

There is a new man who has entered my life. For what reason is this? I am seeking clarity around how much of myself I may safely share with him. Is there something about him that I am not seeing but would be wise to look at? If so, what is it?

He has entered your life for the same reason all beings enter your life. To be a part of your growth process, to offer you an experience for growth and expansion. This is an opportunity for you to express yourself......that which you are afraid of.....that which you are uncomfortable with.....that which you are feeling within you, allow yourself to go there. This is a process.

He is providing an opportunity for you to face and walk through some of the issues that have surfaced for you, to move beyond your current limitations. This is what you have been wanting and this experience was called forth by you. You can choose to utilize this opportunity in whatever way you wish. There is no set experience that must be encountered with this person.

You come together as desires for an experience match up with your wanting and their wanting and a co-creative process begins. And it is continually changing. As you experience, as things shift, so does what you are wanting. It is a continual process of creating that which you want to experience in the moment. Allow it to flow with ease.

What is going on with my friendships? Can you confirm for me the nature of the seeming transitions?

You have already stated they are transitions. You feel these transitions occurring. Friendships, like all relationships, transition. Some continue to flow together and some do not. You will know if you are flowing or not. And those that you are not flowing with will naturally become distant. And those who are flowing with you, you feel and know they are with you. Look to your feelings about these relationships, these friendships? What is it that you feel?

Allow these relationships to flow in and out of your life freely. Allow them to be as they are. They serve the purpose of growth and once that growth has been fulfilled, they no longer serve your process. Some may offer one experience, others many. As your relationships transition, it will be a natural process. You do not need to focus so much about what is going on with them. Just recognize their gifts of growth and allow them to be. They will either flow with you or dissipate. Either way, it is divine. It has all served a purpose. And you can embrace and rejoice in that.

I feel that I am on the verge of a magnificent breakthrough. How can I continue to be open to this new adventure? How do I stay focused, positive and ready for it all? Is it wise for me to create or maintain some steady/regular job? Of course, my regular job has not yielded great results financially, though it is fun.

You stay open to this new adventure by knowing that it is so, knowing that it is happening, knowing that it is occurring, knowing that it is already in the process, in the works and that it is unfolding right before you. It is like a rolling out of the red carpet for you to step onto and into this life. Take notice of what appears in your life. Know this process is in the works and waiting for you.

The energy is in motion and you can step into it and experience all that you have desired when you consciously choose to be aware of your creations. You are creating your life experience. You can create a steady job but is not necessary. If the regular job brings you joy, or gives you comfort in allowing you to be in the space where you are, if it helps you to feel better about where you are then this is always a great place to be. There is nothing you should be doing. It is only a choice of whether or not you wish to experience it. Fun is good.

I feel that I just want to soar into writing more and more and more...is this a good thing? Should I try to balance the writing with other things?

You FEEL that you just want to soar into writing. We do believe you have answered your own question here. If you are wanting to soar, if you are feeling this exhilaration of wanting to soar into writing, then that is source guiding you. Following your desires, your passions, fully and completely, will allow your creations to manifest. Balance is not required, as that is based on your perspective. Everything is always in perfect harmony. If you love the experience of writing, then write.

What causes one person to "awaken" and choose to live consciously and not another? For example, why would I choose to dig for spiritual truths and not my husband? Are we not on similar paths? Does his search only appear different than mine? Is every soul desiring this awakening?

It is not about an awakening. An awakening is here yes, because there is a collective consciousness that is creating it. A large collective that has been seeking and desiring this. But you are all here for one purpose only. Expansion. This occurs with any path you choose. All experiences offer growth. It is not about getting to an awakening. Not every individual should experience this. It is not about looking at another and wondering why they are not wanting this or why they are not experiencing this.

Every beings life experience is about growth and expansion. Choosing to awaken is simply another choice. As this collective is experiencing an awakening and others bear witness to this, many will desire this experience as well and either unconsciously or consciously choose to create it in their life. It is because you desire to experience this that it has appeared in your life. This serves great purpose for you but may not for another. For another, they are just choosing to experience something different. It is still growth for them in where they are. It is just a different path, a different choice and none is better than another.

Who makes the invitation for a human being to know these most magnificent truths? Why does one seek their highest truth and not another?

It is not about seeking your highest truth. It is about the experience of what that is from where you are and the growth in the process. The opportunities for growth appear in many forms and are different for everyone. This is about you now. Only you. You need not worry about anyone else. It is irrelevant whether anyone else appears to be awakening or seeking their highest truth. This is about your life experience, this very moment. What is it you that are choosing for you? Focus on what you are creating and what it is that you seek. It is in this journey that a greater understanding of self and awareness of who you are awaits.

Tidbits from Xander

"Mommy, I love you more than rocks," Xander said. "You do?" I said. "Yes, more than all the rocks in the Universe," he said. "Well, that's a lot of love!" I replied.

Off to Asheville

I leave this morning for Asheville, North Carolina. I am attending a workshop on the twenty-seventh with Abraham, these divine beings channeled by Esther Hicks. I am looking forward to staying with a friend from my retreat and getting a chance to catch up with her. We are also planning to re-unite with two other friends tomorrow. I am excited about this adventure.

I arrived at my friend's house after a five and one-half hour drive through the mountains. It was an absolutely splendid drive. I enjoyed taking in all of the beauty before me. I left early and got in at 2:00 this afternoon. We talked and laughed all day. It was fantastic. We went to a great Italian restaurant for dinner and then headed back to her house for more chat. She did speak with Jacob at the end of the evening. I have no idea how long the conversation lasted. It felt like a while. We need to get up at 6:00 a.m. to be ready for the workshop tomorrow. Or should I say later today as it is now 1:00 in the morning. How did that happen? I am off to bed. This has been a wonderful day!

10/26
Can you tell me if I'm getting closer or further away from where I am supposed to be?
You are not supposed to be anywhere. It is about embracing where you are in this moment of now. Rejoice in where you are. It is perfection.

Then can you tell me why I feel like I am supposed to be someplace?
This feeling is a result of everything that is going on around you. Paying attention to others that hold the idea that you are supposed to be somewhere, get somewhere, do something. It is only about you choosing what you wish to experience, and choosing to fully embrace this in every moment. It is not about getting anywhere. You are already there. It is for you to recognize this. Every experience is of your choosing and you will continue to choose another and then another and another. It is never ending. So you will never get there because there is always another "there" to experience. And when you realize this, you can begin to embrace where you are and enjoy the process. You are always "there" in every moment. Wherever that is for you.

Can you explain to me why I seem to make choices that are not to my benefit?
What choices have you made that you feel are not beneficial?

When I sever my connections to people that I care about. When I sever my connections to spirit. When I isolate myself. When I dwell in a depressive state instead of looking toward the positive.
You are just disconnected from who you are. Forgotten how magnificent you are. Allow yourself to be where you are. And from this space choose where you want to go. Then you can begin to create something new for your life experience. The same experiences will continue to appear

in your life to give you the opportunity to respond differently. As you do, a shift will occur and you will no longer draw the experience as the growth in that process would have been fulfilled. Yet you have continued to respond in the same manner and therefore, continue to create the same experience. Why do you think you have continued to choose this for your self?

Well, I am not sure. It does not seem like a conscious choice and yet it appears to be a repeating pattern.

You do not have to be consciously aware. On some level, you are always choosing. You are always choosing as it is being created in your life and you are creating all it. As you choose to become more aware of what you are creating, you will then make a conscious choice to create something different. And this is where you look within, look within yourself to really connect with you and that which you are wanting. As you consciously become aware of what you continually manifest in your life and recognize the parts that are what you no longer wish to experience, you can then begin to create change. By choosing something different. Consciously choosing a different experience.

So, awareness is a large part of the process?

It is the entire part of the process. It is awareness of who you are. When you know the divine being that you are, you can make choices from this space. And know that you are creating everything. And that when you acknowledge that you have created all that has transpired in your life, all of the seemingly unpleasant things, you then wield the power to create change and can begin to create the joy in your life. The power is within you.

I have had many people tell me that I need to take leap of faith and yet I am very resistant to that idea. Part of my resistance is taking leaps of faith in the past and ending up falling and not having a success with it.

Well you don't need to just jump off the cliff. If you are jumping off the cliff not sure if your parachute will open, that's not a place that you want to be. You want to be in a place that feels good to you. So you pick a place to start. Just a little at a time. And begin to open yourself up to this new world that is awaiting you. As you state what you desire to experience, opportunities will arise for you to shift your beliefs about where you are, shift your perspective, and release congested energy. You then open the flow for that which you desire to appear in your life.

So you're saying that the leap of faith is actually many small steps? Yes **Oh, I like that.** *And it is different based on the each individual's life experience. Some can take larger steps and some smaller but it is all within their comfort zone. It is what is feeling good to them and only they can know what feels good to them. And as they continue they will begin to move beyond that comfort and expand beyond their current limitations to experience more of what is available to them.*

Okay. Well, that is comforting in itself. I know that the two people in my life that encouraged me to take a leap of faith have taken their own leaps but they have the support of husbands and financial stability.
And this is also where they are. It is just where they are. And as many others may want you to get to that place of joy, want you to be there, you will experience it in your own time, in your own way. The answers are within you. We are here to guide you back to you. You are guiding you. YOU are guiding you. And when you look to yourself for that guidance, when you allow yourself to really listen to what it is that you are wanting and consciously choose from that space, you will bring forth the experiences that you consciously desire. Stability is an illusion and is only as you define it. You are source expressed and all is possible.

I seem to have a hard time listening to what it is that I really want. And it is almost like an idea will come to me and I deny it very quickly.
Why do you deny it? **Well, what just popped into my mind is that I don't feel like I deserve to have what I really want.** *Know that you are a magnificent being and that you are worthy. And that everything is awaiting you. It is all right here for you. And it is not about deserving or about worth. It is about a choice. You can choose to be in a place of depression, you can choose to be in a place of struggle, or you can choose to be in a place of joy.*

Imagine yourself on a path and you come to a fork in the road. One side leads to a path of depression and struggle and the other side leads to a path of joy. And if you can choose either one without having to do anything, it is not about deserving...it is not about anything else, but if all you had to do was push a button to choose your path, what path would you take?

I would like to think that I would take the path of joy, and many times I do. But there are times when it seems like I am attracted to the other path.

What is it you are receiving from this experience that continues to attract it? And is it confirming for you the lack of worth that you have felt?

Well, that would fit. It would.

And then you continue the cycle. I don't deserve this and then I create things in my life that confirm for me that I do not deserve it. And when I experience this, I confirm this even more for myself. And then because I am feeling so strongly, this is the vibration I am sending out and this is what I continually draw back into my life. And I create it again and again and again. As you shift your perspective about how you feel about you, you can choose to create a different experience in your life.

So it doesn't really matter where those ideas originated from, I mean, I don't have to analyze why? *No*

I can just choose to make different choices? *Yes. You can choose in this moment. Past experiences do not define you. They simply offer growth. Ask yourself, what is the growth in this for me? As you acknowledge the creation and embrace the growth, you release resistance to what is, which creates a shift in your vibration to attract other experiences you seek.*

While I am grateful for you being here. I understand that I am surrounded by what I call spirit guides. Do I have a special group that is sort of watching out for me?

It is you. **It's me?** *It is you. This is who is guiding you. And some may call it spirit guides, some may call it many things, but it is always you. There is only one source you see. Source may manifest in many forms to offer this guidance. We represent one form of this guidance. And we are here to guide you to a greater awareness of who you are.*

So I find myself making choices that are not beneficial, and it is almost like a weaving in and out of what choice do I make today? How am I going to act in the world today? Who am I? What am I doing? How am I going to be? I often feel swayed by the people who surround me.

As you begin to make other choices that bring you to the experiences you desire, those who surround you will change. You will draw to you those who support you and love you for where you are. And we would like to point out as you use the term beneficial, that every experience in your life is of benefit to you. Even though it may seem unpleasant at times, this is only because you do not understand it. Every experience serves great purpose and as you come to a greater understanding of the process of your life experience, it will be more enjoyable to you. Growth and expansion. This IS the purpose of life. Expansion for you, expansion for the collective. It is not necessary to beat yourself up over where you are. Where you are is a wonderful place. It may not feel as good to you from your current perspective, but it is indeed beneficial for your growth. Rejoice in where you are. It is perfection.

I feel in my mind that I would like to make choices of connection, connecting to source, connecting to people of like mind. *What do you feel is stopping you?*

Mostly just me getting in the way and just..........sometimes it's a matter of just being distracted. *You are creating the distraction.* **Right.** *What are you afraid of?* **I guess I am still afraid of rejection, although I have learned to deal with it a little bit better in the last couple of years. I don't enjoy dealing with that.**

When you understand that there is no rejection, this will be of great peace to you. As you connect with who you are, know who you are, really know the magnificence that is you, you will not allow others to define you. And you will not allow others to affect you and how you feel about you. You feel about you how YOU choose to feel about you. And you will know that when others speak of things to you that appears as rejection, it is only saying everything about where they are and nothing about you. So what appears to be rejection is simply them showing you where they are in that moment. This is also an opportunity for growth for you. An opportunity for you to choose to feel good about you regardless of what another feels about you. And when you do, these experiences will no longer serve you. Enjoy the process of exploration, observation, and creation. Embrace where you are. It is perfection.

That's a concept that I need to spend more time getting to feel comfortable with. I understand the wisdom, but I'm not sure how to bring it into my life.

Well let's talk about this. What is it that is so hard for you to wrap your brain around so to speak?

I'm afraid that my definition of myself is………. well, I feel like I'm rejecting myself. *Yes. Yes. We would agree. And that's okay. Embrace it. Acknowledge it. It is the experience that you seek. Just even having the awareness that you are feeling this way is the start for creating great change. You can choose to embrace yourself. Why do you feel you are rejecting yourself? What is causing this?*

I don't know. I feel like I was conditioned that way at an early age. *Conditioned by whom?*

Family and difficult school situations. I've dealt with a lot of people telling me that I wasn't good enough.

So these experiences that you've had helped you to confirm feelings about you. But these people who were telling you this were not in a place of love. They were not connected to the awareness of who they are. And they were putting off on you how they were feeling about themselves and where they were. And in that moment, you chose to believe it. You can shift your perspective by understanding that they were simply doing the best they could, knowing what they knew. It created an experience for you, which built a foundation for growth.

You can say – I no longer choose to believe this about me because I know that it is not so. I know I am kind, gentle, loving and a caring person. I have all of this love inside to give and I want to share it with others. I want to expand my awareness to understand and know that I am love. Feel the love that you are and allow it to be expressed. Allow yourself to embrace the divine source that IS you and leave behind what no longer serves you. It served great purpose to bring you to where you are now but you do not need to carry it with you any further. It is your choice.

You can choose to still bring that baggage along or you can drop the bag off. You can say – I'm tired of carrying this. It no longer serves me and I choose to let it go. Imagine a new backpack and start filling it with all the things that you want to take with you. Anything that does not serve you, just leave it behind. Then welcome experiences in your life that will give you the opportunity to declare that you have released them. When they appear, recognize them for the gifts that they are.

I find myself experiencing that other people seem to like me more than I like myself. Does that mean that my true essence is able to shine through despite myself? And is that why they are able to see it even though I can't?

They see who you really are. They experience your source and it is for you to come to the awareness of it. Those open to the love cannot help but see the love in another. It is a reflection of self.

Is my rejection of myself keeping me from being able to connect with others?

Absolutely. You cannot connect with others until you connect with yourself. It always starts with the self first. When you connect with your self, allow your love – the true essence of you to be expressed, then you expand out to fully connect and share that with others. Share all of who you are.

Do you have recommendations for things that I can do to be able to get there, to do that?

Take time for yourself. Do whatever feels good to you. And ask these questions of yourself. State – I want to know who I am. I want to connect with my higher self. I want to know and feel the love that I am. I choose to love me. I welcome the experiences in my life that will help me create the changes that I desire. I choose to acknowledge them when they arrive so that I may receive the benefit from the experience and enjoy the growth process.

So my higher self has the answers, and it will help me to connect?

Yes. All the answers are within you. Others offer you the experience of what you desire, but only you can know where you are in all of it. You are continually choosing and creating your experiences based on what you feel in the moment. Look within for clarity. As you ask yourself questions, the answers will come through for you when you quiet your mind and listen. Allow the connection to flow through and pay attention when it does. It is your desire that will create it. You can say – I want to know who I am and I choose to be open. And an energy shift will be put in motion. You can start there.

You can also begin to be consciously aware of the choices you are making. And if a choice is not yielding the result that you thought it would, you can take a closer look at what the experience is offering you.

You asked why you continue the same cycle. Because you are giving yourself the opportunity to make a different choice in order to create change and experience growth. Yet you continue to respond in the same manner. And until you choose to consciously create change, these experiences will continue to show up in your life. And as you make a different choice, the energy hold around it dissipates.

It is not something that is going to keep hitting you as you ask yourself why? why? why? Why is this in my life, I don't want to deal with it. Until you do deal with it, you will not expand beyond it. Release resistance, face what is, embrace it, and utilize it as an opportunity for growth. Once you do, it will no longer serve you.

As things surface for you, it is a wonderful opportunity to grow and expand your current frame. Instead of seeing it as – why are these things coming up for me, I don't want to deal with these feelings, I don't want to look at this, welcome the experience as an opportunity to create change. Know that when they appear, it is your grand opportunity to release them. *This is the experience that you seek. You are just not consciously aware of what is being presented to you.*

I find that I have made choices in the past that were very painful, very difficult. It was a conscious effort to stop the drama. But then I ended up going too far in the other direction and remained stagnant for a long time and I was hiding. Obviously, I still have a lot to learn and I am very interested in learning. I am more interested in learning in more subtle ways though. Is it possible for me to get the most out of the experience without the high drama?
If there is drama, you are creating it. Anything is possible. All is accessible to you.

Yes, and I don't feel the need to do that anymore. Do I just stop?

Embrace the experiences and choose to respond differently. As you make another choice, a shift will be created and the experience will change for you. This drama is there because you have created it and you can just as powerfully create something different. Acknowledge the growth in the process and begin your next creation. Enjoy this process.

So there is still value in less dramatic lessons?

Yes. There is value in all experiences. Every experience is an opportunity for growth. It is how you perceive the experience. Many are drawn to drama and get caught up in it. You get caught up because being caught up in the drama allows you to not have to look at yourself. You become so caught up in everything that is going on outside of you that you do not look within. And when you realize you want to look within and connect with the source of who you are, then you won't need the drama. The drama is a distraction from awareness of self.

Yes, it was a huge distraction for me. It was ridiculous.

I feel like I'm on a path that is working for me. I have allies in human form, I feel like I have a spiritual connection that's there for me if I choose to acknowledge it. It really does come

down to the matter of what choices do I make on a daily basis. And do I remember to make the choices that I really want.

And also allow yourself to be where you are. This is so important because if you are not embracing where you are, you remain stagnant. If you are still beating yourself up over not making the right choice, over not already being somewhere further along in your framing, then you are resistant to the process and cannot create change.

In those moments you can say – I made this choice and it was not what I consciously wanted, and I feel gratitude that this experience is showing me more about where I am. Instead of looking at it and asking – why did I do that again? Be grateful for the experience and the opportunity to gain clarity and rejoice that you can make another choice. As you continue to look at your life experiences in this manner, you will continually shift your energy for the growth and expansion of your current frame.

I have made poor choices in the past and that does stick with me. I'm afraid that I'm going to make poor choices in the future.

There are no poor choices. They are simply choices, choices that did not yield you what you consciously thought that you wanted. Therefore, you define them as poor. But they are not. These experiences are manifestations of your creation based on what you are choosing. It may have been your unconscious choosing, but it is a choice that became a manifestation in your life experience. That's all it is. It is divine because you created it. It is divine because it is source expressed. There is nothing but perfection in that.

So you can say – I made this unconscious choice and it was not what I thought I wanted. I will utilize what is showing up for me as a tool of information that tells me more about where I am in my life experience and what I am inviting in. I can then consciously choose to create change from a place of greater understanding. And this will be perfection as well. One choice is not better than the other. It is simply an awareness of a different choice. That you consciously want something different is what makes it seem better to you. It is you who defines it. Acknowledge your creations. They are all divine.

I understand that and I've certainly learned a lot from all of the choices that I've made. But I don't want to make choices that are that painful again in the future.

And that is wonderful because you are having clarity about what it is that you are wanting. You know that you do not wish to experience that pain again. Did it not serve great purpose for you? **Yes.**

So taking time for myself and just basically learning to care for myself will be steps in the right direction? *There is no right direction. But it helps guide you to what you state you want to experience.*

Well I've gone through phases like that and it certainly does make a huge difference. I'm not sure why I stopped doing that, but I guess that's not important. I can just start doing it again.

Yes. Whatever has caused you to stop in the past is irrelevant. It is about where you are now and just being aware. Ask yourself for clarity. Say – I want clarity on this. I choose to be consciously aware in the moment. And if something appears in my life that triggers that old pattern to surface, take notice of it. Acknowledge, embrace, and release it. That is your moment of power.

That would be extremely helpful, because so often it seems that I just slip back into that place unconsciously. If I had an awareness of it more immediately instead of letting so much time go by, then I would feel better about the process.

End Session

My friend's cat curled up on my lap the moment Jacob flowed through. He stayed there for the duration of the conversation. I definitely think he was drawn to Jacob's energy vibration. Another interesting thing is that the moment the session was complete, the tape recorder clicked off as it had just reached the end of the tape. We both laughed at the timing of it.

A Day with Abraham

The workshop was held at the hotel on the Biltmore Estate. When we drove onto the property, a sense of peace came over me. I told my friend that I would love to tour the Biltmore House. She said we could go the following day. That's great, I said. Our other two friends arrived at the workshop before us and they saved us two seats. We were in the second row and I noticed Jerry's chair was right in front of me. The room was filled with about 200 people. It sounds like a lot but it was actually very warm and inviting and I found it to be very cozy. Perfect for me.

I was sitting in my chair just feeling excited for the day when all of the sudden I see Esther and Jerry walk in and stand right in front of me. In that moment, I was overtaken by emotion and I burst into tears. I was overflowing with gratitude. Esther then sat down in "Jerry's Chair" and began to sing the joy song. She was smiling and so joyous. Her chipper spirit just beamed right out at me.

Jacob was present and I sat there with a feeling of total bliss while the tears continued to stream down my face. I cried the entire first segment and I do not know a word that was said. I realized in that very initial moment of emotion that I was not there for Abraham, I had come for Esther.

The first break came and my friends were wondering what was wrong. Was I okay? I explained the sheer gratitude I felt for the extraordinary, joyous life I am living now and how much Esther and Jerry were both a huge part of that creation. And even though I created this in my life, they were co-creating participants in my major life-changing experience. I was just so grateful. I can't even begin to describe what flowed through me. I wanted to hug Esther, hold her and thank her. Of course, I wanted to thank Jerry too. I have just felt a close connection with Esther with what I have experienced. I am grateful to them both.

After the break, I thought I had gotten myself together. I sat with Jacob in bliss again and Jerry began the second segment talking about their products and somewhere along the way he mentioned Neale Donald Walsch. I immediately burst into tears again. These were the people in my life who participated in helping me to experience and create this incredible life I have now. I was boo-hooing over my gratitude for Neale and I thought, is this what will occur at the Holiday Retreat I am attending in December?

I can see it now. He walks in and I start crying. At least they will be tears of joy rather than the tears of pain I once expressed. I know that he will allow me to hug him and tell him I love him. For this I am grateful. So there I was, tears streaming through the entire second segment. I just stared at Esther. Yet again I heard nothing. Not a word. Nor did I need to. It wasn't about that for me.

Lunch time: We were told if you have a blue ticket to go next door for lunch. Everyone else was to go downstairs to eat. The three friends I was with all had blue tickets. I did not. I caught one of the staff members heading to lunch and asked about it. They said they were just splitting up the group. I explained the situation and she gladly gave me a blue ticket. I ended up sitting at the table next to a lovely man and his wife. I began making conversation with this man and he brought up The Monroe Institute. I don't even know how that conversation got started but I was taking notice because I have wanted to go there since I was a kid. I had previously looked into attending the Gateway Journey, which is a weeklong experience.

This wonderful man was sharing many of his personal experiences with me about his trip there and the family members he had talked to on the other side. I felt like it was an "in my face" and a loud and clear sign telling me to go. And go I shall. It was so very interesting. He then began to tell me about the remote viewer, Joe McMoneagle. I knew exactly who he was. I had read his book *Mind Trek* (which I thoroughly enjoyed) and I took notice of the significance.

It was absolutely fascinating that I was aware of everything he was talking about. It was a conversation just for me. And I wasn't even supposed to be at that table! I was supposed to be downstairs. I just love how everything unfolds. It is a great joy to witness and acknowledge the beauty of the process.

You will love this one! After we finished lunch, we still had thirty minutes before the next session would begin. My friends and I decided to go outside. We walked down to the other end of the hotel and out to the patio. There was a table with four chairs at the far end of the patio that I gravitated to. Everyone joined me.

We were talking and taking in the scenery when an Abraham staff member came out of the door and headed across the patio and right up to our table. She said a client had given her an extra ticket to the Biltmore House and asked if anyone could use it. Then she literally handed it right to me. My friends all stood there in amazement. They said, "She came right to you. I mean right to you." They couldn't believe it. Remember, this woman had to pass by pretty much everyone as she walked all the way to the other end of the hotel, out to the patio, and all the way to the far corner to get to me.

The only one who was not surprised by this was myself. I knew immediately that I had created it and had been open to receiving it. I acknowledged this magnificent manifestation of my desire and was grateful to all those who participated in the co-creation of it. It was only after receiving the ticket that I found out the cost was $49. No one had told me that.

The interesting thing here is that the cost never even crossed my mind when I decided to go. I never even thought about it. Logically, of course there would be a charge, but I truly never thought about it. My focus was on what I wanted to experience and I always hold the intention that abundance will flow in for whatever I wish to experience. I knew I wanted to go and chose that experience and just like that, a ticket appeared.

Now many months ago, before my transformation, my first question would have been, how much does it cost? I would make my decisions based on cost rather than joy. Now I rejoice in knowing the contrast. I rejoice in the experience of it. And I love leaving the door wide open for how it will manifest. People often limit their possibilities by trying to figure out where the money will come from, their job or wherever. And it is so very limiting. When I allow for all possibilities, I have experienced that things flow into my life in the most glorious and unexpected ways. In this case, it was not in the form of physical money, simply a ticket. Money was never even in the equation. Isn't that wonderful?

The afternoon segment begins. I sit as Jacob flows through me. Observing. I think it was more that I wanted to experience this happening with them. In total bliss, I was zoned out. I think the streams of tears finally slowed but I was still only taking in bits and pieces of what Abraham was saying. I heard very little. It was just the best feeling though to sit and feel these vibrations, peace and love.

The third segment flew by. When it was over, my friends both mentioned they had gotten really hot. The staff member at lunch commented that most people get cold as they keep the temperature low. I was sitting between the two of them and I wondered if the heat they were feeling was Jacob. Many times they raise my temperature and I feel as though I am radiating intense heat. I definitely sensed it was their presence.

Last break of the day. I went outside and sat in a chair on the porch. There was a wonderful breeze and I closed my eyes as I felt the heat of the sun upon me. In that moment, I came to the awareness of why I was there. What this was really about for me. Esther was showing me what was possible for me. By watching and being present in this process, I was seeing what I could offer to others. Others who were seeking to know more about who they are. Others who were seeking to understand their lives as I had been for many years. Even though I knew this, the magnitude of it had been hard to let in.

My friend was sitting next to me and so I shared this with her. The moment I voiced this to her, a huge surge of energy (that was Jacob) shot through my body so intensely and they were yelling

Yes! Yes! You've got it! They were so thrilled that I got this. And it was a huge confirmation for me. Wow. Thank you for this gift of clarity.

The last segment begins and I am just focused on enjoying the moment. Basking in all of it. Feeling the bliss. The love. As it came to a close, I was so uplifted, connected, fully aligned, energy bursting out of me. Esther and Jerry took off very quickly out the side door. I never really had the chance to speak with them. (And yes I know, I could have created it.) But it just didn't feel like the right timing to me. Too many people around and not the way I wanted to approach them.

I know the moment will come when I will share all of this with them. Perhaps they are reading this now. I am open to however it unfolds. I have greatly enjoyed this experience and I am grateful for its many gifts.

After the workshop, we all went back to the house where I was staying and enjoyed a lovely dinner together. After dinner, we sat around the table talking. The discussion led to many questions, which began to draw Jacob out. I could feel them and welcomed them to join us. They talked with Jacob for quite a while. I did not have the tape recorder out because I did not anticipate this experience. I was delighted that the opportunity arose. Everyone seemed to enjoy the experience.

We also experienced other visitors. There were two black bears we could see through the window. They had climbed up into the pick up truck and had gotten into the trash in the back. My friend had mentioned before my trip that the bears often visit her. When I expressed my desire to experience them, she said that she would see if she could manifest that for me. How delightful! Thank you for that gift.

They were beautiful. I had never seen bears in the wild before. We were all excited at their appearance. We continued to talk a little more and then our two friends headed home around midnight. I was definitely feeling tired by then after only four hours of sleep the night before. I got comfy on the sofa and was out for the night.

Jacob who?

The next day my friend was sharing her experience in an email to our entire retreat group. It was funny because she mentioned that Jacob came and that we were working together.

Most of the people in my group do not yet know who Jacob is. And the way she wrote it made it sound like Jacob is another person. I am sure people will be asking about Jacob. Perhaps wondering if he is a new man in my life. Well, sort of yes. I got a great laugh out of it.

10/28

This morning we were headed out to the Biltmore House when we noticed that the air in my front tire was a little low. We went to stop at a gas station to fill the tire. I had no idea how to do this. (I am sure you are laughing now.) I have never put air in the tires. I have always had a man in my life to do this for me.

So we pull up and there is a lovely man at the air pump filling his motorcycle. I begin to check the tire with the gauge, which I wasn't doing right and I couldn't even find on the tire how much air to put in them anyway. All of the sudden I look up and this man had finished with his tire. The air was still running and he came over and asked me which tire needed air. I pointed and he began to fill it for me. He asked if it was the only one and I told him I didn't know. I wasn't sure what they were supposed to be at. He then proceeded to check all of my tires.

It was oh so joyous. When he was done, I thanked him and asked if I could give him a hug. He got the biggest grin on his face and said yes. It was so great. So without having to verbally ask, I had manifested the help I desired in the most delightful way. It was beautiful to watch it unfold. My friend sat in the car watching it all transpire. It was really something. I take notice of the perfection of it all.

I shared this experience with a few friends. Some were delighted and others felt only concern for me. They let me know that I better learn how to do this or I may be in big trouble next time. To them I asked if they could look beyond the surface appearance of what many define as "practical" to the beautiful process of creation. It was wonderful to experience and a great joy to witness the process.

The Biltmore House

My friend and I arrived at the Biltmore House and I was so delighted that I got to keep my ticket. (I have since laminated it and hung it on my vision wall.) We had a wonderful time touring the home. It took several hours to make our way through all of the many rooms. I enjoyed taking in all of the architecture. I was looking around to take in every little detail. I appreciated all that went into the creation of it. Beautiful. It was a fantastic day!

We headed back to her house for a final dinner together. She cooked spaghetti which was delicious. It was dark by the time we were done. We hugged and said our good-byes. I gathered my things and was on my way.

Where Am I?

I left my friend's house at 7:30 p.m. I had called several people on the way home and since I knew it was a five and one-half hour drive, I kept telling everyone I would be home at 1:00 a.m. Well, I was on Interstate 70 and needed to get onto 81 North. I completely missed my exit and went way out of my way by many miles. I finally got off at an exit, turned around and headed back to look for the right exit. I was chatting on the phone with Jan at the time and he asked if I had found my exit. I said, "I don't know where I am. I'll look at the next sign and see." The next sign said I was already on 81 North and close to home. What? How can that be? All I can tell you is that I never got off on that exit and I know I must have been behind about 45 minutes due to getting lost. Yet do you know what time I got home? That's right. 1:00 on the dot! I think I had so clearly stated my intention for 1:00, and because I was so focused on my discussion with Jan, I had no awareness of time and was able to create it to be. I had no thoughts of disbelief of this possibility to block the manifestation of it since I was not focused on the time or my trip at all. I was just enjoying my conversation and then wham – I'm home. Who knows? I don't know for sure what happened that night but I do know that it was something really incredible. Maybe I'll set the intention that it will only take me four hours next time!

10/29

After being gone for several days on my trip, I was looking forward to spending the day with Xander. We had a great time playing some of his favorite games, Chutes and Ladders, Sudoku, Bingo and Chess. We talked about his weekend and all the fun he experienced. We went to Waffle House for dinner because he loves the chocolate chip waffles. After playtime in the bathtub, I tucked him into bed.

We read a few books and I sang his favorite night, night songs – This Old Man and Hush Little Baby. I enjoy that so much. I told him how much I love him and what a joy he is in my life. I thanked him for choosing to be a part of my life experience. He told me he loves me more than anything in the whole universe. I told him that was a whole lot of love. And then he thanked me for choosing to be his mommy. So cute! What a great day.

In this moment, I take notice of how normal my life is to me. I am a mom who takes her son to school everyday. I take him to the park to play on the playground. We go for walks on the nature trails. We play games. I talk to him about anything he is interested in. We have wonderful communication. And then I also have what I guess could be called my work with Jacob.

This is just my life. I embrace it. I have become so used to it that I forget that it may sound strange to others. And sometimes it sounds strange to me when I say it out loud to another explaining about what I do. It's like, umm, well, I am a stay-at-home mom during the day and I communicate with this group of entities who speak through me at night. Say what? And even though it still sounds odd at times to describe it, it is completely normal for me to experience it.

A Contract on the House

It took several days but we finally heard from our agent that the buyers had accepted our counter offer on the house. We were thrilled. However, closing the end of December would still not resolve our financial situation for next month. Yet, all was falling into place. I told my former husband that it would all work out. That I wasn't thinking about the "how." I just trusted that something would unfold. This was again another wonderful opportunity for me to experience peace in the moment. What a gift!

10/30

Today one of my dear friends is leaving for a three-week trip out of the country. I just read my final email from him until he returns. I feel a sense of loss, yet I know all is well. I have just really enjoyed his presence in my life. He lights me up. This is an interesting feeling for me. I am not sure what to do with it.

We have built a beautiful friendship in a very short time, in just a few weeks actually. He just recently entered my life but I feel as though he burst into it with a powerful energy that I could not take my focus off of. At least, I did not want to.

He fascinates me, amazes me, continually surprises me, and I am just captivated by him. He can grab my attention at any given moment. Why is this? I am not sure. I know I feel wonderful when I am in his presence. Even if that presence is just through emails. I have only physically met him once. He does not live in my state. I have enjoyed the most delightful conversations and experienced very stimulating discussions with him. He has brought so much joy into my life and has offered me tremendous growth. Hmmm, I do believe I just answered my own question.

Of course, I am drawn to the growth he offers me. He has stimulated me in a way that no one else has. I welcome a continued friendship. I sense there is much for us to experience together. I am open to what will unfold and I am excited to see what will be revealed.

So Much Love

I often tell others how much I love them. Not just family and friends, but people I just meet. It has become such a normal part of my life that I have almost forgotten what it was like to not say it. And how odd it might seem to others when I do. Some welcome it; others are unsure of what to do with it. They are not sure how to respond. If they are male, they cannot help but read this as a romantic interest on my part.

My love is pure. Love is who we are. It is simply the essence of me expressed. And that is the joy. It is a great joy for me to express my love (myself) to others. I see others through Jacob's eyes. Jacob has great love for all. I see the love, the pain and sadness that one carries. I feel it all. The pain is not painful to me – it is more that I feel and am aware that it exists for that individual. This only makes me want to love them more.

So I may not know the person all that well, but I do know his or her soul through Jacob. I feel it all and it is incredible. It overflows for me and all of this comes pouring out to all I encounter. With Jacob, it is all pure and very real.

They cut through the barriers. All the stuff that people put up for protection dissipates and all I see is the source of who they really are. This allows me to make an instant connection with people. Which, of course, is perfect for this work that I am doing. I have embraced many who I have met for the first time and told them how much I love them. And when they looked into my eyes, they knew. And I could see the tears of joy in theirs.

It is the most amazing feeling I have ever experienced. I have great love for all. Every being is glorious. Magnificent. There is none that I would consider dark, only those who are lost, angry, or in pain. Confused about who they are. They are just as beautiful as anyone else. They are just further away from knowing this. And because I know this, it is easy for me to reach out and love them instead of judging or reacting to the anger being displayed.

Tidbits from Xander

"Mommy, thank you for coming in my life. I am enjoying this experience. I want you to stay in my experience forever."

10/31

I just spoke with my friend with whom I visited in Asheville. The evening we all had dinner together, I had originally sensed that Jacob would not be interacting with them because I was not feeling a receptiveness to it. And as they say, it is for the asking and those who wish to participate. I was not sure why I was feeling this but I have learned to trust my senses.

During the dinner, discussion began and I felt they were drawing Jacob out with all that was being said and so I let go and allowed it to flow. In that moment, it felt right. And the conversation, communication began. It wasn't until now that my friend informed me that before we all met, her husband did not believe that I was experiencing anything. He doubted the whole thing. I was delighted to hear this because it was a huge confirmation for what I had been feeling.

During the experience when he spoke with them, there were tears. Having experienced it first hand, he apparently changed his mind. She said he did indeed experience Jacob. I think if one is even a little open to it, you cannot help but feel the love of Jacob's presence. I felt it so strongly for him so I knew he had to feel it too. It was just pouring out of me.

Happy Halloween

My former husband and I took Xander to walk around my old neighborhood as there are a lot of kids there and it is a great place to trick or treat. My sister and her husband (whom she is separated from as well) joined us with my two nephews. Xander and his cousin were both Ninja Turtles. Xander was Raphael. His cousin, who is the same age as him, was Leonardo. His older cousin was The Flash. They were all so excited. It was so much fun.

What a beautiful night it was. I looked up at the sky and the stars were so bright and fully present. You can't always see them so clearly here. At least I had never seen them it that way. Perhaps it was I who had changed. Did I mention that I used to want to be an astronomer? Yes, I had many dreams. The thought of them being possible just wasn't a reality for me at the time. I enjoyed walking for hours this Halloween night. It would have been quite the romantic walk. People had their bonfires in their front yard and it is just a magical evening. It is wonderful to watch the excitement of all the kids and their zest for life. What a great evening!

Jacob, Jacob Everywhere

A friend of mine just called me to share something interesting that she had noticed lately. And that is the name Jacob. A couple weeks ago she was in church and the entire lesson that day centered on Jacob. One of the things she remembered is that Jacob's story in the Bible was meant to represent the consciousness of humanity. Then last week when she was researching a woman who is an attorney at the law firm, she noticed that the woman is involved with some organization called the Jacob something or other. And for Halloween, when the trick-or-treaters came by, of course she heard one of the kids being called Jacob. She said she heard his name repeatedly and it was just so obvious. Then soon after, she picked up the book, *Many Lives, Many Masters*. It was recommended by one of the women at a meeting she attended last night. This was not the first time this book came up and so she figured she should pay attention as it keeps entering her awareness to notice it. She opened up the book to a random page and just happened to open it to a page about a young man named Jacob who had a near death experience in 1975. She said she has had a few more Jacob sightings but these are the ones that stand out as she is now paying closer attention. She thinks it is just the excitement of bringing them into her conscious awareness. She said that even though they are communicating through me, she still feels they are with her, helping her, guiding her if she needs reminders. She said she adds Jacob to the legions of people who are helping her achieve what she desires.

What can I say but how awesome is that? Jacob began popping up for me a lot in the beginning too as I desired confirmation that they were really with me. Aside from the obvious Gym Jacob, which was a big sign right in my face, I remember a commercial on TV and JACOB appearing in big bold letters on the screen. I don't even remember what the ad was for. And I rarely even turned on the television and usually fast-forwarded through the commercials when I did. The fact that I even saw it tells me it was clearly Jacob just saying hello.

Health Insurance

We have officially lost our health insurance coverage. We could no longer afford the monthly premiums and I received a notice that if we did not pay it by October 31 that coverage would be terminated. And so it is. To be honest, I was delighted to receive this notice. I had felt for a while that it was no longer necessary. Yet I could not bring myself to actually cancel it. There was still a part of me holding on. So instead, I created a situation where it was terminated for me. The manifestation flowed through for the experience that I ultimately desired. I acknowledge the creation and rejoice in it! I understand that this may sound crazy to many of you, but there is something in the releasing of what society has defined as my way of life that is so freeing. The idea that I can create a different way of life, one filled with love and joy and not based around fear of what will "happen" to me, is glorious. To just be able to let go and know that all I need is me. I have me, the awareness of self. That is all the security necessary. Anything else is just an illusion.

11/01
    A friend of mine sent me Phillip Daniel's CD, *The Theory of Life*. He thought the song "Look Within" could be Jacob's theme song so to speak because looking within is part of their message. I wasn't aware that Jacob would be in need of a theme song but who knows, I take notice as it has appeared in my life. Now I am not usually a music person. I have never been one to just sit and listen to music because I usually like to be alone and present with myself and my thoughts. However, this music was different. It touched my soul. I completely fell in love with every song. The songs are so uplifting and a reminder of the divine beings that we are. I have been listening to them every day and it is just amazing. I feel so connected. I can literally feel Phillip's soul as he sings. It radiates throughout my being. There is something very special here. (My first experience in awakening to music was with Cathy Bolton at the retreat. I experienced it in a way that I never had before and have been enjoying this divine connection ever since. Thank you for this gift.)

Change in House Closing
    We were supposed to close on our house the end of December but the buyers called and now want to close the end of this month. Without even doing anything, the financial abundance was making its way to appear sooner in our lives. Of course, we agreed to this change. How fantastic is that? Just holding the thought that it would all work out beautifully was all that was necessary. There was nothing else required in the "doing" department except to allow it in. Being open to receive the creation in order for it to manifest. And manifest it did!

11/02
    This has been a fantastic morning. The sunrise was amazing. The clouds were in beautiful swirl shapes all over the sky. The sun was still hidden behind the mountains and as it shined upon the clouds, it gave them a tint that looked like a deep pink color. It

was absolutely beautiful. I love those moments. I would love to just lie down on the mountainside and take it all in.

I was at my old house today and found all of the brochures and paperwork for the Monroe Institute. My application had already been filled out to attend the Gateway Journey Program. So I asked myself, why didn't I actually go? At the time I think it was the money and a feeling of guilt to take a whole week to myself. Yet when Neale's retreat came up, I was so compelled to go, knew I had to be there, that all those thoughts got pushed aside. I had to make it work. And it did, to perfection. And now it appears to be the perfect time to experience this Gateway Journey. I am open and ready for the full experience.

My Father

My sister just told me she had a two-hour conversation with my father. She has a connection with him that I do not. She talked about Abraham and he seemed to really want to embrace the idea and wanted to know more. She also told him about Jacob. He was excited. He actually wants to talk with them. I have many feelings in this moment. As I mentioned earlier, my father was always angry. I was a constant disappointment and never good enough. I felt like he thought I would never amount to anything. How odd to now finally be coming around to a full circle moment where there is much to be offered and shared and he is open to embracing this. It is odd but glorious. She told me this was the first sound of hope she has heard from him. I never would have imagined I would be sitting with my father as Jacob speaks but then so much is shifting within and around me now that they are here. I would love nothing more than to share in this experience with my father. I know there is much growth in this for both of us. He lives in Richmond. It is a two-hour drive. I am not sure when I will see him for this to transpire. This is a grand opportunity. I will just let it unfold. Apparently he has a long list of questions. Whatever happens, it is going to be quite interesting. Wow, I am continually amazed at the joy in my life.

11/03

I was up late last night and decided to watch a movie. I realized I have been so busy that I hadn't seen any television or movies in a while. It felt like a good night to relax and flow into a story. I ended up watching *Anna and the King*, one of my favorite love stories. A beautiful story in general. It was a nice evening. Just by myself, enjoying the moment.

Voice Recognition What?

I'm excited that I am now using my new Dragon Voice Recognition System. It just arrived in the mail yesterday. I spent most of the late evening doing a tutorial and trying to figure out how this thing works. The software is pretty fantastic. I am hooked. I have a headset that I speak into and it types everything for me. I am a hunt and peck gal. And with all of the conversations I was transcribing, I thought, there must be a better way. Just then, a friend recommended it and I was like – what, it can do what? I had never even heard of this before. And voila! There it is. Thank you for this gift.

11/04

I had an interesting experience typing up the following conversation. I started at 3:45 and when I got done, I thought the typing from the software was amazing because it only felt like maybe 15 or 20 minutes had passed. I thought I did great! I then looked at the clock and it was 5:00. How can that be? I thought. I feel like I completely lost time. How could I be sitting here for over an hour and not know it. Things just keep getting more interesting. The following is what I got lost in transcribing. I hope you enjoy these. I know I did.

What about the statement that people make about something being "meant to be"? Is there any such thing as that?

Meant to be can be. You choose what you want before you even come forth. As you come forth you continue to choose in every moment and at the same time having the opportunity to choose what has already been chosen. As you choose in the moment to continue with what has already been chosen, it is in that moment that it becomes what was meant to be so to speak. But you always have the choice in the moment. You can always choose something different. You will feel compelled to choose and go forth in the direction of what you have already chosen because this will resonate most strongly for you. You will feel this as it aligns. And this is what was meant to be. And if you choose to change it in the moment, that too is meant to be. It is all perfection.

Many new people have entered my life this year. Is there any significance as to why this is so at this time? *Many enter your life because you are creating major shifts in your life experience. It is only natural that those who are a part of helping you to experience these shifts will appear in your life. You are saying – I am ready for this now and welcoming the experiences. And all of these beautiful beings are flowing into your life to offer you the experiences you seek.*

Is it true that a soul will orchestrate the times they will want to encounter certain other souls while on earth?
Your being will always orchestrate the timing of encounters. Always. You are always choosing in every moment. You need not concern yourself with it. Enjoy the moment. Enjoy it all. Everything works to perfection. You are always choosing, always creating.

What is the place of self-confidence in a person's life?
Self-confidence is nothing more than an awareness of who you are and where you are in your life experience. When you embrace this fully, you are confident in you. And that is divine.

Talk to me about the difference between spirituality and religion. How might I better understand and share these concepts about the spiritual nature of human beings?
Spirituality and religion is simply an evolution. The only difference is what you know to be so for you. You are all where you are and it is ever changing. Both offer you an opportunity to declare where you are. How wonderful to have such glorious choices. For you to be able to experience

and decide what it is that you choose. You get to experience knowing how you feel about all of it. This is the growth and expansion. There really is no difference, only a different experience that is being offered and created by you.

You need not explain this to anyone. It is not to be explained. It is simply for you to experience and come to a greater understanding of where you are. You are experiencing. This is the purpose. We tell you that if you wish to explain, to ponder the difference, then share your perspective of your own experience. This will capture the attention of others as they decide how they feel about where you are, which will help them to gain clarity about where they are.

What does it mean to feel inspired and is there value in waiting to feel inspired before deciding on a project, activity, or goal?

Inspiration is experienced as a rise in your current vibration. Your frequency is enhanced as you come up with new ideas in which to express the source of who you are. Conscious expression of source is exhilarating. Connecting with you is the greatest most divine guidance you could ever seek. As you connect, you are guiding yourself.

Yes, wait, listen, hear, connect and be with you. Allow your self to flow and be in that space. As you feel a raise in vibration by your excitement of new thought, allow it to be fully expressed in whatever form feels good to you. There is much joy and tremendous value in this.

Is it possible to trigger inspiration?

You can trigger inspiration at any given moment. Simply ask to connect with you, to access your divine source.

Is it possible to literally create the life I want?

You have already done so. You are just not consciously aware of it. It already is. We understand that you are talking about your conscious awareness of it. Creating the life that you want from that perspective is simply shifting into consciously creating rather than unconsciously creating. You have created your current life experience. Begin by acknowledging your divine creation even if it does not appear on the surface to be what you were seeking. Consciously choose to create the changes you desire. Welcome the experiences that show up in your life to facilitate this process and you will no longer ask this question. For you will know first hand just how magnificent the process of creating your life experience really is and how easily things can flow into your life when you are consciously aware of the process.

How will I know when I am making decisions that are in alignment with my higher, wiser self? How do others affect my decisions?

You will know when you feel joy. When you feel a sense of peace. You need not worry about anyone else. At times when you think you are making the right decision for you but you are feeling angst, that feeling may be coming from concern of what others will think of your choice. It does not necessarily mean that your decision is incorrect for you. It simply means that you are caring about what others think and are allowing it to affect your experience. It is for you to come to know and understand what you feel and where you are. The only effect another can have on your decision is whatever power you give to it. You can release those thoughts knowing that you are here to experience what you desire for your growth. This experience is all about you. Do not deny yourself full expression of self. If you feel joy in the moment, if you are drawn to an experience, let go. Release, and allow yourself to experience that moment. No matter what another may think of it, this is your life experience. And no one else can ever tell you what is right for you. Only you can ever know this. As you align with you, you will gain clarity on how you feel. Focusing on being clear about what you really want for you and paying attention to the source of your feelings that surface for you will help you in this process. This too is an experience you seek. Enjoy the fine-tuning of it. Rejoice and love yourself for the magnificent being that you are. You cannot do any wrong. Choose as you feel guided and then EXPERIENCE, EXPRESS, EXPAND.

Change in House Closing Again

Our agent contacted us again because the buyers now want to close next week. My former husband asked me how I felt about it, as we would have little time to get everything moved out. I told him that the universe works to perfection and that we created this. Financially we had no idea how we would pay our rent or mortgage or other bills for November and here, without doing anything but knowing and feeling all was flowing beautifully, they want to close even sooner. Not once but twice changing the date. We have equity in our home so closing sooner means financial abundance flowing in now. I know there is so much more to come. It may be a little crazy trying to get everything moved out in such a short time but I am game. I might be off my rocker for the next few weeks, although many think I already am. Ha! Ha! Seriously, I know all will go smoothly and I choose to enjoy the process.

Weight, Body, Self

I went to my old house today to get some clothing for wintertime. The weather has gotten cold all of the sudden. I found a dress in the attic that I had worn for New Year's many years ago. Oh, how I would love to wear it again. I brought it home with me. At some point in my marriage, I came to a great place with my body. I was in a great spiritual place and felt connected to myself. But then I experienced some turmoil in the last few years and put on 50 pounds. What is weight anyway? It's all just energy. Surely I can shift the energy.

There are endless reasons of why I think I might have manifested this weight. My unworthiness manifested a protective barrier, a way of not attracting attention from other men so that I would not be tempted to get from them what was not received from my husband, or a way to hurt myself because I was in so much pain. All of these reasons are irrelevant. I have tried working out and eating all the "right" things and yet my weight has not budged. I am aware that it's not about the food or about the exercise, but about my embracement of me.

I have been resistant. I do not like what I see. I know this is my vehicle through life but this one has been a long struggle for me. I know there is growth in this process. I know I need to love myself, just as I am. I asked Jacob about this. They told me that when I release resistance, it would be and that it served purpose for my greater growth and to enjoy the process. Gee, thanks. That's not feeling so helpful at this moment. Although I know there is wisdom there. I don't think I want to receive it just yet. I am not sure how to create that shift. I am just intending for it to be. I am excited about the growth and creating change. It is just hard for me to imagine how that will come to be. But then it is also those thoughts that have hindered me from shifting beyond this. I choose to let go and allow for all avenues for a shift to occur. I intend to remain open to this process.

Hello from the Trees

Yesterday morning I arrived at Unity Church and there were only a few cars there. I went in and the band was practicing. No one else was there. Then I realized I had forgotten about daylight savings time and I was an hour early. Oops! Since I had this extra time. I decided to go visit with the trees behind the church. It is the most beautiful little forest. I hugged some of the trees and felt their love. They had the most beautifully colored leaves. All of the leaves were at the very tops of the trees and they had very tall trunks. As a leaf would fall, it would flutter so freely down, each one floating along as if dancing. It was wonderful to witness. I said hello and I asked the trees to give me a little wave and in that moment, they began to sway. It was amazing.

Notes

As the time has changed, I am missing the sunrise now. I loved watching it rise over the mountains every morning on the way to school. I will embrace the mist on the mountains. Although not the same, it is still a magnificent view. After all, it's what is.

I am at the gym and I feel really great. I desire to release some of these thoughts about myself. Part of me wants to get in great shape and feel fantastic again and I think part of me is resisting the conformity because of how others may view me – that I will somehow be better thinner rather than seeing the perfection that I am now. This is clearly an issue for me. Yet I know that what others think of me is really irrelevant. It is only what I think of myself that matters. So why don't I think good thoughts of my body? What is this about for me? I haven't a clue. I really need to look within and find out what this is REALLY all about. Whatever it is, I am holding myself back. I can feel the resistance as Jacob mentioned. I know that when I am ready, a shift will occur. I had too many years of buying into the idea that I wasn't good enough. I know the rest of me is glorious but there is a separation in my mind about my body. My body is like this other thing in the far corner by itself. I know it is all one. Yet my mind has created this. I am aware. I am open and creating change. I choose to enjoy this process.

My Sister

It's another beautiful day as always. I had the most wonderful talk with my sister last night. She has been struggling. She opened up to me, shared her fears and how lost she was feeling in that moment. She said that she hears people telling each other that they love one another, but she has a very hard time believing that the love is real. She does not know what love is. And she creates distance between us. I was just so happy that she felt she could share this with me. I so want to love her, embrace her, let her know that there is so much joy here for her. So much love just waiting to flow into her life if she chooses to open the door and let it in. She knows the love I have for others is real. She knows the love that I receive from others is real. Yet when it comes to her own life, she cannot imagine it being a part of hers. It feels odd to be in this position because part of me desires to reach out to her, yet the other part knows that this is her life experience and that she will experience it as she chooses for her greatest growth. I rejoice in knowing this is so.

Fun at the Dentist

I like to think that any experience can be enjoyable, that it is up to me and how I choose to experience it. I had a dentist appointment today and my mother met me there to watch Xander in the lobby. I have to say this was the best visit ever. It was just a standard teeth cleaning and the woman who does it is always enjoyable to talk to. This time she was telling me that she just had a big lunch and that her stomach keeps growling. Normally this is the kind of thing you just try to pretend like you don't hear. But her tummy was making all these sounds and she just started laughing and apologizing and because she was laughing, I started laughing. We were both laughing hysterically and couldn't stop. I wasn't sure if we were going to get through the cleaning because it kept happening and the laughter continued. I told her this was the most fun I had ever had at the dentist. Then I thought, everything else is so joyous in my life that it only makes sense that the visit to the dentist would be too. Isn't that great? I thought so. You really had to be there. It was funny!

A Disconnect

My mom and I had lunch after the dentist visit but we haven't been able to connect. I feel like she is so distant. I would really like to have a relationship with her but I am not sure how to do that except to keep sharing with her where I am. I feel like I don't even know her. And I know that she does not know me. I rejoice in the gifts she has given me and I honor her path and allow it to flow, as it will. I know that this is a co-creation and that I am every bit a part of it. I know there is much growth in this process. I am open and excited as to what will be revealed.

I Lost my Debit Card Isn't that Great?

I have another fantastic and fun experience to share with you, although you might not view it that way. A few days ago I misplaced my debit card. Now this is a situation where I could have freaked out, called to cancel the card right away and worried about it.

But that just isn't my life anymore and I am so glad I got to experience this. I felt peace that all was well and it would turn up. So I did nothing but enjoy the peace. I thought something good is in this for me. Well, I was in Charlottesville and needed gas money so I started calling my credit cards to see if I had any available credit.

They had all been at their maximum limit the last time I checked but I just thought, you never know. And sure enough, I had $200 available. I don't know how but I was grateful for the gift. If I hadn't lost my debit card, I never would have checked. I felt peace all week and today, when I put on my coat, there in my pocket I found my card. All was well, as I knew it would be. I understand if it might sound a little crazy to you, but to me it is absolute perfection. It really is.

And it is a wonderful way to live and experience life. No stress, no worries, just freedom. The freedom to just be carefree, to laugh, have fun, enjoy life and experience nothing but peace. It is so magnificent!

Tears of Joy

The sky was absolutely beautiful today. The clouds were like streams across the sky. It brought tears to my eyes to witness such magnificence.

11/06

I have had quite a few questions flow in for Jacob this week. It has been really great practice and a wonderful opportunity to explore this more. Much growth. I am enjoying the process. I tried to have them speak directly into the microphone for the voice recognition but that didn't quite work so well. I am still tape recording it and then speaking it as I play it back to transcribe. That's all right with me though. It is still so much quicker than before and a lot of fun.

11/07

Today we have begun preparing our house for the big move. My former husband and I decided to rent a truck and start clearing out the garage stuff and moving it to a storage unit. We spent all day working on it and still didn't get it all done. Tomorrow we have a packed attic to go through. It is a little more challenging because we have to get everything down the ladder stairs. I am enjoying the process. There really isn't that much left inside the house besides furniture. I had already cleared out a lot when I moved to my apartment. I am very excited about coming to a closure with all of this.

It is more of an energy closure. I can feel the energy shifting as we are clearing the space. It really does feel like it was a lifetime ago that I ever lived there. It even feels like I am almost observing someone else's life. My life has changed so drastically that I still cannot believe it has only been a few months. I barely even remember that life.

This has helped me gain a better understanding of the concept of time. My consciousness shifted so much that the time frame felt of great distance to me. I experienced such a huge shift from where I was to where I am now that I could no longer relate to that life. Therefore, it had to be a long time ago because it is the only way for my mind to process it. This feeling was immediate. It did make it easy to continue living my joy without experiencing any grief over the relationship. People would tell me the time would come. That I would deal with it. I told them there was nothing to deal with but I could tell this was hard for them to understand. It's not something that can be explained.

The experience provided me great clarity and that was all I needed to be free. There was nothing to grieve. I had been living in the pain. Now I was free of that. I have felt only joy and excitement for life. I am feeling so incredibly happy in this moment.

I am happy for my former husband and the new adventures to come for him and I am happy for me. I am delighted in knowing that I am finally living the life I have always wanted because I finally allowed it in. I look forward to every moment and to experiencing this exciting new world that has opened up to me. How great is that?

Opening Up to Connect

When Jan first suggested I think about visiting again I told him that if he opened up and began to fully connect and share with me that I would think about it. And do you know what – he did. He has shared much with me and we have had some really fantastic communications. I know there is much more there that I can connect with. It has already been a wonderful healing process thus far.

His comments to me were a co-creative process that I know I called forth to surface my stuff that I have wanted to release. And he has been supportive and present for me, as we have participated in this together. And this has also been a great growth experience and opportunity for him to look within as well. Some really great things have been occurring. I also asked him if I came for a visit what he envisioned the weekend would look like. He said a lot of talking and sharing and some lovely food and wine. I liked his answer.

A Roommate for Oregon

Now that we are about to close on our house, I finally went ahead and made my hotel reservations at the Ashland Springs Hotel in Oregon for the Holiday Retreat. I had been telling my Freedom Family all along that I was going to go. I just knew that I would somehow create it to be. And here it is. Delightful! MaryAnn, a friend from the Freedom Retreat, called me and said she would like to be my roommate. That was a pleasant surprise. I have only spoken to her a couple of times. She is sweet. I had left the roommate spot wide open to whomever came my way. I knew the first person who said yes, I want to be your roommate, would be the person I would spend this special time with. There is much opportunity for growth and a grand experience. I also spoke with another friend and I am planning to fly in a couple days early to spend time with him. Things are getting very interesting. I love how it is all unfolding. It is so great to just let go and allow it to flow in to perfection. It is going to be one fantastic trip!

11/08

After I pick up Xander from school today, I will be off to our house to clear out the attic. I am not really looking forward to the physical labor part of it but I choose to focus on the joy of this experience and the energy that is shifting as this space is released. Yeah for that! This is the most time I have spent with my former husband since we separated. Much clarity has come to me as I have been around him and view things from this new perspective. I am glad to be where I am. Delighting in my life, my freedom to be all that I am, do all that I choose and know that I no longer care what others think of my choices or my lifestyle. This is my life experience. I am the one living it. And I choose to live fully, completely, and put myself out there to all. I am grateful to him for that gift of clarity.

My new motto is this: "If I'm not embarrassing myself every day, then I'm not fully living!" It's been great. And the moment I feel embarrassed, I am immediately thinking – "YES, now this is living!" and I rejoice in the experience. I say and throw things out there and I have the most amazing experiences. I never know what may come of it but that is the fun of it. Where will this roller coaster go to and who wants to hop on board? Yippee!

Now I know there are those of you who are thinking, why would I be embarrassed if I do not care about what others think? This is just about me moving beyond my own comfort zone and how I feel about it. Others reactions are irrelevant to me. I may have a brief moment of "Okay, that was really embarrassing." And then I rejoice in that! Because I know that I have chosen to experience something beyond my previous limits, limits that were only set in place by myself. I am expanding. It is joyous.

It's the Thought that Counts

I am feeling especially chipper this morning. It is a beautiful day. I am eagerly waiting to hear from a dear friend who went to New York to attend a party. She has written a book and there may be contacts at this gathering that may lead to her getting it published. I was so excited for her. I had wanted to send something to her hotel room to celebrate this adventure of hers but she was staying at The Ritz and I figured they would charge $100 for a few mints or something.

So I just kept sending thoughts. Intending for something special. Well, when I finally spoke to her, I shared with her my thoughts. She said, well now, it IS the thought that counts. And she meant literally. She proceeds to tell me that she received a bottle of champagne from the lady at the front desk. She had told them about her book and then they sent it as a best wishes gift.

We both acknowledge the manifestation of my intentions and that it showed up in the form of delivery through someone else. There were two glasses. I told her the other one was mine. She toasted to both of us and drank one for her and me. Isn't that fantastic!

11/09

Today was another day of packing. We only have a couple more days to go. Almost done. Time to go to bed early. We start moving the big furniture tomorrow into my former husband's new place.

Goodnight Jacob

I have been missing Jacob lately with being so busy with the move. I asked them to come and just be with me last night. I haven't had time for much interaction with them recently. I just wanted to be in their presence. We chatted briefly and then I basked in their peace and love as I fell asleep. That must sound a little weird but I am just so used to it now. It's like having someone hold you and feeling safe. It is wonderful.

11/10

I am still feeling super-charged from Jacob. Wow, that interaction last night was so fabulous. Do I really even need a man when I have them? Well, yes, because I can have both. Yeah for me! (Are you laughing? This is my humor.)

Falling in Love

Someone asked me today if I would like to fall in love again. I would like to experience a relationship. I know it will be an incredible experience and I welcome the man who can step into my life fully. Completely. Connect with me on all levels. I look forward to that moment. I am open and will just let it flow. I know that all will unfold to perfection. I rejoice in where I am.

11/11

We got a lot done at the house today but there is still so much more to clear out. My former husband and I have been laughing a lot and talking about funny things we remembered from our many years together. It was really nice. There were some good times along the way. I have much love for him and it is wonderful that we can enjoy this experience together and maintain a friendship. But then, that is what we have had for all these years, a really great friendship and nothing else. I am now ready for so much more. I am excited, as I know it is already there for me. Just waiting for me to step into it.

I talked to Jan for about four hours last night. He and I have built a very lovely relationship since my trip there to see him. We have been talking for many hours several times a week. We also laugh a lot. I love that. It is so wonderful to laugh together and enjoy the bliss of life. I still don't know what you would call our relationship. We consider ourselves to be friends who enjoy engaging in physical pleasure when the opportunity arises. It has been interesting who has appeared in my life. He has had past experiences in his life that were similar to my husband. But because he was no longer in that space, he has been able to help me to walk through some of those things. It is wonderful to have someone communicate with me. I have gained a greater clarity and understanding about where I was and where I now am. I am grateful for my interaction with him.

Notes

I had a fun-filled evening with my friend this evening. I took her out to Red Lobster for her birthday. It is her favorite place to eat. We had a great celebration and it was a lot of fun. We plan to go swing dancing this Saturday.

I also had a great conference call with the gals in my Freedom Circle. There was a lot of laughter, joy, love and support. It is so wonderful to come together with them every week. I am grateful for their presence in my life.

Tidbits from Xander

Xander went poo poo on the potty today. He was so excited. Then he flushed the toilet and waved good-bye as he said "Bye-bye poo poo, have fun with your friends." I am sure we will be laughing at this one for a long time! It was just too cute.

11/13

What a glorious day this is! A dear old friend of mine just recently contacted me. I haven't spoken with her since last Christmas. It's been almost a year. We worked together about six years ago when I lived in Virginia Beach. She was the first person I felt a deep spiritual kindred connection with. Yet, she was brought up a strict Baptist and very religious. I always respected her beliefs and she allowed me to be as I was. I would talk about my meditations and my spirit guide Ariel as she listened to all of it. (I had done a past life regression session when I lived there back in 2000 and I ended up meeting Ariel. I talked to her often and this brought me to a great place of connection during that time. I have since come to understand that Ariel was another form of me, of source, and that I was guiding myself.)

We may not have agreed on everything, but it didn't matter. She knew my soul. She knew I was nothing but love and had nothing but love for her. I know this made her question her beliefs. When I asked her if she thought I would go to hell, she said, "Yes." Although she did express feeling conflicted at trying to understand how someone so loving and kind could be sent to hell. Yet the rules were the rules; I did not meet the criteria. I didn't mind that she thought this because I understood. How could she not think this based on what she had been taught her whole life?

After a long friendship and as she really got to know all of me, she told me she thought I was her angel. How interesting that I went from going to hell to being an angel. Well, when she called and asked how my life is going now, I told her. I told her all about Jacob, my free spirit living, and how extraordinary my life has been. She was intrigued. She wanted to know more. She had many questions. It was so delightful to speak with her. I knew that as crazy as it may sound to her, that she would listen because she knew me. I told her to send me some questions. I have no doubt they will all be based on the biblical teachings and wanting to understand how that fits in. I am very excited about this process. I know that she will ask the questions that no one else has. She was fascinated by the name Jacob and kept asking me if it were different than in the Bible. I told her I did not know. I know nothing about the Bible. All I knew is that this was the name that was presented to me as Jacob made their introduction.

I told her that I would not want to offend her by sharing some of these things with her because I knew it would contradict her beliefs. She told me that nothing I could ever tell her would affect the love she has for me. That she would always love me because she knew that I had always respected her and her choices. What a great friend she has been to me. I can see so clearly why she was my very first kindred soul connection. She was the first one to really see me for who I was, to embrace me for me as I embraced her for her. I am so grateful that she has re-appeared in my life. Once again, I take notice of this. This is significant and I am excited to see what will unfold from all of this.

She sent me the questions and they were indeed religious-based as I expected. I immediately did the session with Jacob, as I was so eager to know the response to these myself. Wow, prepare yourself. I felt the most powerful surge of energy flow through me during this session. It was the most wonderful feeling. The love and peace is just amazing. It IS heavenly. I know this may be a lot to digest but I made a promise to share whatever came through for all those who are asking.

What do you think of the name Jesus Christ?
It is a name like any other. It is not about a name, it is about who you are and where you are in your life experience. What you choose to experience. A name is just a word. It is irrelevant. It is the essence of what is being shared that is for you to take notice.

Do you believe that Christ came to set us Free?
The only one who can set you free is you. This is what we are here to guide you to. He offered an example of freedom. Showing others what was possible. Showing what was accessible to you and what you too could bring into your life experience. It is for those who observe it to decide how they feel about it. The framework of your perspective through which you observe it will bring forth an experience. That experience will be different for everyone.

We are here to guide you back to you. There are no external parties involved. It all begins with you. You are focused on Jesus Christ. He is no different than you. The only difference is that he was aware of who he was. He was aware that he was a part of God, of source, a part of all that is. And he shined his magnificence for all to see, for others to awaken to their God self. This is for you to come to know, you are just as magnificent. You have that shining light within you. You are part of God, source expressed, all that is and you can shine your light to others. You can set your self free. And what does that mean? Allowing the fullness of you to be expressed without fear, without worry, but just allowing all of you to be shared.

You are the only one who binds you. You are the only one who puts the chains upon you by the thought you hold about your life experience.

And you, in turn, can choose to be free. To allow yourself to awaken to the magnificent being that you are. As you open up to greater possibilities of what can be, you then open the door to allow it into your experience as it becomes part of your reality. You can awaken to this at any moment. It is at your choosing. You are always free to choose. Know this, you are glorious. We have only love for you.

Do you believe that Christ Jesus walked the earth as a man but ascended to Heaven?

And that the Holy Spirit resides on the right hand side of God the Father and dwells in the temples of the people (The Human Race)?

He was a man of awareness as many are today. He knew who he was. And yes he walked upon the earth, but again there is no difference. He ascended to the same place that you all will and that everyone does, back to source energy form. He was source, God expressed in physical form just as you are source, God expressed in physical form. We are all manifestations of source expressed. We are all one you see. There is no difference. And when you come to the awareness of who you really are, you need not put anyone on a pedestal. For you are just as glorious and magnificent. Each and every one of you is just as glorious and magnificent. And you are all here to experience growth and expansion. THIS is the purpose of life. And it is at your choosing. It is all perfection. It is beautiful. And you have chosen your religious path as an experience. It created a foundation for your growth. And now you are choosing this interaction with us in this moment.

It is all a co-creative process. Always. Every interaction is a co-creative process in which all parties involved are participating. You have drawn us to you, and we are here for the asking because you want and desire to know more. And why is it that you are asking? This is the question to ask your self. What are you seeking? What does this tell you about where you are? You are having this interaction because you have a desire for more. There is much that you want to know and understand. You have had many questions. And we are here. Here for you.

Do you believe that between God and man there is only one mediator and that is Jesus Christ?

There is no mediator between man and God because you ARE God. God is source. You are all God, source expressed in many forms. You are part of the magnificent source of all that is. We are all one. Like rays of sunlight shining out, you are having these different experiences for growth and expansion. There may be many rays but the sun is still the sun, the whole, and one source of these light rays. Expansion for one is expansion for the collective. God source is pure love. Love IS who you are. You have come here to create and experience those creations. You need not look for a mediator because it is you. There is no separation between man and God except that which you believe in your mind it to be. The power is within you. You have always had access to source but in believing that it requires another to make that connection, you have not brought the experience into your reality. All of the power is within you to create whatever you choose for your life experience. You need not look for God outside of yourself. For God is always within you. You are a divine expression of source. Rejoice in where you are. It is perfection.

11/14

I have been at the house all day and we have finally gotten everything out and cleaned up and we are done! We said our goodbyes, thanked our home and wished it well with the new family. We were supposed to close on the house this past Monday. I knew by the end of last week that we could not get everything done by then. So what did I do? I simply held the thought that all would unfold beautifully. I was at peace. The next thing I knew, we were receiving a phone call from the buyer's agent to push back the closing to Thursday morning.

It's now Wednesday night and we just finished up at 8:00 p.m. so it couldn't have worked out any better. Now could that be any more perfect? I mean really. And YES, I totally created that and I love to watch these creations manifest so beautifully. Isn't it wonderful?

Breathtaking Beauty

I want to share with you an extraordinary experience I had today. We were coming back from the storage unit and the sky was dark and cloudy. Then I looked up and there were these most magnificent rays of light shining through the cracks of the clouds. It was heavenly, absolutely divine. The rays created these circles and there were several sets of them across the sky. I got tears in my eyes from the sheer beauty of them. I have never in my life seen anything like this. Then, after staring for a while as my former husband drove along, I remembered what Jacob had said last night in our last session about the rays of light and the sun.

I was like, wow, they are showing me. I take notice. They are really showing me this. It was just such an amazing feeling. I am so incredibly grateful and happy to be me. I am still and continually in awe of my own life. I know this can be perceived in many different ways and it is in no way a comparison to anyone else's life. It is only a comparison to my own. For me, it is about my experience of shifting from a place in my life of such despair in not wanting to go on to a place of enjoying the beauty in everything. I cannot help but be in awe of that. It's just where I am.

Big Closing Day

We signed all the paperwork and officially closed on our house today. My former husband and I were talking and laughing. We rejoice in how we have chosen to handle our relationship in the midst of a "split." It is beautiful. I was feeling peppy all day because I could feel the release of the energy as this phase came to completion. It just felt great. I am beaming, glowing and radiating light, love, and joy.

He surprised me with a card at the closing. The envelope said: "Happy Closing, Wonderful Life." Printed on the inside of the card was: "It was your moment to shine, and you did it so beautifully!" He wrote: "You are sunshine! Thank you for sharing your life and blending your light with mine. Thank you for blessing me with your friendship. I appreciate you."

It was this part of him that I loved for so many years. The part that I knew was within him but he wasn't able to fully open up and let me in. Let me in to fully share a joyous life together.

I would just get tidbits here and there. I know that he did the best he could with where he was and so did I. We created many wonderful opportunities for growth together and I am so glad that I can finally recognize the beauty of those experiences now. This was a beautiful moment and I am so grateful for him and where we are now. It is a great friendship for a lifetime and then some. I am grateful for his many gifts.

I am celebrating and having a wonderful evening just relaxing at home and being with my happy, joyful thoughts. A new condominium complex is about to be built next to Xander's school. There is still just dirt right now but the sign got my attention and I am now enjoying envisioning this as home, at least a home base. There are lovely mountain views and it is a great location with easy access to everything. And it is close to the airport for all of my many travels to come.

I love my dream and even just the experience of the vision is extremely enjoyable to me. I look forward to the manifestation but at the same time, I am open to anything and am always living and choosing in the moment. I am aware that vision can shift and change and I allow it to freely do so as I continually come to greater clarity about what I want to experience. It is always exciting to see what will be revealed. Life is magnificent!

11/16

What a great day this has been. Xander had a school concert today that was really fun. They sang songs and the older kids did some drum and sword dances. They had a potluck lunch afterwards. All of that keeps me grounded. It was very nice.

I picked up my check from the title company this afternoon. I headed straight for the bank and it was so much fun to deposit that money. The next thing I did was to schedule my flight to Oregon for the Holiday Retreat. I had trusted that all would unfold for this trip to come to be and here it is, in this glorious moment. I love this process.

Now that my house is complete, I am sitting in a huge mess heap at my apartment. I moved more here than I really wanted to. I need to go through all of this stuff. I can't say I am feeling motivated at the moment. It is a bit overwhelming because it is so much. Today is Friday and Xander has already left to stay with his daddy for the weekend. Now would be the perfect time to organize it and yet I desire to just relax and do nothing. And what will I do? Live in the moment with what I am feeling right now. Perhaps tomorrow I will feel inclined to go to it. Before, this mess would have bothered me. In this moment, I feel only joy in allowing myself the freedom to just be. It is truly wonderful.

11/17

Today is Saturday and I am having fun going through things at my apartment. I brought my Phillip Daniel CD in from the car and I'm listening to it as I organize. I got a strong sense last night that I am supposed to meet him. There is something very special there. At the place where I am now, I am aware that every person who appears in my life is of great significance. And I am paying attention to what I am feeling. So I emailed a woman I thought might have his contact information. I didn't know if she could give it out so I asked her if she could give him mine. I was hoping there was a website or something. Ultimately I know it doesn't matter because if I want to meet him, I know the possibility is there for it to manifest in the most magnificent way. I am excited for that day. Although what would I tell him? I haven't a clue in this moment. Probably what I just told you. That I felt we were to meet and see what unfolds. Pretty interesting. I spent the day cleaning and I truly had the most joyous time. The last time I cleaned the toilets it was really fun. I was laughing and I shared this with my freedom circle. They were laughing and invited me to clean their toilets too. Ha! Ha! It really is about choosing the joy in every moment and so it was. I had a great time today.

Tonight I went Swing Dancing and they had a special dinner for Thanksgiving. I was supposed to attend with my sister and another friend of mine. My sister called earlier today and said she was sick and then my friend called once I was there and said she worked hard today with no breaks and needed to go home. So I ended up being there by myself but I embraced the opportunity to meet new people. It was nice to have the dinner first because I got to talk to people and get to know them a little. The dance lesson they did was the Country Two Step. I actually really liked that one. The men have their arms around you a lot. That works for me! There were more men than women there tonight which they said was unusual. It was nice to have so many people to dance with. I had the very best time.

Ready for Jan

I talked to Jan last night and he asked me to come for another visit. I could feel the anxiety arise in me, so I said "Yes." I knew that going beyond my comfort zone is where the growth is and I welcomed the opportunity. I booked a flight for next week. I have no expectations. I only want to connect as I feel there is much possibility for growth for both of us. I am living in the moment and in this moment I desire to go. There was no hesitation when we spoke about it this time. We had come to a great place during the many conversations we have had with one another. There is something very special that I cannot explain. I am excited to explore this further.

Phillip Daniel

What a beautiful day it is. I started this glorious day with an email from...........Phillip Daniel! Yes! Apparently the woman I contacted had just forwarded him my email and I am delighted that he chose to reply. He said he wanted to say "hi" and told me how much he appreciated my enthusiasm for his music. He also told me to feel free to write back. Well that left the door wide open so of course, I stepped in. I was so excited to hear from him. Then I thought, what do I say now? So I just shared exactly what I had sensed. That I felt drawn to meet him and that there was a greater purpose for him appearing in my life. I invited him to communicate with me so that I could get to know him and have the purpose revealed. We'll see what he says. Regardless, I am so happy to have had this interaction. I rejoice in knowing that reaching out to him was something that I never would have done from my old space. The contrast is beautiful. And I am so grateful to my friend who first gave me his CD and brought the awareness of him into my life. The series of events are always incredible. Thank you for this magnificent gift.

11/20

I had my Freedom Circle Call tonight. It was just three of us. The other two could not make it. It is the first time any of us have missed the call. It felt a little odd but, of course, it was perfection. We had some really great conversations. I always feel energized by our calls. They are so uplifting. Even though I start the call feeling great already, there is no end to how great it can be. The energy vibrations just continue to rise as we uplift and connect with one another.

In Tune with Another

I had a dream last night, which is the first I have had in a long time (that I can remember anyway). It was about my friend who had gone to Africa. In my dream, he walked through the door and he was home. I gave him the biggest hug and I didn't let go for the longest time. I think we stood there for hours. I just felt the energy flow. And then I looked into his eyes and the awareness of self was there. It was amazing.

I received an email from my friend this morning letting me know he had returned last night. He had never told me the exact date he would be returning. I didn't know when it would be and yet, apparently I did as he returned in my dream. I am paying attention. I have felt very in tune with him. Clearly I am. Amazing! To make it even more interesting, I had shared with him about the magnificent sunrays I had witnessed about a week ago. Well, he had taken pictures on the exact same day of ………you guessed it, sunrays! He sent me the photos. How divine! I take notice.

I stopped at 7-Eleven this morning for coffee. When I got up to the register they had these safari pens for sale. There were giraffes, lions and zebras. Of course my first thought was of my friend again who had just returned from a safari. I take notice of even the smallest of things. These are things that many might easily dismiss or more likely, never even notice. I see the beauty in it. I see its significance. And these wonderful little "signs" continue to appear in my life. Reminding me of where I am and how perfect it all is. And yes, I did buy a pen. The giraffe. One of the most magnificent creatures I have ever seen. Of course, all of the animals are magnificent. I just feel a special connection to the giraffe. I am not sure why, but so it is.

11/22
What is a collective consciousness?
A collective consciousness is many parts of source, expressions of source that come together as one collective. It is a group that chooses to come together. We are a collective and have come together because we are all choosing to participate in this process. Choosing to participate with Kayite and choosing to interact with you, with all who are asking. We have come together as a collective for the purpose of participating in the growth and expansion.

Was the collective consciousness that is Jacob ever in physical form like spiritual guides or always non-physical like most angels?
It is a variety. Some have experienced the physical and some have not. But in our non-physical, we choose to come together in this manner.

How is our inner being also a collective?
Your inner being is a collective because there are many parts to you. You are experiencing many lives all at once, many expressions of source. It is the collective of all of these expressions that come together as one source, which can be referred to as your inner being. There are different parts of you experiencing growth and expansion, source continually expressing in many forms. It is all occurring in this moment.

Is our inner being our soul?
Yes. This is the source of who you are. Love. This is your soul. Source expressed in physical form to experience life, grow, and expand.

What is the role of guardian angels and spiritual guides in the overall growth and expansion process compared to Jacob?
We have a very similar role. We are all here to offer guidance. Your spirit guides and angels are none other than your self. Source expressed in this form to guide you. Reminding you of what you seek to experience. And though they may remind you, you always have a choice in this moment.

I assume all are in touch with source and is source another word for God?
Everything is source expressed. Anything that you can imagine is manifested from source energy. That manifestation is an expression of source and is simply source experienced in a different form. Everyone has access because everyone is source expressed. You are source. There is no separation. Yes, source can be another word for God. Though we would say that God is another word for source as the idea of God is an expression of source. Those who are seeking God are seeking source.

Is there anything else that you would like to share with me?
Everything is within you. You have access to all that is. You are the creator of your life, your world. Choosing in every moment to create it, as you will. We are here to remind you of this. For you to know that you can experience life as you choose. There is no right or wrong choice. It is simply a different choice of experience. We are excited for your growth. We are excited for right where you are in this moment of now. There is nowhere else for you to be. You are already there, experiencing, expressing, growing and expanding. This is the joy. Embrace all of who you are. Allow yourself to shine unto the world. To allow the full expression of self to shine through and in this, joy is experienced. You are glorious. Know this.

Thanksgiving

We spent Thanksgiving Day at my mom and stepfather's house. My former husband joined us along with my sister, brother-in-law, nephews, my stepsister, stepbrother and his wife. It was a wonderful union. I enjoyed every moment of the experience. It was great to come together, to talk and share and enjoy a lovely meal.

11/23
We are here. What would you like to talk about?

The thing I am thinking most about is that I feel lost and at times stuck. And how.....how can I get past that? Feeling so good on some days, and feeling so bad on others.
Why do you feel you are stuck? What is holding you back?

Being...... being angry. And getting stuck in old patterns. I think because I...
What are you so angry about?

I don't know. It's like there is...... I know it has always been that there is never enough time for me. And I just sucked it up. But now I have time for me, and it still seems to be that there is never enough. So everyone is still getting in my way instead of adding to my joy, which is what I really want. And it just keeps spiraling downward from there. I don't know why I still feel like there's not enough time.
Do you feel that you have lost time? That you have not gotten where you have wanted to go? Done what you have wanted to do? Completed what you have wanted to accomplish?

Yes. How do I get through that to be in the now?
You are in the now. There is nothing to catch up to. There is nothing lost. Every experience has brought you to this moment of now. You can rejoice in this. You are here.

I can rejoice in that!
The only thing for you to choose is where to go from here. What do you want to experience in this moment?

I want to stay there. To stay in the moment somehow.

There is only this moment of now. It is for you to be consciously aware of this. You can take small steps.

I want to take small steps and I feel like that's what I've been doing but now I feel like I've been going backward small steps. And maybe it's just as simple as I have been doing that and now I need to go forward again. But then I think I just get so caught up in why am I going backward that it takes me further backward.

Yes. Although this is not about a backwards or forwards as only energy in motion exists. Everything that appears in your life is an experience for growth and an opportunity for you to create the change that you desire. As you recognize it when it shows up, acknowledge its gifts, you will create a shift to release the energy. This is the purpose it serves. It is not backward at all. It is just your view of it from the framework of where you are. As you allow for greater possibilities, experiences will show up for you to shift and expand your framing in order to experience this differently. Embrace these experiences and utilize them as the tools for creating the changes that you desire.

That's really good. If my kids could follow I guess. I really worry about them.

They are doing just fine. They are having their own experience. You need only concern yourself with you. And as you live your life, they will get exactly what they desire. You are always creating together. All is perfection.

I want to be with them instead of always doing around them. I'm trying to focus on that.

And what is keeping you from doing this?

I don't know. It............ good question..... what is it........ I'm not sure. I can't.....I.........I'll feel so good and then I'm looking at conditions basing how I feel on how they behave. Which of course is only getting worse if I am reacting to them instead of being. And I know that. I know it. I just have been feeling a little powerless.

You feel if they behave in a certain manner that you are controlling the power?

Well, if they would just behave...... you know if they wouldn't...... but I know that doesn't make any sense. If they would just....

You desire control but if you are connecting with you, with who you are, and you experience the power of the being that is within you, you would not be looking outside of yourself to gain the control. You would wield the power within you for that and you would easily be able to release that part of your self and allow them to be as they are and be joyful in that. And then you will naturally connect because you will not be so focused on how they are behaving but instead be rejoicing in them being where they are.

But your question is how to get there and we understand that. It is a process. It is the experience that you seek. It is this process that you are seeking and it is the experience along the way that offers the growth. It is not about getting there. The joy is in the journey of expression. As you desire to create change, experiences will show to provide you that opportunity. It is for you to recognize them when they do. Embrace exactly where you are. It is perfection.

I feel like they are more stuck with the things that I am wanting at this age in their lives but....

It is all a co-creative process. And as you are growing, they are growing with you. And they are creating with you as you are creating with them. Always.

I really feel that a lot.

You need not beat yourself up over it.

My little one really seems to be teaching me more than anything. He is so wise.

They are all teaching you, everyone who appears in your life. Every being that you encounter is offering you an experience for growth.

My anger could be as simple as still trying to control the conditions of how they behave. I'm trying to figure that out.

I'm trying to control how they behave and I know that I have thoughts of why do they do this to me? Those are the kind of thoughts that bring about anger for me.....and all I really want is to be their loving mother. And allow them to be who they are.

Then allow yourself to be where you are. **Right.** *It all comes back to you. Because when you start with you, all the rest will follow. When you allow your self to fully be, you allow everyone else in your presence to be as they are. That naturally follows. You do not have to try to make it happen. It will be. Focus on you.*

I was thinking about a retreat that I went to and my reaction to all the egos in the room. And I was really wondering if you had anything to say about.........well people were talking that they felt this person should leave because he didn't follow the rules and I literally, my whole body started to pulse and I remember my heart felt like it was going to explode out of my body. I've never felt anything like that physically before and I just felt like I needed to leave. And then when I left I felt such joy and freedom and clarity but I still wonder about that because I've had reactions to egos before and I just wondered what that pulsating was. It definitely seemed to be telling me to go. And I thought, was I running away again?

What did you feel in that moment?

Free.....and clear and happy and wanting to be.....wanting to enjoy the trip without all of what was going on around me.

What was going on?

The hour and a half of "you did something to us." All of these people telling this one person, you did something to us. I really didn't like it. I just didn't want to be there. I didn't want to be a part of it. I didn't want to be around it. Apparently it was affecting me very physically but I don't know why....

What emotion did this experience trigger to surface for you?

Well, I remember that I wasn't really angry like I thought that I would have been. Like what's wrong with these people.

I wasn't thinking those thoughts. But I was thinking, this is such a negative space. This stuff coming out of these people is so negative and part of me thinks should I have been sitting there trying to see the good? I mean I guess the good was that I got out of there and felt great. When I left that was good, but should I have stayed?

There is no should. You did exactly what you felt in that moment. And if you were experiencing joy in that moment, if it felt good to you, then embrace that. You followed what you were feeling. But what you were feeling does not mean that it has to continue to be in this moment of now. As you continue to grow, your perspective will change and you can allow yourself to be open to something different. And that what you experienced then was right for you in that moment because that is what you wanted to experience for your growth. All is perfection. You need not doubt what has already been. Only ask for clarity in what growth was in it for you. Utilize the experience to your greatest benefit.

That makes sense.

It does not serve you to look back and say what if. It has already been. Embrace it as it was created to be. For the divine co-creation it was. How do you choose to experience it now?

That's pretty neat because it's not about regret. And I don't really have any regret when I do think about it because I do feel so good about how that went for me. And I felt like it was amazing and then on the way back, I had a fearful experience on the plane. I have never been so scared. I was scared and missing my kids and thinking what if I never saw them again. Which was so out of alignment with what I knew to be true, that life is eternal and that I'm always safe. But I was so scared and I have felt that way in my car a few times since then. And I don't know if that's anything...

This is a big transition for you. You are on the verge of creating great change in your life. You are right on the edge. And these scary moments are experiences that are telling you – I am scared to make this leap. I am scared to make this leap because I don't know what is waiting for me. These thoughts have created confusion for you. We are here to tell you what is waiting for you. Joy. Love. And if you allow yourself to make that leap, to walk through your fear, you open up the door to experience all that you seek.

Yeah, I think I was so joyful over the summer because I was looking forward to the retreat and it was easy for me to think more joyful thoughts and stay in a positive space. Because anything negative I would just say, I'm working/headed toward this retreat. And then when I came back, it was so wonderful the whole week. And it makes sense the fear of coming back is of the change I am bringing into my reality, my daily life. And then I don't feel like I have anything I am looking to....like I'm almost scared because the New Year is going to come.........I know that I don't need to have a time....it's probably good that I don't have a time because as long as I keep the time in the future like I'm looking toward the New Year or I'm looking toward June or whatever it is, then I'm putting my good in the future and I'm still not living in the now.

The year is irrelevant. The day is irrelevant. There is only this moment of now. And you do not need to set yourself up for this goal that is only going to bring disappointment. Embrace where you are. You are setting your self up by saying – If I don't get to this space that I have somehow failed – and then beating yourself up by saying – why can't I get there. Not realizing that you are already there. YOU ARE ALREADY THERE. This is the journey. You are on it. You are not here to cross the finish line. You are here to run the race. Allow yourself to be consciously aware of the process and enjoy the run. THAT is being in the moment.

I feel it now. Sometimes I feel it so strongly and sometimes I don't feel it at all. I just feel anxiety again. Like I haven't had in a long time.

The anxiety you feel is because you are on the verge of shifting into a new vibration and you are resistant. You are scared because this space is out of your comfort zone. It is a place that you are not familiar with and you feel uncertain. You want control. Yet the control of your life is there for you. You have absolute control of how you choose to experience everything. And if you embrace this, that you are creating your life in this manner, this is a grand form of control that is joyous rather than coming from a place of desperation. It is more glorious than anything you think you can control outside of yourself. It becomes a struggle when you want to change others, or control things outside of you. And then you will feel off balance when it does not occur the way you would like it to. When you consciously control how you choose to experience what shows up for you, you will experience the harmony that exists.

I'm just realizing that I haven't felt so out of control in a long time. The more that I have been trying to control my conditions again. That makes a lot of sense.

And we would say to you that when you feel this anxiety, when you feel any sort of resistance, that is the moment to say – onward bound. It is uncomfortable for me but I choose to move beyond this feeling because that is where the growth is. You can say – as scary as this is for me, I choose to see the growth in this and I choose to respond differently to create change.

What are you so afraid of?

I really have gotten on my journey for abundance and well-being and I realize one of the things that holds me back is something that I think of as a secret. My husband.......I haven't been honest with him about how we've been able to maintain our finances. And he'll probably never have to know what I've done to maintain our finances. And if it weren't for him, I'd feel totally fine with the way that I am managing things. But this is the hugest thing. It's something that carries me down.

It's so funny, I hadn't even been thinking about it this week. I pushed it so far down. It's the one thing that just doesn't feel right to me. And I can't...I know they say everybody lies and I can go on about how he doesn't take any responsibility, he doesn't ask questions, he doesn't even seem to want to know. But I still feel like, well I know. That he wouldn't do this. It would be risky for him. Yet his choice is not to participate. But then I am constantly saying I feel great about this but then it's still tied to him and I don't know how to let go.

Know this, he is participating. It is always a co-creative process. He has participated in all that has been created. Even though it may appear that he is not a part of this process, everything that has occurred he has created. And you have many choices here. You can share with him all that has been occurring if you feel you wish to do so or you can simply choose to look at it from a different perspective. Changing your own view of the situation can release this for you. This financial situation is about the experience. Everything is just a different experience. It is a growth process. This is growth for you and the growth being none other than how you choose to view it and expanding your frame. As you shift your perspective, growth and expansion occurs. You are feeling that it had to be done a certain way because of how he views things. But you do not have to live your life based on another's view of anything. This is your life experience, your creation. You create it as you choose. And you can release this as you choose. You are doing the best that you can. This is just where you are. This is what has been created and there is no specific way that it has to be. Embrace where you are. What do you choose for you?

For once I totally get this. It's hard because I know I'm not suppose to care what he thinks but because I know that the fact that I'm scared to tell him means that I'm not letting it go. The fact that I know he would feel betrayed and never forgive me. That's all I'm thinking and it's hard for me to figure out how to let that go. It makes me feel like I'm not a trustworthy person when I know that I am. But then I think, well on this issue I'm not. And that I'm afraid with the whole fear of telling him....it's just gotten so complicated for me.

And if he were to feel betrayed, this would simply say where he is. It is not about you. You would be setting off a trigger point for him for this feeing of betrayal to surface. But you are not the cause of it. This would be an opportunity for growth for him. An opportunity to release the congested energy that activates his trigger point.

That felt really nice.

And this experience has been created for you as well. What growth is in this for you? Embrace this as an opportunity for growth, instead of something negative. An opportunity for you to let go of another's view of you, to let go of basing your value from another's idea of you, allowing him to define you. He does not define you. You define you. You know who you are. You know the magnificent being that is beaming from within.

I really felt that while you were saying it.

Allow your light to shine. It is a brilliant light that is waiting to just burst out of you. And for so long you have allowed others to define you. Taking in what they are telling you about who you are. No one else can tell you who you are. You are the only one who can define this. And as you gain greater clarity about where you are in your life experience and expand your awareness of self, you will radiate to others and declare – this is who I am. And maybe they will see it and maybe they will not. That is dependant upon the framework through which they are experiencing this world. This is about how you experience yourself. Make the declaration for you.

I have to get a tissue. Thank you. That really is it. That's what I'm so angry about too.

(tears....pause....more tears)

Are you still there, Jacob?

We are here.

That's really it. I've always cared what everybody else thought. I didn't realize that was at the core of all of this. I have known that my biggest resistance was that I didn't want to tell anyone, that I didn't know whom to tell about this.

You do not have to be afraid of being who you are. And as you begin to express that, this is part of moving through the fear. Beginning to express to others who you are and where you are in this life experience. And as you express to another, you are stating it to yourself. Rejoice in you. Empower yourself. What another thinks of you is irrelevant.

I have been worried...not only about the betrayal but I am also worried that everything that is going on is holding me back. I've just been worried on every angle.

And it is holding you back but only because you have placed yourself in a box. Understand that as we use the term "holding back" that it does not mean that where you are and have been is not all right. It is perfection. It is always perfection. We simply use the term to relate to you and what you are feeling about where you are. It is a hold back from where you want to go as you do not allow yourself to open the door of this box to experience more. The box was created by you and can be dissipated by you as well. This is all part of your experience. Growth is offered in the seeking to open the door. Growth is offered in the seeking to shift the box. When you release resistance, recognize and embrace the growth, you can create change.

It's so true. It really is an important part. Because honestly, I look back on my life and I want to see I have done nothing wrong. And this is something that glares at me as maybe something I did wrong. And that in itself is not a way to live.

You can do no wrong. That is simply a term that was created and is defined by each individual based on the framework of where they are. There is simply a different experience. And anytime you have those thoughts, remind yourself of this. Anytime you are questioning if this is right, should I be doing this, you can say – this is simply a different experience and what do I choose to experience now? Do I want this, or do I want something else? The choice can be as easy as that. Instead of it being about right or wrong, would this be okay, would that be okay, make a choice from a different place. Make a choice based on what you want to experience.

I wish our money weren't tied together.

If you did not want it to be that way, it would not be. And if you really want to experience something different, you will create it. The only thing holding you back is your thoughts about it. It is the thought about it that creates it. Your perspective of it can change and it would no longer be an issue for you. Welcome the experiences that will shift this perspective.

I've seen the magic of things. I know it's there. The ways finances stretch and wellness becomes better.

And do you not believe that you can create this too?

I do. I do.
   We are excited for you.
   End Session
   Tape cut off. The rest of the conversation was not recorded.

Trigger Points

A friend of mine contacted me and told me how she has really been enjoying her spiritual journey to know herself. That at times she has hit some of the highest of high moments and they are remarkable when they happen. The flip side of that is, there are some pretty strong things the universe is throwing at her regarding finances.

She said she has come to grips with understanding that this piece is truly hers to figure out and it is a gift, not a burden. She is strongly focusing on her money experience and doing her best to get clear about what it is that she wants. She has those "human moments" as she calls them, when she does buy the illusion and all that goes with that in terms of fear, worry and all that. She does her best to make the best of those moments when they come which isn't always easy. She has noticed that she is not staying down as long as she used to.

   The following is my email response:
My Divine One,

Things sound wonderful for you. I would like to share with you some of Jacob's Message as this feels like the right moment. When you said you are still being thrown experiences regarding finances, I felt compelled to share. Every experience that shows up in our life is here to offer us growth.

   Now, from past experiences we have chosen to hold onto energy from hurtful and painful experiences and carry it with us. As we hold onto these energies, they become congested and manifest in the form of physical and mental dis-ease. Jacob refers to this hold of energy as "congested energy." As you desire to create change, you must first release that congested energy. (Many do so without the conscious awareness of it.) Experiences offer us the opportunity to do that. Others appear in our life as an opportunity to do that. They appear and set off "trigger points." These are feelings that arise from past experiences that have caused you to feel concern in the now. When a trigger point is activated and these feelings surface, this is a wonderful opportunity to release them. There is much growth in this process. It requires an experience to create a shift and set it free. Jacob calls this "walking through it."

So the financial issues keep coming at you because you are holding energy around it that has yet to be released. There is resistance to the process. I have walked through many of my own trigger points with another and set myself free of the congested energy. I could feel it shift and then it allowed for what I desired to flow in. And once it dissipates, similar experiences will no longer activate these feelings, as the trigger point will be gone. Then they will no longer serve purpose to show up in your life. However, they may still show up a few times to let you know you have shifted. This has been my personal experience. When you have an experience and realize that it no longer triggered the response you would have previously had, this is how you will know things have shifted. You acknowledge, say thank you for the gift of clarity of where I am, and bye-bye.

So what exactly am I saying? Look to the source of your feelings around money and what that is about for you. Where is the fear, worry coming from? It's not about rehashing old stuff. It is about acknowledging the source in order to consciously acknowledge your creation of the experience. Many want to acknowledge what they consider good creations as their own but not the so-called bad stuff. They don't know why they would create such unpleasant experiences. It is created on an unconscious level and this is why the acknowledgement of the source is of value. Then rejoice that the issue has been brought to the surface for you because this is the point of power.

There is no need to analyze the past; just embrace the source of it, welcome the growth from the experience in understanding that it is no longer necessary, and declare your current desires. Acknowledging what is coming forth for you, releasing all resistance and embracing what is, will allow things to begin to shift for you. Similar experiences will continue to pop up in your life to give you the opportunity to respond differently. As you do, the congested energy will be released. When these experiences arrive, instead of thinking – "not again, why is all of this happening all at once?", welcome these experiences for the gifts that they are. Consciously welcome them and the growth in that will set you free. I know you said you understand that these things are a gift but perhaps this will show the gift in a different light.

As I have worked through some of my past issues, I have felt the feelings of past hurt that surfaced while at the same time feeling the joy of the process since I was consciously aware in the moment of why it was occurring. That to me is peace in the moment. Peace in knowing that what I am feeling and experiencing is important to my growth process. And I was aware that the feelings coming up were not fully present in my now. They were leftovers that I forgot to throw away. I recognized them and said, "Oh yes, I don't need you anymore," and in the trash they went. I really enjoy the process. Embrace it as it is for you and allow it to flow. Know that it's all right to buy the illusion. This is the experience that you seek, the divine experience of shifting from illusion to clarity. And there will always be something else after that. Enjoying the beauty of where you are and the process as it unfolds is the joy. Embrace where you are in this moment of now and you will experience great joy in your life.

Much Love, Kayite

My Goody Bag

After sharing the last exchange about the stuff that comes up for us, I want to share more about my experience of the "stuff" from the framework of where I am. We all have stuff. I have money stuff, relationship stuff, work stuff. It is how we experience our stuff that is different. I experience my stuff as a big ole goody bag of growth. I get excited to open the bag, take out a new gift, and open it to see what will be revealed. How will I choose to experience this? How can I best utilize this experience for my greatest growth? I may not have an answer but I do enjoy thoughts of – what would happen if I responded in this way or that? And then I'll just give something a go and see what transpires.

Whatever the end result, it cannot possibly be considered a "failure." It can only ever be an opportunity for greater understanding. At least that is my perspective. And I can honestly say that I haven't gotten a crappy gift yet! (Smiling)

This is because the box is never empty. There is always something there for me. And I am open to expanding my frame by responding in ways I never thought possible before. It is the most exciting game I have ever played. There are so many choices, so many ways in which I can experience a single event in my life. This viewpoint makes life so much fun to experience. Have you looked in your goody bag today? I know there is something really fantastic waiting for you.

11/23

My sister is coming over tomorrow to speak with Jacob. We had that one experience together and then she canceled the next two times because she just wasn't ready for the stuff that was coming up for her. She said she knows she has been resistant. She feels things have gone downhill for her since because she has been resisting so much and she can't take it anymore. I told her this was a good thing.

She is finally at the end of her rope and now she is at a place where she will really ask the questions that maybe she would have been too afraid to ask before. She is at the breaking point. But the breaking point can also be the break through point, the point where one can burst through to the joy on the other side. I am really looking forward to this experience with her.

There is much growth in this for me as well. And I felt Jacob most powerfully when I was with her. I would love to feel those intense vibrations again. It is always different so we will see.

Taking Notice

I recently shared with a friend of mine about Jacob. I explained that things really began to open up for me after my retreat with Neale Donald Walsch. She had not heard of him. I told her about the *Conversations with God* books. She was very interested.

Right after our discussion, she went to visit a friend at her house. Her friend said that she had a great book for her to read. She got it off of the shelf and handed it to her. And what was the book? *Conversations with God.* Then, she was talking with her sister-in-law and asked her what she was going to be doing over the weekend. She responded that she was planning to watch some movies and that there was one particular movie she had to see. And what was this movie? You guessed it, *Conversations with God*.

Keep in mind that my friend had never even heard of this until I spoke with her. She was amazed at how it was just everywhere she turned. Surrounding her. She began reading the book and she is going to watch the movie. I told her that things like this occur in my life every single day because I take notice. These beautiful messages are always there for all of us. I am enjoying this process. It is beautiful to witness.

11/24

My sister finally made it over to speak with Jacob. She experienced a huge breakthrough. She burst into tears and just kind of let everything flow out. Things came up for her that she had not anticipated. She said she just felt safe with Jacob. That she knew that it would be okay. She felt their love and peace. It was really wonderful. I did not experience the intense vibrations as I did the last time, but I was in a very blissful state.

She desires to keep this particular conversation private and I honor that. I can share with you that she called me later that day and told me that she felt a weight had been lifted off her shoulders. She was feeling so glorious. I rejoice in her process.

Tidbits from Xander

Xander and I were sitting at the breakfast table this morning. I said, "Good morning handsome." He smiled and looked at me and said "Hi, beautiful."

11/25

As I am writing my first book and attempting to learn the so called rules of publishing, I want to know if it is possible for me to achieve my current goals within the world of publishing as it is seen and defined by so many others? In other words, do I need to play their "game" with the rules they have established?

You can achieve your goals in whatever way you wish. You do not need to play someone else's games, someone else's rules. You are creating your own rules, your own game. This is your life experience, your reality. You are the creator of everything in your experience. If you believe that you must follow others' rules, then this will be your life experience. If you indeed believe that you can create and manifest your book in your own way, then it can be. There are no limitations. The only end to what is possible is that which you believe in your mind it to be. It all comes back to your belief system, which has molded the current framework you have created through which you experience your world. Open up to greater possibilities of what can be. It is only when you allow for the possibility that you can then invite the experience and allow it in as part of your reality. Anything is possible. We would say to you, follow your own guidance of what feels best for you. This book will manifest. It is already there. You can experience it however you desire. That power lies within you.

I am enjoying this process of creating my books, contacting others who are co-creators, etc. I am sensing the possibilities despite the current "reality." Is there a way of managing the timing of it all? May I say, "I would like to have a six figure publishing deal before the end of this calendar year," and have that as a real possibility? How much control do I have in this process?

You have all the control in this process. Now you may say that you would like to have a six figure publishing deal before the end of the year but the question is, do you really believe this? Do you believe it is possible? Anything you choose can be but you must believe it to allow it in. If setting that goal seems so far out of reach for you, if you feel this is too big of a goal, then it will not be.

You may want to start by releasing your focus on a specific amount and time and instead focus on knowing your book will be published and abundance will flow in. Know that this book is a wonderful masterpiece that many will love and embrace. The abundance will flow from the passion and desire that you have for this creation. And you do not need to have a time-line because a time-line can create a roadblock. The closer you get to a set time frame, the more nervous you become and begin to doubt your creation. And because you start to doubt and worry about it, it does not manifest. You will feel disappointment and then this experience will affect your belief system for the next creation you desire.

We would say to you, believe in what you have created. Know that this book is brilliant. Start with thoughts that you feel you can embrace. Something that feels good to you. And not having a specific amount in mind will actually allow for more to flow in. If you release all limitations and allow for great abundance to flow in, you may find that you will receive more than you ever imagined in this moment. Expand beyond the horizon. Much is awaiting you.

I have been talking lately about the concept of time. How can I more clearly understand the concept that "there is no such thing as time?" Is there a way to understand this that helps us with our every day decisions and things that we have intended but not yet seen?

Choosing to live in the moment and enjoy the moment. As you are enjoying the moment, you're not so focused on what is ahead, on how much time there is, or on what you think needs to be done. There is nothing that has to be done. There is nothing that has to be accomplished. It is the experience of the process that you seek. This is what you are wanting. It is not about the book being published, but the experience of writing it, the experience of seeking publication, the experience of sharing the manifestation. Release the end result and allow yourself to experience where you are, right now, this moment.

And yes the manifestation of your creation will be joyous, but it is about the journey along the way. You can say – I embrace where I am right now in this moment, this is the joy of my life force expressed. Being in the moment is the process and you will not focus so much on time when you are consciously aware of your presence of being in the moment. Shifting your thought from day-to-day living to just being present now can expand your framing to experience life in an entirely new way. Embrace everything around you and feel gratitude for what you have created. Consciously choose in every moment what you want to experience. As you are cycling through this particular life experience, you are creating the pressures of time. There is an abundance of time. Your lifetime here is but a blip, a snap of the fingers. And you can live it again and again and again.

Your opportunity for growth and expansion is never ending and therefore time does not exist. With your everyday decisions, decide what you want to experience and allow yourself to consciously observe the process of what shows up for you. What you have intended and not yet seen manifest is a clear message to let you know where you are. Enjoy the experience of taking a closer look at your thoughts that have created this to be. It is a grand opportunity to consciously be aware of your continual growth.

Focus on this growth that is always successful in your life, always will be as it is a continual process, and you will not concern yourself so much with the details of the end result. You are not here to cross the finish line. You have already done that. You are here to run the race. Already having your trophy, allow yourself to slow down and enjoy the run. Enjoy all the many magnificent experiences along the way, moment to moment. As you release and let go of time, things in your life will flow much smoother. It is the focus on time that hinders you because you are trying to get somewhere else and feel the pressures of time to do that. You are here. The only place you can be. It is for you to awaken to where you are. Everything always occurs in the perfect moment. You cannot go wrong. Enjoy where you are, right now.

The books I'm creating cause me to look at the human population and the ways in which we have divided ourselves. One of my goals with my writing is to invite others to step outside of their current reality as it appears and consider the larger picture of why we are here. Can you speak to this topic? I do understand that this is MY passion, and my purpose as I have defined it. But, there must be a reason why I would have this particular desire.

You are here for growth and expansion. A population divided is a population that can come together and in this the contrast and a foundation for growth exists. You have this particular desire because it gives you great joy as you are guiding others to unite. Your passion is your greatest desire and when you follow this you allow the fullness of your life force to be expressed with no resistance, a beautiful flow of expression, which is the joy.

You desire to create great change in your world, to create healing. You are creating a space for others to step into, for all those who have been asking. You are answering and agreeing to participate in the experience in this manner because it feels so good to you to express the fullness of you in this way. This is why you have chosen it. There is much growth in this for all of you. It is a collective creation. Enjoy the process.

Speak too of the unique place of the African American population in this country. I know, we are all one, but obviously giving that advice is not sufficient for addressing the issues of that population. I am here to serve, with delight and according to what pleases me. And, I desire to be a voice of love and possibility. What can you tell me to assist me with this dual purpose?

It is your perspective that the African American population has a unique place in this country. Every being and every experience is unique, each creating your own experience for growth and expansion. Each choosing how you want come forth into this world based on what you wish to experience. All beings provide a contrast and point of growth for one another. All beings provide the opportunity for continual growth as source continues to be expressed in many forms for this growth.

You have chosen to be part of this population for the experience. And from this experience, you have come to be where you are now. You desire to be a voice of love and possibility and this experience has provided you the foundation for what you are wanting. You already are a voice of love. And you are showing what is possible just by being you. You are powerful. As you look for assistance, we would tell you to fully express all of who you are. If you want to be the voice of love, express love to all. If you want to be a voice of possibility, then go forth and experience and show others what is possible. Live it. Be it. This cannot be denied and others will take notice. This is what will create the change you so desire.

And regarding my every day life...what can I do to allow any bodily conditions that I do not enjoy to no longer be a part of my life experience? What do I need to know about my body that is causing it to feel the way it feels...not at optimum health and vitality? What do I need to know about this? It seems that there are two desires at work, here. Can you elaborate on that?

What we would tell you about the bodily conditions that you do not enjoy is to look within and ask yourself why you do not enjoy them. What is it that you desire to change? And can you embrace where you are right now? It is your thoughts about your body, your health, and your life that is creating your current manifestation. As you shift your thoughts about you, you can create the health that you want. It is a natural flow. It is simply for you to remove the blockage you have created.

There is nothing that you need to know about your body, there is much for you to know about you, how you feel about you, and how you are choosing to experience your life that is causing you to experience a decrease in health and vitality. Look to the source of the congestion. Coming to a greater understanding of what has been created and why can open you to expanding your frame and creating change. There is great purpose in every experience. You are asking the questions. In doing so, it brings forth thought and creates the desire for change. With that desire, your energy is already in motion for the manifestation. It is for you to allow for the possibility in order to invite the experience into your reality as you expand the framework of where you are.

11/25

I ended up at Unity by myself again. My friend that I normally meet there had trouble with her heating unit at her house and she needed to stay home to meet the repairman. I was sitting in the middle of an empty row when a lovely woman (in her 70s) came and sat in the chair right next to me. I had not met her before. She beamed a huge smile and said "Hi" as if I were a friend she had not seen in a while. Her name is Ella and she is just delightful. There was a special guest comedy singer who was performing and his songs were so hilarious that Ella and I laughed the whole time. It was great. When the service was over, I gave her a huge hug and thanked her for her beautiful presence appearing in my life. It was so great, again, always perfect.

I was able to finally meet up with my friend this afternoon. We went out to lunch and then went shopping. Now, I know many women like to shop but I am so not a shopper. It is not my thing. Well, unless it is a spiritual store. I suppose I could spend hours there. I was more company along the trip as my friend was getting some things she wanted for herself and I just enjoyed spending the day with her. We went back to her house and talked for several hours. We had a very long conversation about love. It was fascinating and it offered me a wonderful opportunity to gain clarity about where I am and to declare it. From her perspective, she thinks there would naturally be a big difference between my love for Jan and my love for my other friends. Which I understand because there is sex involved and would be what most people consider a romantic relationship. I told her love is love to me. Jacob has said that love is who we are and that love is just expressing ourselves.

So for me, from my perspective, my love is the same to all because I am open and fully expressing my love, myself to all. Now I may choose to experience that in different ways, such as a sexual interaction, but it is still just another expression of self. In knowing that love is all there is, and that we are all one source expressed in many forms, I do not hold one relationship more sacred than another. I have created the most incredible relationships and each one of them is so vastly different. It is wonderful to have the conscious awareness of what each brings into my life. Some I am drawn to more than others but each is an important part of my process. I am so glad this love thing came up. I think I will start to ask everyone about what love means to him or her. This will be very enlightening for me. I am excited.

Computer Glitch or Divine Creation?

I have been working for hours on a Jacob transcription. I type it in an email and save it as a draft as I continually add to it. Well, I'm not sure what happened but I was almost to the end of the tape, almost done, when I somehow lost everything I had spent the last few hours working on. The thought of doing it all over again just made me want to cry. I contacted a friend and just shared. I centered myself and just said, "All is perfection." I know there is something wonderful in this for me. My friend and I had a really beautiful interaction.

So what did I gain from this experience? I came to the realization that I didn't even care that I had lost it. It only felt like a loss in the moment but nothing was actually lost at all. What I came to understand is that I had been offered an experience with my friend as a result of what appeared to be a "loss." I chose to move beyond the surface appearance to reveal the beauty of what was being offered.

And after our discussion, I have now learned about a program that may be very beneficial to me and to my work to come. It is all so divine. And after all, it's just what is. I embrace it.

I have also noticed that there are times when I cannot log into my computer. It just isn't having it. I welcome the computer glitches and rejoice in what will be revealed in the experience. I take notice of all the little things that show up. They are easy to dismiss but when you begin to consciously take notice, you can then begin to experience just how significant they actually are.

11/26

My sister has said that she has felt a huge shift occur since talking with Jacob. Things have been going really great for her lately. She feels good. I am excited for her process.

Love Continued

As I was asking others about the meaning of love, this is one response I received: Most people look at love in many different ways from romantic love for someone, to loving a family member or best friend, to loving life, their job or something similar. In other words, love is compartmentalized and not unconditional in most cases. I guess I fit into this category based on my life and personal experience.

11/27

I have had discussions all week about what love means and then one of the women in our Freedom Circle just happened to come up with a quote to share about love on our call tonight! She was not aware of my discussions. Very interesting. I take notice.

Vulnerability

You know, even though Jacob has opened me up to a whole new connection with others, I had already become very open at expressing my feelings after my experience at the retreat. Before, I had felt like I was dying. Actually, I felt like I was already dead. (At least in the awful way I used to view it. Now I know death is beautiful and I can only rejoice in it.) I just existed, but nothing in me was living. (Of course I now know this cannot be. Existing is living. But that was my perspective at the time.)

I felt like I was given another chance at life and I chose to fully express myself like never before. I chose to live. I chose to just go for it. Put everything out on the table and see what manifests from that. (So many glorious things.) We had an interesting discussion with my group call tonight about being vulnerable and others wanted to know how I was able to open up so freely.

I can tell you that I experienced more hurt and pain being disconnected from myself and hiding from others with a barrier wall up than I ever have at being fully connected and open. There really is no vulnerability in this space because when I put everything out there and state this is who I am, I feel only strength in that. It is extremely empowering. Many might see it as a weakness, but there is truly great strength in being open and expressing you. That is source expressed with no resistance.

Can you imagine just how powerful that can be? I know who I am now and am no longer looking to someone else to define me. So it does not matter whether someone else will embrace me. I embrace me. I do not need to look for love or approval from anyone. I am the love. I am the source. The joy flows through me in this space. And when the joy is flowing, there is no room for anything else.

11/28

I am off to Florida tomorrow. Excited about my trip to see Jan. No expectations. I am just choosing to be in the moment. No matter what occurs, I feel there is much growth in this experience for me. I am looking forward to it all unfolding. It has been a month since our first visit together. I had said that I felt anxiety when I agreed to the trip. Well, as the time grew close to my going there, I have become sick. Physical manifestations appeared, all of which I acknowledged and shared with him. I can see so clearly the relationship between the physical illness and what is going on with me. I cannot help but think will he again feel disappointment?

It is a scary thing for me, but I am choosing to walk through my fear. I know that as hard as it is to do, that this is the experience I am seeking. I also know that on the other side of the fear, joy is awaiting me. That if I stay with it, allow myself to expand, anything is possible. Ultimately, this is not about what he thinks of me, disappointed or not, as this is irrelevant. It is about how I will respond to the experience and the acknowledgement of how I have felt about myself. It is about me loving all of me and embracing myself fully.

Lack of Preparation or Gift?

Let me tell you about my fun adventure yesterday. Well, I got lost on the way to the airport and missed my 12:45 flight to Florida. I know that some of you might be thinking that I should have planned better. But the unfolding was truly divine. The next flight left at 5:15 (which is when I was initially intending to arrive) and would not arrive in Florida until 10:00 p.m. This flight went to Atlanta rather than through Ohio. Now here I was at the airport with four and one-half hours to wait.

As I sat there, of course I was thinking about what this was about. I knew that I was not supposed to be on that flight. That this was to occur, but why? What was I to receive from this experience? There were many gifts. The first was being able to experience where I am now. I was at peace and felt great about the whole thing. I was actually laughing. I thought, maybe I'll sit next to someone on this next flight and have an enlightening conversation. I am always looking at it from a most beautiful perspective. And I could truly appreciate this because of the contrasting experience I know I would have had many months ago before my transition. I know that before I would have cried right there at the front desk. And I really would have boo hooed when they told me it would be an additional $115.

I might not have even still gone on the trip. And then I would have spent the whole time at the airport beating myself up over not getting there sooner. I would have thought if I had only done something different. And feeling so upset that I had missed five hours of fun on my trip that I would have allowed that to be my focus, it would have expanded, and infiltrated my thoughts throughout the entire visit. And the whole thing would have been "ruined."

It is so ridiculous to me now but it was true. And many of us do this all the time. We allow one little thing to offset us rather than just embracing a so-called unexpected opportunity that has come into our lives. How much we allow our thoughts to completely run our lives. Just by becoming consciously aware of my thoughts, I am now running the show rather than it running me. At least that is what it felt like for a very long time. I was lost just being "in" my life, in all the stuff, rather than observing and experiencing the joy of it. I couldn't even see what was happening because I was too deep in the crap. Stepping back and observing my life allowed me to see that the crap wasn't actually crap at all, but beautiful opportunities for growth.

My awareness of that changed everything. A whole new way in which I could experience life was created. My framework had been expanded and my view of my life and my world completely shifted.

All of this was great for me to know and as I came to a greater understanding about myself and where I am in my life experience. I am delighted to know that the experience of missing my flight could occur and that I could feel just fine in the process. More than fine actually. I felt incredibly excited to see what experiences my little detour would bring.

And what were the other gifts of this experience? Did I end up meeting anyone? Have any great conversations? Well, yes! On my layover in Atlanta I went and sat at the bar at Applebee's and ordered something for dinner. There was only one seat available. Just for me.

I said hello to the man next to me and asked where he was headed. His name was Gary and I think he's in his 60s? We started talking about life, where we have lived and then somehow we got on the subject of my book. I shared with him about my life transformation and what it was all about. He said, "Good for you." It was great. I was so lost in the conversation and we talked so long that, oh my, I almost missed my connecting flight. Five minutes to go and I am jumping aboard.

This was the biggest airplane I have ever been on, the kind with two aisles, a 767 I think. I felt like a kid in a candy store. Looking around excited about all the features. I ended up sitting on one side in an aisle seat next to a most wonderful man named Jack. He was about 70? And do you know where he was on his way back from? Africa! He had been on a two-week tour and told me all about his trip. He then shared about previous trips to China, Laos, Cambodia and many more. It was fascinating.

He encouraged me to do a lot of traveling and stated that there was no better way to experience life. I have long desired to travel and I have noticed that I have drawn into my life those who are experiencing a lot of traveling in their life. They are showing me what is possible. I take notice. Pretty fantastic!

I had such a great time that I could not imagine my day unfolding any other way. This beautiful perspective is how I choose to look at everything in my life. It really is about being in the moment and knowing that everything is occurring for my own growth and greatest benefit. It has certainly been a wonderful way of life for me.

Allowing Others to Define You

I was having a discussion with a friend of mine and she expressed her desire to let go of what others thought about her. She has continually allowed their thoughts of her to impact her life in a way that didn't feel good to her. I know it can be a challenge to overcome comments from family, friends and others. I myself had allowed other people to run my life for many years, the first thirty-four to be exact. I was always concerned if others would approve of my decisions, how I chose to live. And I believed all the things they told me about who I was. I allowed them to define me. I chose to believe that what they said about me was true. Now I know my own truth, the only truth there is. And it was inside of me all along.

When I connected to this, all of that other stuff became irrelevant. I live for me now. I still listen to what others have to say about me, but I no longer immediately take it in as my truth. What I once considered an unpleasant interaction – those telling me how to live, what to do, who I am – I now consider a wonderful experience where I can utilize the information to gain clarity about where I am and what a wonderful opportunity it is to declare it. They had been offering me a gift all along, but I just couldn't see it, until I did. And in experiencing it, I was able to allow the full expression of self to shine through. How freeing it has been to just be me.

If you can relate to my story of feeling run by others, know that the joy of the expression of self is waiting beyond any fear you might have to create change. We are the only ones who place ourselves in a box and we are the only ones who can set ourselves free. Our own fear keeps us in the box. Fear that is just an illusion but we cannot truly know that until we choose to move beyond it to experience it. Fear is very real and scary in our reality while we are still in the box.

As you unleash yourself, break the dam, allow the fullness of you to flow with ease, your reality will change. Just think of that possibility. Just even allowing for that thought will begin to create a shift. I still have my own fears come up for me and as they do, I continually choose to walk through them.

Walking Through the Fear and Into the Joy

Finally I arrive in Florida. Of course, the first thing that Jan told me was that I looked beautiful. Did I believe it? Not at the time. I thought he was trying to make it easier for me. I was nervous. It was just the two of us, no other friends there this time. I had no idea where this would go but I just focused on the growth. I felt open to what was to come. I definitely felt there was something powerful being offered in our experience together. I didn't fully understand what it would be and how it would show up, but I just continued to follow my guidance and allowed the space for it to be revealed.

We headed home from the airport and got back to his house at 11:00 p.m. We ended up talking and sharing until about 4:00 a.m. There were tears for both of us. I could feel something shifting for me. There was a connection that transcended everything. We ended up making glorious love all weekend. I wasn't even sure if I would be able to go to that place with him. Yet when I was there, in it and he was fully present, any thoughts of concern just dissipated. My own thoughts about my body began to shift. I even ended up walking around the house naked.

That was a huge step for me. Having not felt comfortable with my body, to be fully naked in front of someone, anyone, just standing there, was magnificent. I asked him to draw a sketch of me like in the movie Titanic. It was about the experience of it for me. It was so very freeing to allow myself to go to that place.

11/30

Jan and I drove to Orlando today. We stopped for lunch at BJ's Brewhouse and I had a chicken Caesar salad. We had great conversation throughout the meal. I loved the way he looked at me. His eyes drew me in. His smile exuded joy. As we left, I noticed the beautiful architecture of a store across the street. It had a unique design. I said, "That's what I want for my house." I would like to build something like that. We didn't have a camera with us but he said the next time he was in the area, he would get a picture of it for me so that I could add it to my vision wall. My vision wall is a wall filled with all the many things I would like to create and experience in my life.

After lunch, we went to Ikea. This is the reason we came to Orlando. Jan was doing some renovations on his home and wanted to get some ideas with what products the store had to offer. We walked around for several hours and it was a lot of fun. We headed home and I was falling asleep in the car while he was driving because we hadn't gotten much sleep the night before. When we got home, he cooked dinner for us, and we ate while watching the movie *Elizabethtown* with Kirsten Dunst and Orlando Bloom. It seemed quite fitting for the moment. Our perspective was that it was about a free gal (me) showing someone (Jan) how to live in the moment and be free. We both really enjoyed it and got the deeper meaning that was relevant to us. Perfection.

It was getting late. We headed off to bed for some more fantastic lovemaking. Yes! This was very exciting for me considering I had left a sexless marriage and I had already had more sex in two days than I had experienced in many years. (I want to be clear that the issues in my marriage were something we both created together and my former husband is a beautiful man. We were unable to connect with one another because of our past pain that had created barriers. That disconnect was not conducive to inviting and creating physical, pleasurable interaction. We both remained distant. I have tremendous gratitude for the experience he offered me to know more about myself.) And this was not just any sex, but the most fantastic, glorious pleasures I have ever experienced.

There was an amazing energy exchange and I was aware of it. I acknowledge and talk about the physical pleasure because this was a point of growth and expansion for me to allow it into my reality, but what I experienced with Jan was far beyond the physical; it was a combination of all that we shared that made it incredible. It was possible to experience because there was a deep level of connection that already existed. I had desired this connection for a long time but did not know how to make it happen. Then I discovered I didn't have to "make" it happen but rather "allow" myself to receive it. When I opened to allow for that possibility, Jan showed up for me to experience it. Thank you for this gift.

12/01

Jan and I went out to breakfast and had a great conversation with a lot of laughter. We then we headed off to the beach for a long walk along the shore. It was a beautiful sunny day. Warm but not hot. There was a wonderful breeze. The water was a bit too cold for swimming but I enjoyed dipping my feet in and walking along. We looked at all of the houses we passed and he described what he liked and didn't like about each of them. I then described all that I liked about them. Of course my perspective was so very different. It was a fun exchange.

We spent a glorious afternoon talking, sharing and exchanging love energy. Later that night, we watched the movie *Reign Over Me* with Adam Sandler and Don Cheadle. We cried together. We held each other as we shared about what we felt and experienced. The connection was beautiful.

We then headed off to bed for more endless hours of incredible lovemaking. (After having that deep connection during our time of sharing, it really opened the space for an amazing physical experience.) I did not even know this was possible before. How did I not know this? I think I had always convinced myself that it was normal for the sex to dwindle after a while in a relationship, although it was never really there to begin with in my previous marriage.

At some point, I realized that as soon as I desired more of a connection, more intimacy, anything more than just a physical act, my former partner was not able to connect (because of what we had created together) and became distant. I had tried for years and was continually rejected. At least that was how I chose to experience it at the time. I felt awful about myself and did not understand why he did not want to be with me. I thought that it must be me. And it was. Just not in the way that I thought. My actions, responses, did not create a space for us to connect, nor did his. We created an environment of chaos, which was not inviting of a pleasant physical connection. I am aware that I still carry rejection issues but I am beginning to feel those shifting for me as well. I know that I was not actually rejected. I was just receiving a clear message about where we were yet it wasn't clear to me at the time. I didn't know how to read the message.

Eventually I came to the point in the relationship where I had no desire for physical contact either. Even the interaction we had felt very empty at the time and that has helped me have a greater understanding of why I was okay with not having it. It was empty because there was no emotional connection. He wasn't present because he did not know how to be. He did the best he could with where he was. I was no help in that process either as I was just as confused, lost in my own pain and doing the best I could as well. I know that we created that experience together as a foundation for growth for both of us.

It's pretty amazing when I think of it in this way. We actually offered each other something really wonderful. That foundation was huge for me and I would not have been able to experience the sheer bliss with Jan had I not had that glorious foundation to launch my desires to create that in my reality as well as use the foundation as a comparison for my own growth. My divine husband, I thank you for this gift. You are beautiful!

12/02

I awaken to more pleasure. What a great way to start the day. Jan asked me to join him in the shower. I felt a bit of discomfort again at the thought of just standing there, naked. Although I had made some previous progress in shifting this type of discomfort, there was still an energy hold present around this issue for me. So I went for it! I knew this was another opportunity to create change. I was ready. We shared a beautiful moment. There was something so special about that experience. Something pure, innocent, my vulnerability exposed and he knew this. Again, I felt something begin to shift for me.

We got dressed and headed off to the First Unity of St. Petersburg, the church he regularly attends there. We stopped by Einstein's Bagels for breakfast on the way. I got a cinnamon raisin bagel with cream cheese. Something I have not had in a long time. It was delicious. The service at First Unity was amazing as always. It uplifts my soul to be in such a wonderful environment. A place filled with love. We went to the Cajun Café for lunch afterwards. The meal was great. I had spicy chicken.

There were a few hours before my flight. I asked how far we were from his house. "Ten minutes," he said. Of course, all I could think about was more love making. I just wanted to spend several more glorious hours in total bliss, fully connected, experiencing the pure pleasure of our energies combined as one. And that we did! Wow. The touching, caressing, loving. Just being fully present in the moment. It was amazing.

It was finally time for me to quickly pack up everything and head to the airport. Jan dropped me off at the curbside check-in. He walked me to the counter and gave me the most beautiful kiss good-bye, a kiss for all to see. He was feeling the love. He wanted to express the joy in that. I was excited for him and the growth I witnessed in him throughout this past month. I waved good-bye as he drove off. This visit has shifted something for us. We both are amazed at what has transpired. It was just so unexpected. That's the only way we know to describe it. Unexpected. And delightful!

My flight to Atlanta was quiet. Everyone seemed tired. I just looked out the window and thought about the wild, passionate love that had transpired. I was dreaming. Before I knew it, we had arrived in Atlanta. What a great way to enjoy the trip. I had about an hour layover. I called my sister but she did not answer. I called my former husband and we chatted for a little bit. He knew that I had gone to Florida. He knew Jan was in Florida so I assumed he knew I went to see him. He never really asked so it didn't come up.

He asked who else went on the trip and I said "Just me." He said, "Oh." He was okay with it. Fine. He just didn't know. In fact, he was happy for me. I was so glad we could talk about these things, that we can maintain a wonderful friendship. He too, is dating and I can only feel joy for him in whatever he desires to experience.

My flight to Charlottesville was delayed an hour due to weather conditions. As I waited, there were several people from a Double-Dutch Jump Rope Competition and they were practicing in the waiting area. It was great entertainment. They were doing flips and jumps and spins. I enjoyed it very much. I had my own little private show. It was delightful. I heard the boarding call and awoke from the captivating show to make my way onto the plane. The flight home was in the rain. There was darkness with flashes of light. Even this I thought was beautiful. I just stared out the window in awe of it all. We finally arrived at 10:50 p.m. I got my baggage and headed to my car that I had left in the long-term parking lot.

I still had an hour drive home from the airport. I called Jan to let him know I made it back and he chose to stay up and talk with me the whole way home. We had more glorious conversation as we were connecting and really getting to know one another. I felt very wired up. My head was still spinning from this magnificent weekend.

I am usually interacting with people through emails every day and so even though it was late when I returned home from my trip, I felt a desire to check my email to get back in touch. I ended up staying up until 4:30 a.m. Phillip Daniel had written me back accepting the invitation to communicate with me and explore this opportunity. How wonderful!

12/03

MaryAnn was to be my roommate at the holiday retreat but she has left me a message that she cannot go because financial things have come up. She has continually expressed to me the desire to go. I felt compelled to participate in helping her to experience the retreat if she chose. I felt in that moment that I wanted to pay for her trip. If she really wanted this, then I wanted to help her make it happen. I called her but she did not answer the phone. I left her a message on her voicemail.

Tidbits from Xander

Xander has been making up songs lately. He likes to sing them for me and tells me they are all about love and joy. He sings about being who you are and loving yourself. I just love it!

12/04

MaryAnn called me back today. She explained again how she is not able to go on the trip. I asked her if she didn't have to pay for anything, just make arrangements with her family to be gone, would she go? She said she didn't see that happening. I then shared with her that I would very much like to pay for her trip. That it would give me great joy to do so.

I felt the tears begin to flow as I expressed how grateful I was for my own retreat experience as it had changed my life. I had always thought what a joy it would be for me if I could be a part of providing an opportunity for someone else to have a retreat experience.

Since we just sold our house, I am in a position to actually make that offer. I was filled with joy in just doing that. Knowing that I could. I didn't once think about what else I could use that money for.

I know that I am continually creating abundance in my life. It flows in and out with ease. There is nothing I would rather do in this moment than to offer this gift to her and share in this glorious co-creation. I told her to think about it as I sensed her hesitation. She felt like it was too much money. The retreat cost, the airfare, the meals. I told her it wasn't about the money. The money was irrelevant to me. This was about an experience.

She said she would think about it. She had to get back to work so we said our good-byes. After we got off the phone, I thought about her for hours. I decided to send her an email so that I could fully share my thoughts and let her know my perspective. Then she could think about it from a deeper understanding of my part in all of this.

The following is the letter I sent:
My Dear MaryAnn,

I have had many thoughts of you today. How wonderful it is that you have arrived in my life. How perfect this opportunity is for both of us. You wanted to create a way for your trip to transpire. Well, you have done so. It is here. I am simply a participant in this fantastic creation of yours.

I understand why many people are reluctant to accept gifts because they often feel that there is an obligation or expectation for something in return. All I want is for you to have the opportunity for this experience. Whatever that may be. This is guaranteed. You will experience something. And I will experience your glorious presence. That in itself is your gift to me. There is nothing to pay back because just you agreeing to go is the gift. It is a joyous gift to me. KNOW this. And if you wish to do more, then pay it forward. Pay it forward to someone else. Shine your light to another. That uplifts my soul.

I think you are amazing. I feel there is much for us to experience together, many conversations ahead. Do you remember at the retreat when you told me you felt a special connection to me? Perhaps because of the similarities with our fathers yes, but consider that maybe what you felt was more than just that. That perhaps you knew that all of this was to come, that we were to experience this journey together. This is your grand opportunity, an opportunity that we have created together for greater growth and expansion.

You created it for the experience of being able to allow yourself to let go and accept such a gift and for the experience of the retreat, which is what you desire. I created it for the opportunity to experience the joy in making the offer, to share in something that was so meaningful to me and to experience this retreat with you. This opportunity is right before you. The door is wide open.

The only question is. .... will you choose to walk through it? Will you take this ride? What is it that you really want? Look within and ask your self this question. Put everything aside and simply ask yourself – do I really want to go? Am I ready for this? You will have your answer. Forget all the practicalities, forget about the money, forget about the reasons why not, what if, how, forget about everything else that is going on. This is about the experience.

You only have to say one word. One little word, "Yes." Just say yes and your flight will be booked, retreat reservations made. That's it, as simple as that and we are on our way. It really can be that easy. It is up to you to allow it to be. You are creating in every moment. This is YOUR moment. This moment of now is very powerful. In this moment, what do you choose?

I love you! Kayite

Notes

Tomorrow is my friend's birthday. I mailed him a card, which arrived a day early, and he thanked me for the nice surprise. He will be even more surprised when he receives the flowers I sent him! He seemed to be a man who had never received flowers before and I always like to offer a new experience. This was my expression of love and appreciation for who he is. I just wanted to brighten his day. He is a beautiful man. Just beaming from the inside out.

The next day, he called me to thank me for the flowers. They were indeed the first he has ever received. This was our first interaction on the phone. We had previously just written daily emails so it was wonderful to hear his voice. We talked for two hours. It was fantastic.

MaryAnn's Onboard

I heard back from MaryAnn and she has agreed to allow me to participate in her process and has accepted my offer to bring her to the retreat. However, she would only agree to it if I would allow her to pay me back. I told her if this is what she truly desires, I would gladly accept her gift.

12/05

We have a critical financial situation in our lives that my sister is trying to manipulate into a financial gain at our considerable loss. Will she back off and release the funds from the Trust without my giving away a major portion of my share?

Your sister cannot manipulate the situation without your participation in this. What is the growth in this for you? Why have you created this situation for yourself? There is much growth opportunity in the experience itself. How do you choose to respond? What is loss? It is only as you define it. You are speaking of money and money is abundant as it is simply source expressed in a different form. Source can be expressed in any form in your life experience and you are the creator of the expression. When you accept, fully know and believe this, this question will no longer be relevant to you. Whether she releases the funds or not depends on your interaction and co-creation with her. You are creating in every moment. It is up to you to choose how you wish to experience this. Can you release and let go of this situation? Can you release the power you give to it? This is the moment to look within and ask your self what it is that you really want.

Release the focus of money. It is not about the money. This is just a surface appearance. This is about your life experience. It is the experience that you seek. In this experience with your sister, this interaction you are having, what do you wish to create as a result of this experience in your life? Whether or not she will release the funds is irrelevant. What to focus on here is how you choose to feel about it. How you choose to allow it to impact your life.

She has no control over you. The only control is that which you allow it to be. The control is within your self because you are choosing and creating experiences in every moment. And you can choose to change what you are creating in any given moment. We would say to you, experience what you will with her and embrace the opportunities for growth that arise from it. You can choose to see them as opportunities rather than problems. With that awareness, you wield great power to create change. Utilize it.

Will the stock market and new job interest support us now or will we have to work into it? These income streams are our life's passions and would give us life's greatest joy.

Following your greatest joy is always wonderful. If this is what you are choosing, then follow what you are feeling in this moment. This moment is all there is. If this is truly your greatest joy, your greatest desire, then what are you waiting for? You are waiting for a guarantee of security that only exists in your mind. There is no real security except awareness to self. Connect with your self, know who you are, and you will have no concerns about what will be. Your passion for this is your life force speaking to you. This joy that fills you up is your source essence telling you that this is the form in which you want to express the fullness of you.

The question is, why are you holding yourself back? Your concern for money and support is a roadblock for you. And as long as you are concerned whether or not you will be able to financially do it, it will continue to be a roadblock and continue to appear in your life. Your current belief system holds you in the state of thinking that it will be hard and you wonder – how can this type of work support me?

We would tell you to begin by choosing to change your thoughts about the situation to allow for expansion of your perspective, the framework of where you are. You can say – This is my passion and this is what I want to experience. And I know that when I follow my passion, abundance will flow in for me as I express love and joy allowing myself to be in a state to receive it. I know that all is perfection. I know that as I spend my time on work that is joyous and fulfilling to me, I feel good about where I am in my life experience. And when I feel good about where I am, I bring myself into a higher vibration. I bring myself closer to allowing full expression of source. And from this place, abundance flows.

As I continue to do what feels good to me, the flow of my life becomes so much smoother. I am easily able to let go and embrace all that comes my way. I know that the experience itself is of great value and I welcome it. – As you begin your conscious journey, things will begin to shift for you. As you recognize the shifts, it will make it easier to believe and trust in the next desire to manifest.

You are seeking these experiences as they offer opportunity for growth and expansion. You are always successful as you are continually growing and expanding. There is nothing else for you to do. You are simply choosing in which manner you wish to experience the growth. You are free to choose whatever experience you desire.

These things are in control of our current moment. What we are currently doing is an uncomfortable method of earning a living and keeps us in the negative. I could do what I really want without ever getting tired of it. It fills my heart with joy at the thought of helping others and bringing them out of despair or giving them the view of eternal life.

These things control your current moment because you allow them to. You are the only one stopping you. And when you shift your perspective, this will change. If you know that you current job is keeping you in a negative space, then you are clearly defining what it is that you do not want. The desire to help others gives you joy and this is your source speaking to you, calling forth an expression of self in this form.

We would encourage you to listen. Source is calling you, but you are distracted by all of the practicalities in this physical world. And if you look at this physical world as simply a manifestation of your creation and everything in it as a part of your experience, then you will understand that you can manifest something different as it becomes relevant to what you are choosing to experience.

All of these wonderful experiences that you have had offer great benefit as you go forth to share them with others. Much growth is in this for them. Much growth is in this for you. We encourage you to embrace all experiences. Even those that may have appeared from your perspective to be discouraging, that appeared unpleasant or painful to you can be experienced differently as you begin to shift your thoughts about them. They have guided you here, where you are right now, and will continue to guide you as you grow and expand.

Experiences for Healing

My experience with Jan is so much more about a spiritual connection and my sharing about the physical part is my desire to share about my own healing. I experienced so much in my past relationships regarding my physical body and sex in which I created a lot of congested energy. I needed an experience to create a shift to release this energy, create change for healing and create the space for all that I desired to fully flow into my life. Jan provided this experience for me. And I, in return, provided him the opportunity for his dam to begin to crumble. He told me that his life began again with me, that I helped him to rediscover the God within him.

In the beginning, he was uncomfortable with others knowing about my visiting him. He did not want to be in that space. He knew his need for privacy was holding him back. That his fear of what others might think of our relationship was creating a barrier for him to fully express himself and he did not want that. By the end of the weekend, that had completely changed. Something shifted within him. I could literally feel the energy shift. There was a huge release. He was able to let down the walls and allow me in to connect with him in a way that no one had. What we shared was so deeply beautiful. We cried together. We laughed together. And we loved together. It was amazing.

Is Age Relevant?

Now from someone viewing my relationship with Jan from their perspective, they might just see age. Several people have asked me about this, as he is twenty years older than I am. To be honest, we don't even notice. It is irrelevant to us. People often ask me what we talk about. They have a hard time understanding what we could have in common. We talk about anything and everything.

The idea that age creates commonality or connection is just another thought that has been put out there and someone has chosen to believe it. Age is a number for the physical body and does not define who we are or what we are capable of experiencing. We only limit ourselves holding those thoughts about it.

Jan and I choose not to limit ourselves. We have had some of the most incredible conversations either of us has ever experienced and I am glad that I did not judge or dismiss him right away and that he did not judge or dismiss me either. We would have missed so much being offered had we allowed the surface appearance of age to run the show. We chose to look deeper, beyond the surface, and connect with the beauty of the soul.

What makes our interaction so wonderful is that he is fully present with me and I am fully present with him. We flow together in harmony as we share all of who we are. As we connect in this way, there are no limitations. There has been tremendous growth for both of us. This is all that matters to me. I know that others will think what they will. That is their perspective and they are free to choose how they feel about it.

All I can say is that I have been having the time of my life and I would not for a moment limit myself from being all that I can be, expressing myself fully, because of the way someone else may feel about it. I am not hurting anyone.

I am expressing and sharing love with someone. And that to me is beautiful in whatever form it shows up in. Just so you know, Jan gave me permission to share anything I wanted about our experiences together. It was his gift of freedom to me, but in offering it, it was truly a gift of freedom to his self. How wonderful!

Another Onboard

Another friend, Melissa, had desired to go to the retreat and heard about my offer to MaryAnn. I offered to help her as well and she accepted. I sensed again that there was great purpose in this. I rejoice in this beautiful co-creation.

12/11

On our Freedom Circle call tonight, one of the women sent us a You Tube video about a guy who had a sign for free hugs. We all watched it and it was so uplifting to see people coming together exchanging hugs as an expression of love and acceptance.

It made a statement about unity and embracing everyone. I just wanted to offer my love and was delighted at the thought of sharing that in the form of a hug. In that moment, I knew I wanted to experience this too. And so I shall. Yes, I am living my joy!

Love Is All You Need

A friend of mine commented that I have moved at light speed in developing self-confidence, wisdom, and clarity about my life that was not there at the retreat. He wanted to know if that transition was all from Jacob or was that only one factor? And how can he experience this for himself?

My response to him is that I would not say I have developed self-confidence, wisdom and clarity. These are not things to "develop." It is something I had all along. Something we all have. It is our true selves shining through. We all have access to it. You just might have created a dam that is blocking this.

The burst of my dam enabled me to connect with my true self and access a deeper understanding of who I am. I did experience this at the retreat. Now, of course, Jacob has brought me to greater depths. They catapulted me into a whole other realm so to speak.

Before I had a deeper understanding of myself and my life. Now I have a deeper understanding of humanity and all creation.

So I am not even sure how to know what the difference would be without Jacob because I am here now, blended with them, knowing what I know. As for you, I would say, love is all you need.

And what is love? Love is who you are. Therefore, all you need is you. And you cannot be without you, so you truly need for nothing. Isn't that wonderful?

Self-Confidence, Self-Esteem

A friend of mine said that she often wonders what self-confidence is? What self-esteem is? What is standing in one's power? What do these wonderful gifts feel like? I thought about this and what's great is that we all have a different idea of what that might be. How we wish to view it.

For me, it was releasing the illusion that what others thought of me mattered. When I came to understand that what others thought about me, thought about my choices, thought about my lifestyle was irrelevant to my life experience, confidence became irrelevant, at least in the sense that I had always viewed it. I wasn't confident because I wasn't sure I would live up to others' expectations of me.

Having often failed to do so, I had little self-esteem. I rejoice in those experiences for the many gifts of growth that I have enjoyed along the way and that have brought me to this place of now. I am grateful to all who participated in offering me those experiences. Now I know who I am and it does not have to be defined. One could say I am confident but it is simply an awareness of self. Confidence is not even necessary. Being myself is just what is. I choose to enjoy the process of my life experience. I rejoice in living my life exactly as I choose and being completely okay with whatever anyone else thinks about it.

I spent my whole life trying to live for others, to make them proud of me and to feel that I was a good person. In this moment, I live for me. The joy and the freedom in that! All that is relevant to me is that I rejoice in me and that I love and embrace myself. For those who might think this is selfish, when we allow the fullness of ourselves to be expressed, that love and joy spills over to all we encounter. It is beneficial to everyone. Suppressing yourself and putting others first may sound noble but it often builds resentment, resistance, and creates a disconnection from others. Expressing yourself fully allows the space for true unity as we can easily connect when we recognize our source in another.

The State of Our World

A friend of mine has had great concern for the state of our world and does not know how to live joyfully when she sees all this awful stuff occurring. I told her that this was her perspective. It is not mine. And that she only needs to concern herself with her own life experience. You can live a joyful, happy, love overflowing, abundant life regardless of what the rest of the world is doing. They are all choosing their experiences.

This does not mean that we cannot choose to participate in reaching out to help others, caring for our planet and desiring great things for our world. There is much growth in these experiences. But it is not about the end result of total peace. If this were what we truly desired, we would not have come forth in this form as a physical expression of source. We are here to experience, to grow. It is in the experience of seeking peace that we grow.

True peace comes from within, connection to self, to source, to all that is. Not from trying to change situations outside of our self. The current state of our world offers us wonderful opportunities to grow. There is much out there for us to observe. Observe and choose what it is that we wish to bring into our own life experience. To decide what we choose to believe, how we choose to participate, and how we want to experience it.

As Jacob says, all is perfection. And I know this to be so. I may not always understand what is occurring but that does not make it wrong, a mistake or imperfect. It just tells me that there is an opportunity for growth, an opportunity to expand the framework of where I am as I come to a greater understanding of what is transpiring in my life, my world. I rejoice in the process.

12/13
Is meditation a way to tap into or find what is within?

Understand that you can experience your life force at any time, doing anything. It is your awareness that allows for the experience of self. As you begin to consciously focus on expanding your awareness, meditation can help in this process. Meditation is a wonderful way to connect with your life force because you can create an environment where you can put aside the illusions that cause a disconnection.

We would suggest that you quiet your mind. Allow your self to just be. Breathe. Relax and feel the peace and love that surrounds you, that IS you, and radiates from you. Feel the stillness, the calm. It is you. As you become more comfortable in this space, with the awareness of how you experience the source that is you, you can then allow for expansion to experience it in every moment. Awareness of self can always be with you.

We are all immersed in a physical world that we chose to experience. How do we follow the advice of Jacob when we are constantly face to face with the realities that the physical world presents to us that run counter to this non-physical input?

You are looking at what is. Instead, choose to imagine what can be. Focus on this and you can expand beyond your current limitations to bring forth new experiences and a greater awareness of what is possible. Intend for yourself what you want to experience. View what is as simply what has already been created by previous thought. In this moment of now, you are creating for the next moment. What do you choose?

If you focus on what already is, you will continue to create more of this and it will appear as if nothing has changed. Change is constant. Many creations continue to manifest over and over again because that is all you see. You see it in your world and accept it as so. Choose to imagine something different, something beyond your current limitations. Allow yourself to wield the power and be the conscious creator of your physical reality rather than living in a physical reality that is defining you and your experience. It can only do so if you allow it to. You define you and your reality is always what you create it to be. There are endless possibilities. Allow yourself to explore them.

Then how do I balance living in the human world in this physical body and also stay connected to my spirituality and true self?

There is a separation that is created when one holds the thought that the human experience is not the true self. The human experience is your life force, the source of who you are, expressed. It is not all that source is, but it IS source expressed. Every part of the experience, whether you are conscious of it or not, is always an expression of self. It can be an expression of confusion, anger, or pain when one does not yet have a greater awareness of self.

All of this is part of your growth process. It is an expression of self in where you are and it is a divine creation. Every experience is a creation of source. Source IS all there is. Observe your life experience and what is being expressed. Utilize what you observe to consciously create the changes you desire.

Know that all of this is part of your process. When you are trying to create balance between what appears to be two different things, you are actually in a state of resistance. You are trying to balance something that is already in harmony. It is for you to come to know and experience this harmony. You can expand your perspective by opening yourself to the idea that your physical experience is a continual magnificent creation of source expressed and that only harmony exists.

The balance is already there. It is just not part of your current reality because you do not understand it. As you open to greater possibilities, you will bring forth experiences that will offer you the opportunity to expand your perspective, the framework of where you are, to experience this. Rejoice in where you are. It is perfection.

I have often thought of changing my career but I am afraid of failing. I feel so overwhelmed with making a decision. I don't want to make the wrong choice.

Failure is only defined by your thought about what is manifesting in your life. Your overwhelmed feeling is brought forth by that thought. As you shift your thought about what is showing up in your life experience, you will create change in your experience of it. Every experience is offering you an opportunity to grow. The purpose of life is growth and expansion. You cannot fail, as growth is ultimately what you seek. How you choose to experience this growth is up to you. The only end to what is possible is that which you believe in your mind it to be. As you allow yourself to expand your thoughts beyond the current limitations that only you have set in place for yourself, then you can open the door to invite it into your life experience. The door to this new career is awaiting you along with many others. You wield the power to open it and allow it in. There is no wrong choice. Whatever you choose, it is perfection.

What is depression? I sometimes feel like maybe I am depressed but I don't like the idea that there is something wrong with me. I feel like I can make changes in this but I am often confused about what I am feeling.

The feeling of depression is suppression of self. When you create resistance in your life that blocks the full expression of self, of source, your light dimmers. Love is who you are. Joy is love expressed. The joy you feel in your life experience is full expression of self as you easily allow source to create, experience, express, and expand as you. You ARE source. Source desires growth and expansion. When you suppress expression of self, you cannot grow. You remain stagnant as the energy congests and the feeling of depression is experienced. We are excited to tell you that you control the dimmer switch. You can begin by becoming aware of your own desires. What is it that you have wanted to express? Do not be afraid to speak your voice. As you begin to express what you truly desire for you, you will invite it into your life experience. Know you are worthy to do so. Your light will shine as you feel the joy in the expression of the experience. There is nothing wrong with you. You are perfect just as you are. This is just part of your experience for growth. Even when you are stagnant, it serves great purpose as you are desiring to create change, and it is in the seeking, the asking, that growth is offered. It is for you to come to know and understand this as you consciously open yourself to expanding to greater possibilities of what can be and a greater awareness of self. The feeling of depression is just a road sign that reads "Suppression in Progress." Allow that feeling to be a friendly reminder that there is something you desire to be expressed. Begin to look within and identify what that is for you. You can then focus on allowing yourself to express it. We can assure you, you will feel better. Rejoice in where you are, it is perfection.

Is there an end of life review to tell us if we have lived a good life or whether we have evolved our consciousness enough?

There is a continual review of your life experience that is performed by you. You are the observer of your life. It is not observed for the purpose of judgment, but for greater understanding of growth and expansion offered and experienced. All life is good life and it is only your thought about it that creates separation as you define your reality. This is part of your growth. Consciousness just is. It is your awareness of it that is expanding. There is no set goal to achieve and you cannot come in behind. It is the experience you seek and that is occurring in every moment. You are not here to cross the finish line. You are here to run the race. Just your participation in it is significant and serves great purpose. Enjoy the run by shifting your focus from the final outcome to focus on what you are experiencing along the way. What do you feel in this moment? This is the expression of your life force experiencing this world.

Tidbits from Xander

A friend recently gave Xander two small teddy bears. He named them Love and Joy. Aw, how sweet it is!

12/14

I traveled to visit my friends Jim and Claire in North Carolina for the weekend. They are a lovely married couple that I absolutely adore. I arrived late afternoon and received a full tour of the house. Claire cooked us a wonderful dinner and then we talked and laughed for many hours. We called Jan about 1:30 in the morning and he joined us on speakerphone for two hours. Jim and Claire went to bed at 3:30 and Jan and I continued to talk all night until about 7:30 in the morning.

Our conversations always flow with ease. I enjoy talking with Jan because there is such a beautiful flow and exchange and it always feels like a time warp as we never feel the many hours we are on the phone. We only experience the joy of the conversation and the time always seems to fly by. By the time I hung up the phone, I realized that I might as well stay up. And so I did. It was worth it. It was a glorious night of enlightening conversation, growth and expansion.

12/15

Claire and I had decided that we would go together to the mall and experience giving "Free Hugs." We knew there would be lots of shoppers out and about preparing for Christmas and thought it would be a wonderful experience. We made our signs this afternoon and then headed off to the mall. It was raining and we gathered under a main entry and joined the Salvation Army guy. We were ready to spread lots of love and sunshine. We received so many hugs.

It was wonderful to watch people's reactions. It was very telling about where they were in their life experience. Some walked right up to us and were delighted to receive a hug. Others were unsure or a little shy but made their way toward us. And then there were those that laughed and walked by and those that looked so scared at the thought of hugging anyone that they walked around to the other side as to not encounter us. (There were only a few of those.) Mostly we witnessed bright smiles and silly grins. We brought cheer and joy.

Even if they didn't get a hug, many thought it was funny and got a great laugh. I rejoice in that. We literally enjoyed hundreds of hugs on this magnificent adventure. Jim took some pictures of this wonderful event. It was great to see so many faces light up. What a fantastic experience this was.

Vincent the Security Officer eventually appeared and was kind enough to give us hugs before he reluctantly gave us the boot. He said that we had to have signed permission to be there.

It was clear that he was enjoying our presence but we understood that this was his job. It was about time for us to go anyway. We were complete. Time for dinner!

We went to a nearby Italian restaurant for a lovely meal and then headed back to their house. Claire spoke with Jacob for about two hours later that night. We were both lying down in the guest bed for total relaxation. It was the longest conversation thus far. She chooses to keep this one private. After the conversation, she and I talked for several hours. It was wonderful.

12/16

Jim took his turn with Jacob this morning. His conversation was only about 30 minutes. He did have a pretty neat experience. He said my face had changed colors during the session. It went from green to blue to silver and then cycled back to green again. Isn't that wild? My experience is always different and I just love to hear things like this! Another one of our friends drove in to visit us for the day. Claire cooked dinner for us and then we talked a bit and took some pictures. It was late in the evening by the time I left. As I drove home, it began to snow. It was beautiful. I spoke to Jan during the six-hour drive. He tucked me in at 3:00 a.m. We continue to expand our connection. I am enjoying the process.

Phillip Daniel

Phill and I have been having the most wonderful email discussions. I had much to share and he was open to receiving me. I shared some about my journey and my experiences along the way. The interaction with him caused me to ask many questions of myself and has helped give me greater clarity about where I am. I just recently checked out his website phillipdaniel.com and noticed that the address said Ashland, Oregon. I was stunned. I contacted him to ask if he were still living there. Indeed he was. Then I announced I would be visiting there in two weeks for my retreat. We agreed to meet.

I delighted at how everything was unfolding. We connected at the perfect moment for the growth experience we both desired.

Although I do not know exactly what growth I was offering him in return, I do know there is always a mutual offering. I rejoice in that. When I first sensed I was to meet him, I had no idea he lived in the very same town I was planning to visit. This union is sheer bliss to me. I am rejoicing in the process, as I am about to experience what I sensed, the vision of it, come to fruition. It is that process of co-creation that is so beautiful to me.

12/17

I spoke to a close friend today and shared that I have been feeling so much come up for me about my body issues. I have processed through so much with Jan and have shared much with others as well. I feel like a big shift is about to occur. I am ready to be free. I choose to remain open and welcome experiences that will help me fully release this congested energy.

Being You, Sometimes?

I recently had a conversation with a friend who was going through what she described as a rough patch in her life. Instead of reaching out to others and me, she first began to hide and become distant. She did not want anyone to see that side of her for fear of appearing needy and weak.

I know from my own experience that I used to hide who I was for fear that I would not be accepted. Only a few people saw most of me, which included my anger, sadness and pain. Even then it was not truly all of me. I never shared that with anyone. For most, I would put on a show. I didn't want them to see the parts that I considered "bad" or "unflattering" to me. I was too concerned about what they would think. I feared being judged, being rejected. But these were all fears that I created. If this is where I was, why not share all of me? It is not "who I am" but rather what I am experiencing in that moment.

This is all just part of my process. And if I shared all of myself with others, only then would I know what the reception would be. And most importantly, it would give me the opportunity of an experience to be okay with me, just as I am. I no longer hold these fears, as I know they are just an illusion. I choose to be fully present and share all of myself with everyone I encounter. If people wish to judge me, I am okay with that. Their judgment is simply where they are. It is not about me.

I spent years looking for approval and acceptance from others. And years feeling like I never measured up. Now I can only laugh at how silly that was for me. Of course I could never meet another's expectations because I was never meant to. It was only for me to know myself. And now, I look only to myself for acceptance. I finally realized that it was me who needed to embrace me. I know who I am and I rejoice in any experience that appears in my life and offers me the opportunity to declare it.

Letters of Gratitude

A few weeks ago I read in a friend's blog about Thanksgiving and gratitude. She recommended for the next holiday that instead of giving "stuff" as gifts to write letters of gratitude. I thought that was a great idea! I knew right away that I was going to do this for Christmas. I have been working on them ever since as there are many to write. I am grateful just to have so many beautiful beings present in my life experience that I rejoice in the fact that it will take me a while to complete them all.

(I did eventually complete these later on and I enjoyed sharing with each person about what his or her presence in my life has meant to me. I must admit that it felt more like a gift to me than a gift for them. But after hearing about how these letters were received, I realized what a gift it was for all of us. And I am so incredibly grateful to my friend who brought this idea into my awareness so that I could choose to bring it into my life experience.)

12/19
What is the point of the name "coincidences" between my friend and me? What purpose does that serve given where we are right now, which is not communicating?

There are no coincidences, only what you have created. The purpose was for you to take notice of this being who was to participate in a co-creation in your life that you desired to experience for growth and expansion. It need not be this grand event for growth to occur. Though there are endless possibilities for all that you desire. You are creating your reality. You created a sign for your self to pay attention. It is for you to know and come to understand what this experience is about for you. It is in this process that growth is offered.

How do I move on, move forward and release this little heart pain I have experienced periodically for the past couple of days?

What is the source of this pain? What is it that you feel you have lost? You are complete within yourself. When others arrive in your life and joy flows through you as you are with them.....connecting with them.....it feels good. And when there is a disconnection, you may feel a loss of that good feeling. Know that the joy that flows through you was not from them. Their presence offered a reflection of the divine being that you are. You felt good about you with this person. You can move onward knowing that there are many to reflect the beauty that is you. Many will flow into your life. You are open. You are growing. Rejoice in this.

What can I say or do to facilitate my healing and growth and his?

Healing can occur as you ask yourself – what is the gift that I have received in this experience? What is the growth in this for me? What does it tell me about where I am? As you come to a greater understanding of what has transpired, a shift can occur to release congested energy and that is the "healing". There is nothing you need do for him. He will create this for himself if he chooses.

Is it wrong for me to keep him in my thoughts if he has said he does not want to be involved in a relationship at this time? Am I interfering with his process by thinking anything at all about him and his journey?

It is not a right or wrong choice for you to keep him in your thoughts. And it is not about you interfering with his process as one person cannot interfere with another's. It is always a co-creative process. What it does interfere with is your connection to you. If you continue to think thoughts of someone who does not choose to participate in the way you would like, it can create a disconnect within your self. Do these thoughts you have feel good to you? Focus on feeling good about where you are regardless of what he is choosing. Allow yourself to feel whatever comes up for you. Use it to guide you. Your thoughts and feelings will tell you so much about where you are.

Should I stop contacting him? Naturally, it is not my intention to make him uncomfortable or to add any pressure. Do my words, my emails help or hurt?

It is your choice. You are creating your reality. Ask yourself how you feel about sending these emails? Does it feel good to you to send them? Do you feel it is helping or hurting you? This is the question. Allow your self to guide you. If it feels good to you to send them, then do so. If it feels good to you to stop, then stop. It is all a co-creative process. You cannot make a wrong choice. It is simply a choice of a different experience created by both of you. Whatever his experience is, it is in agreement with you. You need not worry about that. The only thing for you to focus on is how you want to experience this.

Communication

What is great about Jan living in Florida and me living in Virginia is that our entire focus is on communication. We had been talking several times a week but somewhere along the way it transitioned into four to five hours of nightly conversation. It has been so wonderful.

We talk about everything we can think of, about my life, about his, life in general. Our childhood, previous relationships, kids, all the things we've experienced and grown from, all the things we are experiencing now. We are both an open book and we let each other know that we can ask whatever we want. And we do. We are getting to know each other at great depths. It's fantastic!

Mom Meets Jacob

I went to visit my mom yesterday and she finally spoke with Jacob. It was at the end of the day and she only had about twenty minutes. It was very exciting for me to be able to share with her what has been transpiring in my life and what Jacob is all about. Even though it was brief, I felt intense vibrations just like I did with my sister. I didn't quite get to the g-force stage, but I was almost there. I could feel it getting more intense and I know it would have continued if the session had been longer. So I enjoyed that.

I can't help but take notice that the two most intense experiences were with close family members. Interesting. My mom said she felt the energy shift immediately. That she could feel their intense vibration and it was unmistakable. She said it was very helpful and confirmed a lot of things for her. It was a wonderful experience.

12/21

I think I mentioned before that I have felt a special connection with trees ever since my trip home from the retreat. I have recently been feeling drawn to do nature photography, but then I would ask myself, what would I actually do with all of the pictures I take? I think I am filled with such joy by their beauty that I just want to share it with others.

Well, today a friend of mine invited me down to the outdoor holiday market at the local downtown mall where she has been working. There were lots of vendors. A lot of jewelry and handmade bags and things like that but what caught my attention was the most glorious photo of the sun setting over the mountains and lake.

Then I turned the corner to see the most magnificent photos of polar bears! I cried. I stood there and cried at their beauty. The man who took them is recently retired and started doing this as a hobby about six months ago. He traveled to Canada to see hundreds of these polar bears. It was just fantastic. I took notice of this experience. I said "Yes," to my higher self. "I hear you. I am paying attention."

I bought a few photographs as they inspire me and remind me of this joy. And what did I do next? I went straight to the store and bought a Nikon D40 camera. Now I didn't do any research on cameras. I just let source guide the way. I am sure I will love it. (And I do.)

Well, that was my most enlightening morning. I just love it when all of these events unfold so perfectly and I can see them exactly as they are. And even though I don't know what I will be doing with these pictures, I sense with every part of my being that something will come of it. That this is for me to experience and all will be revealed to me at the most perfect moment. I rejoice in knowing this is so. I am living in the moment and loving every bit.

I'm Sick, Isn't It Great?

I woke up sick the other morning with a sore throat and congestion and I immediately welcomed the experience. I said, "Thank you for this gift. I embrace you." Then I called Jan and said, "I'm sick today. Isn't that great? I rejoice in where I am. It's beautiful. I am enjoying the process." He laughed and jokingly said, "You're weird." I told him I embrace that too. I released any resistance to it and welcomed it for the divine creation that it was.

I had a fabulous day and the next morning when I woke up, it was completely gone. I rarely ever get sick anymore. I used to get sick all of the time when I was in my unhappy, lonely, depressed state of being. Now, when something comes up for me, I always look to the source, and what it is telling me about where I am. The clarity in that is the gift.

12/22

Since I woke up feeling sick, I was not sure if I would be able to enter a session scheduled with Jacob this afternoon. My friend

and I decided earlier in the day that we would just watch a movie. But when she arrived, Jacob wasn't having it. They let me know that this conversation was important. And out they came.
We are here.

I am feeling a lot of energy myself. I want to ask for my friend about obsessive-compulsive disorder and anxiety disorder and taking medications for that. I would like to offer him anything else that you have to say about it.

It is about him being connected to himself. And he is so lost from that in his desire for control, to gain control of himself and where he is, and he is looking outward to doing so. Outward with these physical activities to somehow feel in control of his life…..And that as he looks within to know who he is and to connect to his true self, it will no longer be necessary. He will know the true power within, the true power of self.

That sounds like him……….(long pause)

Ask what you will

I keep feeling this connection to…I keep calling it Shondra, but I lose it…I feel this power and then I feel so good and then I think…the name keeps coming and something feels like it is forming but then it goes away and…

The name does not matter. Just allow it to be and flow and feel. It will stay with you longer. The more that you are trying to hold onto that connection it becomes harder because you begin to have thoughts of losing it and then this occurs. Let go and allow it to just be.

I do try. I get so excited thinking…

Instead, just clear your thoughts and be in the moment and this connection will stay with you.

What about flying, telepathy, all of these things that I feel so strongly about doing?

Your soul can fly all the time, anywhere you wish. Free. Free of the physical body. This is another part of rejuvenation. But you are here to experience this physical world, the growth and expansion is here. Telepathy is part of your natural state of being. You can communicate with anyone, as you are all one source. Always connected. It is for you to come to know and understand how to utilize all that is available to you. You have access to all that is. And it is in your search, your desire to know more, that growth will come. Enjoy the process.

I feel like everything is just flowing. I feel like I am letting it all go. I am inspired to action that is going to separate me from my husband in the physical world and this is feeling so good to me to truly be on my own, because whether I can be on my own…I know that I can be on my own regardless, but I wasn't allowing that. I feel like I am allowing that now by taking these action steps and it just feels really good. And I feel like everything else in my life is beginning to flow with that. That was the big resistance.

Yes. And as you let go physically, you let go with your thoughts, which are creating all of it. Allowing it to flow smoothly, easily. You are only letting go of the idea about what you thought things were. You are releasing the illusion.

Yes, yes.

This was accessible to you always. And everything else, anything you can imagine is accessible to you in the same way.

That's how I feel…….I want so much to share. I don't want to overwhelm my friend or anyone else. I couldn't stop talking. I couldn't stop telling him all of these wonderful things and he seemed really happy to hear them. But I felt the old nagging of – I am talking too much, I am not listening. Umm…

You cannot overwhelm anyone, because it is always a co-creation. They are getting exactly what they are wanting in that moment, even if they are not consciously aware of it.

True. Sometimes I feel like talking and sometimes I feel like listening.

You need not concern yourself about what it will be for someone else. Be who you are and know that it is always perfection no matter what the reaction is. And if someone reacts in what appears to you to be an unfavorable way, you can ask yourself what is this about for you? If you look at the greater picture of things, you do not take it in. You just take it for the experience that it is. Grow from this and move on. But you do not need to take it in and experience it in a negative way. This is never the purpose. You can experience the contrast. You can experience the growth. And you can consciously do this with gratitude for the opportunities appearing in your life in order for you to do so.

And getting beyond...like I feel going to Ireland just feels so wonderful and I want to let it all go and just know that I will be able to pay for it and everything will be fine. And it just seems so awesome and right and great and I know it's going to be wonderful but I still...the slightest little nag of what if I can't make the next payment or what if I can't...

And what if you cannot? Then what? What does this mean to you?

Then I would...Yeah that feels really good [laughs]; I mean it really does. It's like then So What? So what...yeah...

All is perfection. You need not worry about the "what ifs." They are not in your now.

Yeah, that is so...It is my ego that is like I am supposed to be able to pay, I am supposed to be able to...but I am not feeling that inside so much anymore that that's...

And then always knowing that you are creating and always knowing that if for some reason you are not to pay for this, if this trip was not created to be, then what are you creating instead for yourself that is to be for you? Acknowledge your creations, all of them. Utilize them for the purpose of growth and expansion. Welcome all that appears in your life.

Okay.

And it is never about – why could I not pay for this? It is about – I have chosen to create something else on an unconscious level. I choose to consciously acknowledge my creation and look to the growth in this for me. It is an ongoing process. It is not a failure to complete a task. It is not a failure to come up with this money, or a failure to be able go on this trip. It is a change in your creation only. Your creation is magnificent. Embrace it. Enjoy the process.

That is, that's great, because that is what it feels like. I have always been like if I can't do this then I have failed in some way. And I don't think that word, but I feel that feeling of not being good enough, not... but I get it, I get it ... what you are saying. No, there is no failure to complete a task. I am continually creating. Even if is not what I thought it would be.

Yes.

My dad says that he actually sort of lived with these light beings. That he could see them and now he doesn't. And I want to believe him, but my dad is...my dad; he's always been someone who doesn't seem to see things for what they are so I tend to...

He sees the world he has created for himself. This is his reality. As you have yours.

And I don't want to discount what he is saying. I want to believe him that he really sees these things or saw these things and it gets so confusing for me with him having been so sick in the physical world. Sort of when you think of mental illness its as if...

And what would it mean for you to believe him?

That maybe he's not so sick and that would be wonderful. That maybe it's not all about his ego and his... that maybe his ego just is there and gets the better of him sometimes, but that he also has this amazing connection to the spiritual that has caused...well that has been a part of all the problems...the apparent problems in his life, you know, his physical problems come from his mental illness...that he is so connected without support or support from other physical beings. And that would certainly make one sick, because I think I could have been him, I could be him if I didn't have people to talk to about this spiritual stuff. If I didn't have...

What others define as mental illness is simply that which they do not understand. A reality that is so far outside of others understanding is often labeled as something wrong, an illness, or a dysfunction. As you are all coming to a greater awareness of self, these definitions will change. You cannot know your father's reality as it is not your own. He in turn, cannot know yours. You can choose to embrace him as he has presented himself to be. Embrace him for exactly as he is. Just as you would like to be embraced for where you are in your reality. Trust in what you feel. The source of you knows. And what he is experiencing is not relevant to what you are choosing for your life experience, your creation. Embrace what he is saying is so for him. This will feel good to you and help release the congested energy you hold around it.

I would love to see light beings. And I almost feel like something is there, and then I… I am too afraid. Like what would I do if I saw light beings? I feel like I would freak out [laughs]. And I don't want to freak out. I want to see it. I want to feel it. I want to be a part of things. And yet, apparently part of me doesn't want to because I am too afraid. I will get right on the verge where I think something is about to happen and then I will…I can feel myself pulling away.

When you are ready, it will be. If you wish to experience it, it can be if you allow yourself to release that fear, to walk through, to come to that place of inner peace knowing that all is well and that there is nothing for you to fear. The fear is an illusion and part of your experience. The experience of shifting through this, this is what you seek. Not the getting there. Enjoy the process of where you are and this very experience of facing your fears. There is tremendous growth in this. Enjoy it. There are endless possibilities for you.

Yes, there are. (Whisper)

Embrace this moment of now, feel the joy, allow the joy to rise up from within you and [they begin to whisper with such peace] *radiate throughout your being to all that you encounter. Feel that joy and you need nothing else. This is your life force, the source of you expressed. This is the glory of you. There is nothing you need, only that which you want to experience.*

A thought just popped into my head. All this love that I am feeling...

Yes.

Feels so good, um...I have an old friend of mine that I think about a lot. And um...she's not really reaching for this place it doesn't seem and... it's nice to talk to her. I don't know...I don't know what I am asking, I just know I want...

Beings will flow in and out of your life. For your experiences... each offering something different. And as you are moving onward with where you are wanting to go, some will flow in and out more often than others, and some will flow out completely and some will flow in more and stay with you along your journey. You will know as you feel within you this connection and it may become more distant or as things change others will appear in your life at different times. If she is not in the space that you are flowing in now, you will feel this distance, and this is all right. Just acknowledge to yourself that you understand where she is. She does not need to be reaching for the same place. The growth is not in sameness, but in variety. What she is creating for her is perfection and what you are creating for you is perfection.

I am still holding myself back thinking should I be asking about a particular person? Is this okay? I am thinking about a person I met a couple of years ago and I just feel so connected to him. I felt connected to him right away.

It is always okay for you to be where you are. And this connection that you feel is with you connecting with another who is here to offer you the growth experience that you desire.

Wow...

You will continually make connections with others and some will stand out to you more, and sometimes you may not know why. This too is part of your experience. The coming to know and understand these experiences is the growth. This is the reason they stand out to you, because there is much growth from the experience that they are here to offer you and you to offer them and the co-creation as you come together for the experience of it. It serves great purpose. Other friends in your life have already served that purpose for you.

Wow…I am feeling such incredible peaceful loving energy, it's just radiating.

That is the source of you bringing to your awareness that it is so, as you resonate with the truth of who you are.

I feel no worries now. And just yesterday, I was asking myself how do I get back into that space? And last time I spoke with you, Jacob, I spent four days in just blissfulness. And then I began to lose it again and…

You can look within. The bliss is within you and we are here for the asking. And delighted to speak with you. But you need only look to yourself, connect with you to feel this bliss at any moment. You are source expressed. We are source expressed in a different form. The bliss you feel is the connection and awareness of the source of who you are expressed through our form. Begin to allow yourself to experience this magnificent bliss as source expressed through you own form. It is always there for you.

But you create congestion that block this flow. It is more of a removal of the blockage to allow it to flow, but it is always there. It is a blockage in awareness. We are not creating the bliss. You are the bliss. We are guiding you back to you and reminding you of the blissful being that you are. What you feel IS you. The bliss is the essence of you expressed. You allow yourself to be open and express yourself in our presence, as there is comfort here for you. As you allow yourself to be fully expressed in the presence of others, you will experience the joy, the bliss of you. It is a process. Allow yourself to be where you are and enjoy the growth along the way.

I can feel that… and on Tuesday I felt like I started to get it back on my own. I wasn't in the flow though. I wasn't in the flow of it. I felt like things were opening up and it did feel very good today to begin to… feel like I could reach that …connectedness on my own which is how I know it is supposed to be.

If you are starting to feel off a bit, just imagine a bathtub with a little rubber stopper. This little stopper that you just pull and pop it out and let that water flow.

(Laughter) I like that.

You can just envision that. That is you pulling the blockage out of your way. You are pulling yourself out of the way and letting the source that is you be fully expressed and flow through again.

This is great. I'm really starting to feel…I know I was excited about Ireland, but I am starting to feel it. The joy of just being there on the cliffs, being in all that beauty, it's…

The joy of knowing that you are creating it. Your vision, your thoughts, is creating it.

Yes.

Do you feel the divine being that you are?

Yes.

Do you know how glorious and magnificent you are?

I feel that…I do feel that right now. (Laughter) I definitely feel that. It just seems so easy, which is how I know it really is.

And that just being…just being… is so powerful. Your life experience can flow with ease or you can continually resist and create barriers that give the appearance of struggle and that life is hard. It is your choice. Any choice is beneficial. You are growing.

Yes.

You are here in this moment. Rejoice in Ireland but enjoy this moment of now. Create for your life now. Enjoy the experience of right now.

I have something else, Jacob.

Yes?

My friend is gay and he is struggling. Is he choosing this?

It is simply a different experience. And one can feel overwhelmed by this experience in this physical world based on what your society has created. But this is the experience that was desired as it offered much growth. It is a strong foundation for growth and very powerful. You are always choosing every experience.

I want to help him. Should I just let it be?

He is doing just fine. He may not be consciously aware. But the rest of his being knows exactly what is occurring for him. Calling him forth to experience all of this. Calling him forth to connect with you, with us. He will expand his frame in his own timing. When he is ready, it will be.

Yes.

He has created this. Do you not see the magnificence in that?

I definitely felt that. And I told him that today as well. I felt so wonderful to be creating an experience with you Jacob in that...my friend, I told him he was creating the experience of talking to me and of having a friend that he would meet Jacob or... that he was ready to expand or that we would not be talking. And it's just so exciting. And I thought of Kayite and that feeling... of sharing this with somebody else... and it's so exhilarating. It's the most exhilarating that I have felt to share these thoughts and these feelings with somebody else.

Expression of self...your true essence...radiating through..... this is glorious. You can feel the joy because it is you who is shining through.

(Pause)

Are you complete?

Oh my goodness...I was just thinking I am complete. (Laughter) I was just thinking that very sentence. I love that.
End Session

Continued Conversation with Kayite after the Session with Jacob Ended:

That was the most powerful vibration I've ever felt. I mean, I'm still vibrating a little bit and I could feel the current from Jacob.

I felt the most intense vibrations too. My entire face, hands and top of my body are still vibrating. I'm still having a hard time trying to speak because my mouth is numb and I am talking funny. (Laughter)

I thought you were vibrating really hard when you first started. Were you? Or could you tell?
Yes. YEEEESS! I was.

I could sort of…I could see it out of the corner of my eye, because I don't look at you.
You know, when we first sat down, I didn't think we were going to do this today. And then I began feeling the vibrations in my face and hands, that I felt like I was supposed to do this. It felt perfect. It was already starting just by you sitting next to me. And so I felt like something was happening and I was ready to just let it flow. It appears you were to have this conversation. And although I didn't know that, Jacob knew you needed to talk with them. They say they are here for the asking so I guess you must have been wanting, asking…

I really did. It's funny. When you first asked, when you said something I was sort of like, I sort of figured we weren't going to do it, but I realized I was bummed about it. (Laughter) I mean I wasn't thinking about being bummed, but I was sort of thinking oh, it's such a shame we have to wait for a couple of weeks. I just wanted some connection before you left for your upcoming trip. I was sort of feeling like something was missing. And now it's not. (Laughter)

And that was just so wonderfully peaceful and I feel so wonderfully peaceful. And when I watched the movie *Stardust* for the first time, I was feeling in such a great space and I was literally a part of all of the emotions happening and it was a wonderful movie. And I am so excited to be in this space to watch it again. Because it's just so ethereal and beautiful and wonderful…because I am all I need and I have those wonderful feelings and emotions. Whether I'm watching a show or just sitting in the dark or being with other people or whatever it is.

It was just so intense, the vibrations on my face. It went around my jaw line and my ears, this intense vibration on my ears and the back of my neck. It was almost like this pressure on my shoulders as if someone was holding me down, but not in an uncomfortable way. It was a nice peaceful way but as if somebody was just placing their hands on my shoulders and holding me in place just, well, just lovingly. And then these vibrations, not just my face, but my jaw and ears just vibrating everywhere. I am going to have to get on the scale, because I have noticed the past few times I've done this I've actually lost weight and I think all that intense vibration is somehow burning up the calories. So maybe I just need to…(laughter) need to do this everyday instead of going to the gym. (laughter)

You know the words I think of too, I always think of transcending it because it's not about the calories. You know what I'm saying. You transcend the physical.

Yeah, well, I was transcending something.

Because I have been afraid to shine my light to other people, all I think they see and I guess all they can see is that outer shell or sometimes that outgoing person that I can be.

Well, it's not about them anyway, because you're beautiful just as you are…I mean you're beautiful. Everyone will see something different in you so shine your light for you.

The negative thought that I am going to release is – she's got it all together and yet she can't control her eating. When honestly I do realize that I'm not trying to control my eating. I don't want to.

Right, right. You want to change it in a different way.

I'm seeing it through the eyes of others, the way society sees it. You're supposed to control what you eat. You're supposed to

be thin. And if you're not, you're not successful. And that is the thing that I need to let go.

And for me, it's been about growth. It's been about growth in this process. There is tremendous growth in this experience for me. And so I'm grateful for it. I'm still working through that process. It's the growth, the contrast, knowing I love me as I am and that I am beautiful and fantastically funny, and awesome in every way and uh, you know, who wouldn't want to be with me? Come on. I'm pretty great. (Laughter)

That is so true, so true.

12/24

We enjoyed Christmas Eve at my mother and stepfather's house. My former husband drove in with Xander and me. We had great fun during the trip. We laughed a lot. It was really wonderful. The kids played and opened presents earlier in the day. Some other family members joined us later for a lovely meal. It was a fantastic day!

12/25

Xander and I headed over to my former husband's apartment for our Christmas Day celebration. Xander opened his presents from us and we played games all afternoon. I headed home in the evening to get ready for my early morning flight. This has been a very nice day but I could feel a shift in how I perceived the holiday this year. Christmas used to be such a big to do for me but I realize that this was because I had so little enjoyment in my life. Because of this, I put so much focus on looking forward to the holidays to bring some joy. Now that I am enjoying every day of my life experience, I still enjoy the holiday and the opportunity to get together with my family, but I enjoy it as much as any other experience rather than putting it up on a pedestal as a rare special moment in the year.

12/26

I leave today for my trip to Ashland, Oregon to attend the Conversations with God New Year's Retreat. I arrived at the airport at 2:50 a.m. for an early flight. My suitcase was so heavy that I could barely get it out of the car. I finally managed to get all of my things together and make the trek from long term parking to the elevator that led to the main entrance. I entered through the first set of sliding doors but when I got to the second set, they did not open.

It was then that I realized that no one was there. The airport was still closed for the holidays. I had no idea when they would open. I decided to make myself comfortable and went and sat down in the corner of the breezeway. The weather was a bit chilly during the winter season and it was warm inside. I sat for a few moments and all was silent.

Then I said, I welcome someone to join me who will offer a most enjoyable and enlightening conversation and would be very friendly and easy to talk to. In that moment, a car pulled up and several young men got out. One of them said good-bye to his friends, gave hugs, and headed my way. How is that for instant manifestation? He, too, was confused when the doors did not open for him. He immediately walked over with a big smile on his face and sat down to join me.

We introduced ourselves. His name is Quan and he was just here visiting with friends for a week. I found out that he is from China and has been here for six months attending graduate school in Kansas City. And do you know what he is studying? Physics! Something I have been talking a lot about lately. And he wants to be a scientist. He was fascinating to talk to.

We talked for an hour and half before security opened the door for us. The ticket counter was still closed but we got to come inside and sit in chairs. We were still the only two people there. I got a security person to take our picture in front of the Christmas tree in the lobby. (Wish I had worn makeup and did my hair. I thought I was just going to be sleeping on the plane. So be it. I can only laugh at that now.)

We continued to talk until the ticket counter opened at 5:00. I checked in and had to pay $50 more for an overweight suitcase – sixteen pounds too much! Oops. I didn't think twice about it. The old me would have stressed about the money. In this moment, I now rejoice in the contrast and I only feel peace and joy knowing all is perfection. Quan was waiting for me and we went to the gate to wait together. He was going to be on my first flight, which was landing in Cincinnati. We continued to talk and then he disappeared. I didn't know where he went and then all of the sudden he showed up with breakfast for me! A lovely egg sandwich and coffee. How sweet and thoughtful he was.

We just really enjoyed each other's company. When it was time to board the plane, we were seated in different areas. When we arrived in Cincinnati, we walked together to a central location in the airport, said our goodbyes and gave big hugs, and then headed off to our separate gates. What a fantastic experience it had been. I feel tremendous gratitude that he showed up for me today.

A Delightful Taxi Ride

The rest of my trip was very relaxing. I arrived at the Medford Airport and my luggage was already available as soon as I got to the baggage claim. I picked it up and headed outside to catch a cab. There were several waiting but I felt drawn to one in particular. The driver got out and helped put my luggage in the trunk. It was about a twenty-five minute drive to Ashland. We talked and had the most delightful conversation. I shared that I was in town for the Holiday Retreat and a little bit about my transformation since the Freedom Retreat. He shared that he was a recovering alcoholic and had since gotten his life on the path that he desired. It was a very enjoyable drive. It is amazing what others will share with you when you allow the space to invite it and receive it.

Settling In

I checked into the Ashland Springs Hotel. It is beautiful. I have a friend, Ralf, arriving this evening that I was planning to meet for dinner. Several other friends, MaryAnn, Melissa and Silver, are not arriving until tomorrow. I called Jan from the hotel and we talked for a while. Ralf finally called to let me know he had arrived. I was so excited to see him. He knocked on my door and had the biggest smile on his face when I opened it. We gave each other a huge hug and headed downstairs to check out the town.

It was dark outside by then and the Christmas lights were fantastic. We just started walking. We came across a place for dinner. We sat in a back room that had a fireplace and we were all by ourselves. It was very quaint. We talked for several hours and enjoyed the evening. We headed back to the hotel and decided to get some good sleep.

12/27

Ralf and I both slept in as we were adjusting to the time difference. We then met for lunch and took a stroll around town. It was beginning to snow. It was so beautiful. Our other friends arrived later that day and we all went to dinner. We so enjoyed the restaurant that we visited last night that we returned again today. We were seated in the back room again but this time, we were directly in front of the fireplace. It was nice and warm. We all had a great time. We laughed and talked for hours. We were excited to come together again for this retreat.

12/28

We all went to breakfast and then took a walk through Lithia Park. I took lots of nature photos, we hugged some trees, and MaryAnn and I even swung on the swings at the playground to bring out the playful kid in us. There is so much joy in returning to that carefree state of being. We headed back to the main strip and checked out some of the shops. They had some really unique things. It was fun.

We had an early dinner and then headed off to attend an optional nightly seminar with Neale Donald Walsch. We weren't about to miss that! Have I mentioned before that I love this man? Yes, yes. I know I have. And I cannot say it enough. He is beautiful and I am forever grateful for the role he has played in my life experience.

My friends and I sat in the front row in fold-out chairs that were on the floor. We got comfortable and settled in when all of the sudden I began to cough. The cough continued. I got up and walked to the back entry where there was water. The cough still continued and I had to ask myself, why did I create this? I don't know.

What I do know is that I enjoyed the process. I stood at the back entrance and enjoyed the entire seminar from there. So perhaps the creation was nothing more than the opportunity to enjoy it no matter what. And indeed I did. It was fabulous.

12/29

This was the first day of our retreat. I was very excited. My friends and I decided we would not sit next to each other, as we desired to get to know others. The first person I sat next to was a lovely man named Michael. Actually, I was in my seat and he appeared and sat next to me. I told him this was significant. The retreat was wonderful. I just wanted to be in the space and fill the room with love. At lunchtime, I invited Michael to join my friends and me for lunch. I shared with him about Jacob and he was excited. I knew there was more for me to experience with him. (We have since built a wonderful friendship. He has created many changes in his life experience and it has been beautiful to witness and participate in his growth process.)

After lunch, we went by his hotel to see if his luggage had arrived. It had been lost during his flight. When he checked with the front desk, it had not been delivered. He joked that he might have to chew someone out. I told him to just envision himself going back to the hotel later and seeing the suitcase is there and that everything is fine. (He did, and sure enough, that is exactly what happened.) We headed back to the retreat and found new seats. We were all encouraged to switch it up. I enjoyed the rest of the retreat day. I was taking it all in. Just feeling the energy. I enjoyed looking around at all of the people, all the other parts of me. I could feel the energy from each person. It was incredible.

It was late by the time we were done. MaryAnn and I talked in our room for a while before bed. She has desired to create many changes in her life for quite a while now. She says she feels things are beginning to shift for her. She has recently made some major decisions to begin to create these changes. I am excited for her process. We went to bed to rest up for the next full day.

12/30

Today people really began to open up and share. It was delightful. It is my favorite part of the process. I feel an intense connection during this interaction. I am having a great time at the retreat. There are about 100 people. I finally connected with another friend from my previous retreat yesterday morning. She was not there for the optional Friday night lecture. I gave her the biggest hug and, of course, told her we were having lunch together. We had the best time at lunch and then she "outed" me about Jacob to the others at the table.

It was so funny. I guess I was meant to share that part of me at that time. It is not something I usually announce right away. Oh by the way, I channel and communicate these spiritual beings. It still sounds funny when I say that. I really like to give people the opportunity to just get to know me first, just Kayite, as I am. Knowledge of Jacob can sometimes create a separation and others place me on a pedestal that I do not desire to be on. I am just like you. Making my way through the world and having some interesting experiences. My experiences may be a little different, but I am still a woman, a mother, a daughter, a friend, and a human being in this world.

My friend and I had dinner together as well. Each time I invited others I didn't know to join us. It was lovely. I told my friend just how much I love her and how great she is. All she kept saying is that she couldn't believe I even remembered her. I will definitely be keeping up with her. I can't let her get away with that crazy thought! I said, "Of course I remember you!" I remember her dancing so freely, free spirit swaying in the wind so beautifully. That is what I see. She is a glorious woman who has inspired me.

I haven't met up with Phillip yet. He has been out of town for the holidays and is returning to Ashland sometime this weekend.

He is going to contact me when he gets in and we will most likely get together after the retreat ends. He is just so delightful. I cannot wait to give him a great big hug.

My Happy Place

Nancy Walsch led us through a wonderful guided imagery meditation today. I remember I was to walk down a set of stairs to a doorway and that it would open to my special place, a happy place. As the door opened I saw a meadow with bright green grass, beautiful flowers and lots of people. I sensed they were waiting for me. I began to hug each one as we exchanged love energy, the essence of ourselves.

Nancy then said our animal totem might come and join us. I began to see hundreds of butterflies. Then I looked in the distance, and saw that trees surrounded me and that the meadow was in the middle of a forest. A wolf appeared emerging from the trees, then a bear, rabbits, deer, and then all of the animals began to emerge from the forest. They were all flocking toward me. It was amazing. It was one of the most incredible moments of my life as I felt our divine connection and came to a greater awareness of my purpose here.

Inner Child

In another guided meditation, we were to see a child coming toward us. I saw a beautiful, happy, cheerful child who was skipping along toward me. I knew when I saw her that she was me. Just then, Nancy said that this was our inner child. She came and gave me a big hug.

She told me she was okay now, that I had wanted the experiences I had as a child and that I chose them. She said that she was healed now and that I was free. We embraced and then she skipped off toward the light. It was beautiful!

My Future Self

We were then invited to visit with our future selves. I saw myself on a stage speaking to a huge group of people. There was strength and passion in my voice and a confidence and absolute surety that I had not always known. It was powerful, a very uplifting experience. I look forward to that moment coming to fruition.

12/31

I have had the most delightful day. Today was all about sharing. YES! I was home. Connected. Loving. I made sure to hug each person who shared. And I thanked them for sharing and told them I love them. It's been so fantastic. The bigger group is much different from my previous retreat but it offers its own joys. There has been lots of laughter, a room full of many tears together, and we even did a wave! Now that was fun. I have met the most wonderful people and I'm enjoying it so much. One of my friends sat beside me and I held her hand all morning. It was glorious.

An Empty Backpack

Nancy Walsch did another guided imagery meditation for us. When I went through the doors to my happy place, this time I saw a bunch of children playing, laughing and enjoying life. When our totems were invited in, I experienced the same thing as the day before, all of the animals coming to join me. We were then invited to pick up a backpack and carry it up a mountain.

I knew right away that mine was very light and easy to carry. She then said that this was all of our baggage. I carried it to the top of the mountain and then I was told to open the backpack and place the items in a basket that had balloons on it. I just put the whole backpack in without opening it.

I knew it was empty. I let go of the basket and rejoiced in my freedom. It felt great to experience once again the freedom I am already living and to have that clarity about where I am. Thank you, Nancy, for your many gifts.

New Year's Eve

After a fantastic day, we all headed back to our rooms to get dressed for the New Year's Eve Party. There was a declaration of our goals for the New Year (I had none; I was just rejoicing in the moment), a toast, and then the music and dancing began. Then someone started karaoke and it was great! Very entertaining. There was a group of us gals who came together to sing *I will Survive*.

I was smiling and beaming through the whole thing. And by the way, I cannot sing a note in tune. But I sure had fun! It was a wonderful evening with new friends and old and I headed to bed about 1:00. We still had a morning session to round out our retreat.

1/01

It was a beautiful morning. I delighted at what transpired for everyone. So what happened with MaryAnn and Melissa who allowed me to participate in their joining the retreat? I cannot share the details as I honor their privacy in what took place for them. But I can tell you that great shifts occurred and I experienced tears of joy at having been a part of their process. They both gave me great big hugs. They were thanking me and I was thanking them. What an amazing moment. I am grateful to them both for the experience they offered me.

Neale wrapped up the last session of the retreat and I felt calmness, a great sense of peace fill the room. We all exchanged contact information and said our good-byes. Many headed off in different directions. There was a group of us that came together for several photos right outside. After that, about twenty of us went to Louie's Grill for our final lunch together. It was delightful.

My Visit with Phillip Daniel

Phill called at the perfect moment. We were just finishing up lunch on Tuesday afternoon. He came to meet me and I just gave him a huge hug. It was great to finally look into his eyes and meet face-to-face the person I had been talking and sharing so much with. We took a nice long walk in the park and shared some more. He radiates a wonderful light.

We decided to go out to dinner and a friend of his joined us. I was rather quiet as I was in observation mode. I tend to be that way when meeting new people. I learn so much just from listening and feeling the energy.

After a wonderful meal, we went to the local movie theater to see *Charlie Wilson's War*. It was a great day. I really enjoyed his presence. We said we would try to get together again the following day. My flight was scheduled to leave early Friday morning and I only had two days left. I was enjoying every moment.

1/02

This morning I awoke feeling like my time here is incomplete. The retreat has ended but I am sensing there is more for me to experience. I am open to what will unfold. MaryAnn, Silver and I went out for breakfast. We then walked around town for a bit, visited a few more shops and then decided to go see the movie *Across the Universe*. What a great film that was! We all got popcorn (something I had not eaten in quite some time).

After the movie, we took a stroll through the park and eventually got hungry again. We decided to go to dinner but I wasn't able to eat. My stomach was hurting. I thought why did I eat all that popcorn? Phill called and was available to get together so he came and met us at the restaurant. I introduced him to my friends and we briefly chatted. Then Phill and I took off for a stroll around town. The Christmas lights were still up and it was a lovely walk.

I was feeling discomfort in my stomach still but we walked slowly and I was okay. It was very enjoyable. We just talked for about an hour. I just adore him and I am grateful that he appeared in my life. He dropped me off at my hotel and I gave him a big hug good-bye. It was wonderful to connect with him.

Indigestion to Emergency Room

As I headed up to my hotel room, I could feel the pain getting worse. I got into the bathtub and it helped relieve this a bit. Every time I tried to get out of the tub, I could feel the pain more and opted to stay in. I finally made it out and onto my bed. MaryAnn was there and asked if I needed a doctor. "I think it's just that popcorn, I'll be fine," I said.

Ralf came to visit us in our room. As we were all talking, I began to realize that the pain was continuing to get much worse and that something else was going on here. MaryAnn called the hospital and got directions. I was curled up in a ball on my bed. Ralf knew someone who had a car here and he came and drove us to the emergency room. I could barely walk by this time.

What's Up, Jacob?

When I first went to the hospital and had a moment alone, I asked Jacob what this was all about. They told me this was part of my experience and to let go, that I would come back, and that this experience would help me to understand the work we are to do together. I was at peace. I already knew there was growth in it for me. The exact reason was not so important.

Status

My friend stayed with me for four hours. The doctor said he believed it was my appendix. They were going to do a CAT scan sometime during the night to confirm. I finally told Ralf to go back to the hotel and get some rest. I knew I was fine. I enjoyed his presence but I knew he needed to get up in the morning. He was participating in the Life Education Program (LEP), a part of Neale Donald Walsch's offering which lasted several weeks after the retreat. (Melissa ended up staying to participate in this program as well, an unexpected treat.)

The CAT scan confirmed the inflammation of my appendix and surgery was scheduled for Thursday (January 3) at noon. (By this time, I already knew this to be so.) Of course, this meant changing my flight home and making other arrangements. The doctor recommended that I stay at least another week and see him again for a final checkup before heading home.

1/03

The surgery went great and all of my friends and family began calling my room to check in on me. I was continually surrounded with their loving presence. A few of my LEP friends stopped by during their lunch break to see me. It was nice to have visitors being so far away from home. Although I felt so very connected through all of my many phone calls. And the nurses were absolutely delightful. I felt like a VIP.

I rescheduled my flight from Friday 1/04 to Friday 1/11. I would leave early morning time and get back to Charlottesville at 9:12 p.m. and then probably arrive home around 11:00. The airlines gave me a credit for my return ticket and waived the transfer fee but I still had to pay any difference in fare that day. Well, since it was only a week away, the cost was $1250 and with my $350 credit they were telling me it would still be $900. I only paid $650 round trip to begin with.

The person I spoke with was very kind and I could tell wanted to help me. I was at peace. I thought, it's all good. The person ended up handing me over to a supervisor without me even requesting it. The supervisor brought the cost down to $150. How great is that! Had I of gotten upset and angry and put that energy out there, I have no doubt that I would have been paying the $900. When I just let go, everything flows so smoothly. I love this process.

Bridge of Light

When I went in for surgery, at some point, I saw a bridge of light. At the center of the bridge, there was another path leading off into the distance. People began to walk across from both sides. Only, as they were coming together, they were actually meeting the other parts of themselves at the center of the bridge. They were literally stepping into themselves. Awakening to whom they are. Then I saw them walk off on that center path. I came to understand that I was the bridge. I knew this was preparing me for the next phase. I am open to what is to come.

What About Health Insurance?

As I mentioned earlier, I lost my health insurance the end of October. Melissa, who was visiting me at the hospital, knew this. She was very disturbed by my situation. She questioned me about it. She had made the comment that she seemed more upset about it than I was. I told her I agreed, as I was not upset at all. It made perfect sense that as I am declaring that my health insurance is no longer necessary, that an opportunity would show up for me to experience this. "But you did need it," she said. "Did I?" I asked.

The surgery was completed and all was well. I may get a huge bill in the mail but so what. I'll work out a payment plan and so be it. It is what it is. I myself was still fine. It was not the end of the world. This was my opportunity to experience peace in the moment. I never thought twice about it. What a gift this was. Before my shift in awareness occurred, I would have suffered through the pain until my appendix burst before I would have allowed myself to rack up a bill by going to the hospital. That would have been a fear-based decision. I don't live in fear anymore.

So the surface appearance of my situation may have appeared that I "needed" it, but in my reality, all is perfection and a wonderful experience and opportunity for growth was provided. And in knowing that all is perfection, I would have been okay with whatever transpired. If this meant no medical care at all and resulted in me kicking the bucket right in my hotel room, then so it would be. The idea that insurance offers some sort of security is just an illusion. Knowing that I need nothing and experiencing the peace in living this is priceless. I have almost $21,000 in medical bills and this experience was worth every penny. Melissa, thank you for this gift!

1/04

I stayed in the hospital overnight. I talked with Jan quite a bit during my stay. We seemed to be bonding even more during this trip. I could feel something shifting for us again. I chatted with many other friends and enjoyed the process. My LEP friends came to visit me again during lunch. The doctor happened to show up while they were there and signed for my release. It was perfect. They had to get back to class but Ralf, who had stayed with me those first hours in the hospital, again stayed to help take me back to the hotel. Ralf, I thank you for your many gifts!

MaryAnn had packed up all of my things and left them in Ralf's room so she could check out. Her flight left the morning of my surgery and I did not get a chance to say good-bye. I discovered she had paid for our room for the entire week. How wonderful! MaryAnn, I thank you for your many gifts! I got another room and went to relax on the bed. All was perfection. I slept well and felt great.

Scared or Excited?

Numerous people have asked me if I felt frantic or scared about the surgery and medical situation. How awful it must have been, they would say. When I tell them it was for the experience, that I am grateful and filled with joy, it captures their attention. It begins to create a shift as they try to understand this. I was laughing and having a great time at the hospital. The doctors and nurses were so great. I had the very best time. And I do think the physical releasing of this part is significant. It was my experience of completely letting go.

Other things to think about, is all that will transpire this week for me here. None of which would have happened had I just gone home. I got to celebrate Melissa's birthday last night and another friend and I had a really great talk. I am getting to know some of the LEP participants that I would not have had the opportunity to do. I am resting and allowing myself to be in this space. I am writing in my journal. I look forward to what the rest of the week will bring. So I do not know all of the reasons I am still here but I am confident that they will be revealed throughout my time here. Isn't it great? I see the perfection in it. I am not surprised at all. It is just too divine.

1/05

I just finished eating lunch with the LEP Group. I was welcomed to join them for all of their meals. They are taking great care of me. It has been very enjoyable to talk with everyone. A man at the table told me that my eyes were just radiating across the table. Just beaming at him. This was not the first time I have heard this. In fact, I hear this quite often now. I told him it was the love that I have for him. The deep love I have for all. It is the very essence of me shining through.

We had a very nice conversation after that. I shared with him about Jacob. He asked how did I know that it wasn't just all in my head. Good question. How do we really know anything? I can only know what my experience is. Everything has shifted for me. My entire way of life is different. I know what I sense and feel with Jacob, the intense energy vibrations, the information that flows through, and the connections that I now make with others. It is all as I have described it to be. That's all I can tell you. I am not here to prove anything, only to share in my experience. It is what is so for me. What is our reality anyway? Think about it. We all have a different version. Each is just as real and profound as we have experienced it to be. Only in our own experience of something, can we truly come to know and understand that experience.

1/06

I once again enjoyed my meals with the group. As I am interacting with them, I am aware that my presence is not only for my own growth, but that I too am offering them an experience. Of course, the experience being offered is different for each person. I know that just my presence is making a difference and helping to create change.

Phill called this afternoon and we went to another movie. I thought I could handle just sitting in a chair. We saw *The Great Debaters*. It was really good. I cried a lot. I love movies that touch my soul. That reach my emotions and I can just let them flow and feel the experience. It was great to see my friend again. Just being in his presence and having the awareness of oneness was so beautiful. There was nothing that needed to be said. We could just be. I sensed this would be the last time and I enjoyed the process. I gave him a big hug good-bye, although I knew we would remain connected by source. It was so very wonderful to share part of this incredible journey with him. Phill, I thank you for your many gifts!

1/07

I have been talking with many of my friends each day and with Jan several times throughout the day. This has kept me busy in between the meals with the group. I really look forward to the meals and entering delightful conversations. I have gotten to sit with a variety of people. I have been taking it all in and thinking about what is being offered to me with every interaction. It has been wonderful.

Dinner with Neale

When it was time for dinner, I headed to the table that has been my usual table since I have been home from the hospital. (The LEP Group meets for meals at the hotel restaurant.) This one in particular has a sofa on one side with cushions and this was very comfortable and supportive for me during my physical healing process. When I got to the table, I discovered that Neale was sitting there with two others. I was welcomed to join in at the table. How delightful this was.

He told me he had just heard about my surgery and asked me a little about it. I shared with him that I had felt my time here was not complete and that I was excited at what was to be revealed. I went into my quiet observation mode again. I was paying attention, listening, taking it all in, and just basking in his presence. He invited me to sit in on the class for the next two days. Of course I said, "Yes, I would love to." I could feel it all falling into place now.

Joining the Group

As I walked in the room, there was a circle of chairs. I could feel the energy they had created in the space and I got a chair and put it in the far back corner almost out of sight. I did not want to disrupt their flow. Over the course of the next two days, two of my remaining issues (that I was consciously aware of at the time) were discussed and it was perfection. I sat and listened and was grateful. The last day, I sat in the back and cried for a while. They were tears of joy as I was releasing the congested energy. I was enjoying the process.

Now in case you are wondering why I had issues to release when I stated earlier that my backpack of baggage was empty, the reason is because these issues were not baggage to me. Because I was consciously aware of their presence and purpose in my life (for growth), I rejoiced in the process and they were no longer a burden to me as heavy baggage but rather a gift that I gladly welcomed. It was incredible.

1/10

I went for my checkup at the doctor's office. He gave me a "thumbs up" to return home. I now felt complete with my trip. I felt my purpose here had been fulfilled. I still had this final day to enjoy. I was open to what might transpire. It was a relaxing day. I wrote in my journal and packed my bags for a 4:00 a.m. departure. At dinner, I had several wonderful conversations and exchanged information to keep in contact. One of them offered to bring my luggage down for me (I was not suppose to lift anything) and see me off in the morning. Great!

I gave hugs and said my good-byes. Several of them shared how much they enjoyed my presence there and said they would miss my energy. To all of you lovely beings, I thank you all for your many gifts!

1/11

My new friend knocked on my door in the morning. I was all set. It felt great to have an escort on my way out. It would have felt odd to leave by myself as if sneaking off in the middle of the night. There was something special about making that connection. She gave me a big hug and waved good-bye as I got in the taxi. I enjoyed my flight back. I had a long layover in Cincinnati. I was provided a wheelchair and taken excellent care of. I had a nice lunch at the airport and then decided to get a manicure and massage since I had the extra time. This was all a new airport experience for me and I was delighted that I allowed myself to make it a reality. It was wonderful. I headed off on my final flight.

I arrived late at night and my former husband picked me up from the airport along with my son. I was so excited to see my little boy's smiling face. I gave Xander a teddy bear that a friend had sent me while in the hospital. He loved it. He named him Teddy. We still had a one-hour drive home. I was just delighted to be back.

Rest and Relaxation

I spent the next week just resting and relaxing at home and allowing my body to fully heal. I knew I would heal quickly. This was also a wonderful opportunity for me to just spend a lot of time with my son. We played games, read books and talked a lot. It was great to connect with him after being gone for so long. I enjoyed this time immensely. I was up and running and back to my routine in no time.

Walking Through

Jan and I were talking and he told me that he wanted to come visit me at my home in Virginia. I have been to his place twice. I said "great." He booked his flight and all was set. The week before he was to arrive, we both began to experience all kinds of physical manifestations of illness. It was quite funny as we were both very clear that we had manifested these physical things as a result of stuff surfacing for us that we desired to create change in. Our coming together was drawing this stuff to the surface. We understood what was happening and we are excited for the process of our experience together and releasing the congested energy. This was another opportunity to discuss what we were experiencing and walk through it together.

1/22

I saw the most magnificent sky this morning on the way to Charlottesville. The sun was rising and there were clouds in the background that you could not visually see any movement. But just below, and in front of the sun, there were the fastest moving clouds I have ever seen. They were just flowing across with the sun beaming behind it. Clouds filled the entire area ahead as I was driving. The movement was quite incredible. I was captivated yet trying to pay attention to my driving. It was more extraordinary than I can describe. It was a glorious thing to witness and experience.

Joint Meditation

Jan and I did a joint meditation yesterday. We were not physically present together. We just chose a time in the morning to connect during meditation. He shared with me later that day that he had a hard time relaxing his thoughts to go to that peaceful place. I had easily relaxed right into it and had felt his presence.

So this morning I joined him for another meditation, only this time I envisioned holding his hands, then put my hands on his face and pulled him into my space. We sat in the stillness, peace and love. Then I stepped into him, sharing one space. Later that day, he sent me an email sharing his experience. I was delighted to hear he was able to just BE. He sat in stillness. He also told me that he felt us come together as one. Beautiful!

1/23

My former husband and I had a great conversation last night. He came over to go through the finances with me so we could finally separate everything. It was quick and easy. It took all of 10 minutes. We chose to do it in a kind and loving manner and it was such a smooth process. I am so grateful that we have maintained such a wonderful friendship. He then told me about this new woman he has been dating. Here we are separated only a few months after fourteen years together and we can easily share all the details of our new relationships and be the friends we always were to love and support one another. Isn't that great? I sure think so.

1/24

Jan and I talked for many hours last night and I didn't get to bed until 2:00. I was used to going to sleep between 1:00 and 2:00 every night, but ever since I returned from Oregon, my schedule has been off. I am still adjusting but I am enjoying the conversations. We never run out of things to talk about. I love the many endless hours of communication. It has been absolutely delightful and just keeps getting better as we are experiencing and growing with one another.

Tidbits from Xander

"I love everything in the Universe." "You do?" I asked. "Yes" he said. "And I love everybody. It's wonderful to love everybody."

1/29

An amazing gift appeared in my life yesterday and I wanted to share it with you. My former husband had gone through some boxes in the office and found something I had written back in March/April of last year. It was right before the retreat and I had forgotten all about it. He didn't want to throw it away as he wasn't sure if I would want it. I picked it up in the morning when I got

Xander and didn't give it much thought. It was in a bag with a bunch of receipts and other things.

About 8:30 last night I had come to a stopping point in organizing my home and I sat down to check out the bag of stuff before my 9:00 group call. Well, let me tell you, I was blown away by what I read. Not only did I have a clear understanding of how I ended up at the retreat at Black Mountain, everything I had written about has since come to be. Manifested so beautifully in my life.

I created it and hadn't even remembered I had put out the intentions for it. These were written during a rough time in my life yet I had moments of clarity. These were those rare moments. What a gift this has been to see how it all came to be. What my thoughts were that created all of this. How divine! I see just how profound they were. My inner self was shining through. Source was guiding me to the life I stated I desired. Well, I am sure you are curious to know what I wrote. So here goes......

March 12

Today I choose to change my life. I choose positive, loving and kind thoughts and I choose to create that environment. I create my own reality. I am not sure of the direction of my life. I want to reach out and help people. I want to make a difference in this world. But how? I feel I have so much to give yet I have no idea how to share it. I am ready to watch my life blossom as I reach out and create something wonderful. I am ready to break out of my shy cocoon and unfold the love in order to share it with others.

The one thing I have learned is that the people in your life is what matters and how we all interact and affect one another to create change. I choose to give each person my full attention. To take time to communicate, share, and enjoy the experience. Truly sharing who I am with others. Being completely open and true to who I am. Not hiding behind what I believe other people want me to be. I choose to share the bright light of my spirit. The body is just a vehicle through life. I choose to let my true essence shine. To radiate love so that others may feel it.

April 1

I feel joy in this moment. In just being. A part of this grand universe. I often feel out of place. As if I don't belong here in this time. I am not sure how to relate to others in this world. I am not interested in so many general everyday things. I want and desire to experience something on a grander scale. To experience the love of each and every person. To share this when connecting with those I come in contact with each day. For us all to be who we are to the fullest. Can we do this now? Are we ready? Is humanity ready for a tremendous shift in consciousness?

I shared this on my group call. It was the perfect moment for it to appear. I also feel another shift is about to occur. It's already begun. This information arriving is part of that. It is the same thing I felt right before Jacob arrived. I sensed then that something big was about to happen. What I sense now is a shift to the next phase. I am ready and I am excited to see how it will all unfold. At the end of our call, we were to share what we were grateful for.

I said I was so grateful to my former husband for giving me this gift instead of throwing the paper away. It was not in a journal or notebook; it was just a single piece of paper that at any other time he most likely would have trashed. But, of course, he did not as he was part of this glorious co-creation. He has no idea what a gift he has given me. How incredibly significant that one little sheet of paper was. But I will let him know. I cannot wait to see him tonight and share this with him. I am so delighted that he is a part of this process. It brings it all together. How perfect! So Divine! I acknowledge you.

My Perspective on Relationships

These questions arose as a topic of discussion for my Freedom Circle Group. It was the most delightful discussion and offered me the opportunity for great clarity about where I am. I am grateful. Once again, thank you for this gift!

Describe the most incredible romantic love you have ever experienced.

With the idea that love is who we are, the most incredible relationship I have experienced is where love is fully expressed. That is, the other and myself are fully present. We share all of who we are with each other. We are open and honest about what we feel in the moment and are able to meet each other on all levels. We can communicate about anything. Nothing is off limits. We are connecting soul to soul. We consciously choose to walk together through whatever surfaces for us for our greater growth. We honor one another and what we choose for our life experience. We allow one another to be free. We rejoice in this.

Do you think it is possible for another person to make you happy?

No one else can make me happy. It is a choice I must make for myself. I can share in the happiness with another, but they must bring their own as I bring mine.

What is your relationship style? Old-fashioned, risqué, or somewhere in between?

Off the Charts. I choose not to limit myself. I am open to all possibilities.

In your opinion, what is the purpose of romantic relationships?

Someone to share in my life experience for the purpose of offering me the opportunities of growth and expansion that I desire. And at the same time, I am a match for my partner in providing experiences that offer the opportunities of growth and expansion that he desires. And as we desire different experiences for growth, our relationships may change in order to experience these new desires. I allow them to flow in and out with ease.

In previous relationships, what are some of the gifts that you received that you did not recognize as gifts at the time?

My loneliness caused me to desire deep, meaningful friendships. The distance I felt caused me to desire someone who was fully present. The anger and defensiveness caused me to desire someone who was calm and willing to talk things through. The frustration caused me to desire peace. The lack of interest for intimacy caused me to desire someone who had great desire for me and who was willing to go to that intimate sacred space for the most incredible pleasures ever. The lack of excitement about life caused great desire for experiencing the joy in everything. Complete shutdown from life caused me to look within and ask myself what life was all about. I knew there had to be more to life than that. This caused great desire to experience all the magnificence that life has to offer.

I can only be grateful for all of those incredible gifts. I gladly shout from the rooftops – thank you for the magnificent experiences of loneliness, anger, defensiveness, frustration, hopelessness, disconnection, all of which just made me want to end it all. It is hard for me to believe I ever felt that way. But I did. And I sure can relate to a whole spectrum of feelings. I now rejoice in the growth that others offered me. I rejoice that in this moment of now, I am experiencing all of what I desired to manifest in my life. And I am always coming up with more.

Was there something about the man who raised you that showed up in your relationships with men?

Absolutely. I was raised by a man who was unable to express love or share who he was with me. He was completely shutdown from his emotions. In not feeling loved, I felt unworthy. The unworthiness that I felt drew to me those who continued to offer me the same experiences. I could decide that it no longer served me and choose to respond differently to create change, or I could buy into what was being offered.

For a very long time, I bought into it because I was not consciously aware of what was occurring. I stayed in relationships that confirmed for me that I was indeed unworthy of more and that I did not deserve to be loved. When I came to the awareness that I was worthy and that I WAS love, my response to the situation changed and my life experience changed. I released the illusions that I chose to believe about myself and allowed for all that I desired to flow into my life as it matched up with what I now believed to be so.

Do you believe it is possible for men and women to be friends only?
Absolutely. All relationships offer me growth and expansion. Those that offer growth in the romantic department will form into romantic relationships. Those that offer other types of growth experiences, it will be irrelevant, unless it is. I have many male and female friends and they all offer me an opportunity for growth.

Where Does Jan Fit In?

With all of this discussion about relationships, where exactly does Jan fit into my life experience? I am having more and more experiences that help me to gain greater clarity on how I feel about this. I am very happy in my life just with me. And as I have been, things have opened up for me in the most magical ways.

Things have really shifted for Jan and me to another level. It has just been a natural progression. After hours of talking every day, sharing and connecting, we have sort of ended up in a most magnificent "relationship." We have the most incredible communication, which has created great healing and growth for both of us. And the growth just continues which has allowed us to continue together. He asked me an interesting question yesterday. He said, "There must be some part of you that wants the fairy tale."

My response just popped right out of my mouth. There was no hesitation. I told him that I do want the fairy tale but that my definition of what that is has changed. I told him that I am LIVING the fairy tale. Right now, this moment. That's the fairy tale for me, the joy in the moment. And that in this moment of now, he is my "Prince Charming." And that the fairy tale is not about something in the future, not about living together forever or about making a long term commitment or planning everything out. It's about enjoying every moment of this amazing relationship that has appeared in my life for however many moments that turns out to be. He understood and rejoiced in this with me.

Our relationship was very unexpected for both of us. But we chose to go with the flow of things and we are continuing to choose to just let it unfold however it will. We have no idea where this will go, but we are enjoying the now. And many moments of enjoying the now makes for a very happy and joyous life. The other thing I am enjoying about a long distance relationship is that it has shown me by experience just how great the connection can be with another without the physical presence. Incredible.

What's Next?

I have had the idea for a while of creating a website. I don't know exactly what will be on there but I trust it will all just come about and be created to perfection along the way. I thought I was going to wait until I completed my book to focus on that but today I felt a surge of energy around it. I felt a strong sense that now was the moment to get started.

I am excited to share with you that my website **awakeningtoyou.com** is currently in development. (I intend for it to be up and running by the time you are reading this.) I am going to contact a friend who does nature photography about possibly using some of her photos. How great is that? And I am going to start checking out websites to get ideas about what I like, what stands out to me. I am very excited. I can feel the energy in motion.

I have also felt a strong draw to build a Retreat Center in the beautiful Shenandoah Mountains. This has become a great passion of mine. I would love to create a place for others to come and just be. Be with nature, connect with themselves and others and feel the oneness with everything. I envision nature trails, gardens, a labyrinth, meditation areas, a peaceful retreat room, a place for music and dancing, delightful meals inside and out, a spiritual library, and wonderful rooms that are tranquil and relaxing. Xander and I have talked about what he would like to experience there. He is helping me to create this vision to come to be. He is very excited about it. I rejoice in this process.

1/31

My mom's birthday was this month and my sister and I are taking her out on Saturday to a movie and dinner. We are going to see *The Bucket List*. I cried just watching the previews for it so I am sure it will be great. I am delighted at the opportunity to connect with my mother. I am excited about this new adventure. I feel things shifting for us and I feel like our relationship is beginning to blossom. I rejoice in right where we are. It is beautiful.

Investment in Others

I choose what I wish to create for my life experience and I understand that others are choosing and creating theirs. It is just a different experience. I have no investment in what others are doing. I may utilize what they offer and consciously choose to bring it into my experience for the purpose of growth. I welcome the interaction and opportunity for me to decide if I would like to experience what I see in others' experiences or if I would like to use their experiences as the contrast of what I do not want in order to gain clarity about where I am. For this purpose only, are their life experiences relevant to me.

And in every experience, I ask only one question – what is the growth in this for me? Jacob has guided me to this understanding and awareness of the growth process. I have chosen to embrace it as it feels good and I experience great joy in my life in taking notice of what is being offered to me.

When we release investment in others, we release judgment because there is nothing to judge. Only to rejoice in that they are choosing for them as they desire. We release defensiveness, anger and frustration because there is nothing to defend, get angry about or frustrated about. It is when another is not responding in a manner in which we want them to or is not doing what it is that we wanted them to do that we become defensive, angry and frustrated.

For example, I recently asked my former husband if he would be willing to pay half the cost for the oil change for my vehicle because it is used for driving our son to school. I asked with no expectation of a specific outcome. I was fine with however he chose to respond. I was okay with a "no." I had no resistance to the process.

I would also be perfectly fine if he got upset about my asking and began to explain why he shouldn't have to pay. There would be no anger on my part because how can I be angry when I had no expectation of a particular response. There would be no argument because there would be no anger. There would be no frustration for the situation because I did not attempt to control it. I would not need to defend my reasons for why I think he "should" pay because I do not think he "should" do anything. He is free to respond and experience this interaction, however he chooses. And it is my choice how I choose to respond and experience the interaction. I choose to enjoy it.

Now all of this is just my life experience. My perspective. I am not saying that you should believe what I believe or live the way that I choose to live. I am simply showing you another possibility of what can be. It is for you to choose what you desire. I honor whatever you choose for you. I also understand that how I feel about your life experience is completely irrelevant to you. The only relevance it has is to my own life experience. In my release of investment in all of you, I set myself free of all the baggage of congested energy. I break the dam and allow the joy to flow through. I enjoy my growth process and welcome and embrace all of the experiences that appear in my life. And am I saying it is all about me? You betcha!

Selfishness or Growth for the Collective?

I have had people say to me, isn't it selfish to only think about yourself, to only focus on you? Shouldn't you be caring about others? Making the world a better place? My response to that is that we are all one, here to create different experiences for growth and expansion. Expansion for one is expansion for the whole as it affects the collective thought, which includes everyone else. Therefore, by focusing on my life experience, choosing to consciously be aware of and benefit from the growth opportunities presented to me, I am adding to the whole, which IS beneficial for all. We are all creating this together as there is only one source.

Now does this mean that I would not reach out to another who was asking for help? Of course not! I want to be clear that there is a big difference between not caring what another thinks about the way I am choosing to live my life and simply not caring about others. I have great love for all. I just don't look to others for approval in order to experience joy.

Interacting with others is my life. I am here for you. I am here for all who seek me. I am here for all those who seek Jacob. And why? It is because it is a great joy for me to witness the growth of another. It is uplifting and the reason it is uplifting is because as I witness the growth of another, I am witnessing the growth of myself, as we are one. I am more of an observer in this individual physical life experience. I can interact with another without taking investment in what they are doing. Without feeling the need for them to change their ways because of how I view the world. I view it as their life experience outside of my own. I can rejoice in their growth for where they are just as I rejoice in my own. And their growth can come about in any form. I do not judge or define it. It is what it is to them. That is the only relevance.

Jan's Visit

Jan finally came to visit me for the first time at my place. His flight was supposed to arrive at 11:00 p.m. The flight was cancelled due to snow but it worked out perfectly (of course) because he was able to get on an earlier flight that arrived at 9:30 instead. When he arrived, all physical ailments we had previously experienced had dissipated. Everyday this past week, we talked through all the stuff that surfaced for us and immediately released the congested energy. It was a wonderful process. We enjoyed our first night together and got a good rest to prepare for an active day with Xander.

The following day we went to Natural Bridge. Natural Bridge is considered one of the seven natural wonders of the world. It is a bridge that is two hundred fifteen feet tall and ninety feet wide. It is initialed by George Washington and was owned by Thomas Jefferson. It is a wonderful historical place as well as a great place to be with nature. I am grateful that it is just a short forty-five minute drive, a skip, hop, and a jump to a magical place. We had a great time walking on the trails and playing Putt-Putt. On the way home we stopped off at a little town and were just wandering around looking for a place to eat lunch. We saw a sign that said a Joyful Spirit Cafe and it was calling us. Of course we had to check it out with a name like that. They had really great food and a lovely atmosphere. I will definitely be going back there again.

We dropped Xander off with his father later that night and just spent the rest of the weekend at home connecting on all levels. It was wonderful as always and there were many experiences for growth. We both enjoyed the process and enjoyed talking about the process. Jacob appeared for a brief moment. Jan only had one question but apparently that one interaction was very powerful for him and allowed for a huge release. I found myself not wanting to "come back" so to speak. It had been a little while since there had been direct interaction with them and another and I missed the bliss. It was so wonderful that I wanted it to continue. But I was delighted that the experience was incredibly beneficial.

On the last day of Jan's visit here, I realized that I too had a wonderful shift occur. That my perception of myself – how I viewed my body – had changed. I had stated my desire to create change in this and the experience this weekend created that final shift for me. I realized that not once did I have any negative thought about my body. I only felt beautiful and divine. It took the experience for me to really know this. I could think it, but the experience changed everything. And this wasn't about what Jan thought of me. This was completely irrelevant. It was only ever about me feeling comfortable with me. Me loving and embracing my divine vehicle through which I experience this life. Jan just helped to facilitate this process. I was laughing and shouting it out when he was here with me – "I love my body, I am beautiful, and I am free." It was a great moment. My dear Jan, I thank you for this gift!

Embracement of Self

Jan had offered me this opportunity to experience the beauty of my physical body but, of course, the universe was going to provide me more opportunities as well. The first experience was when I noticed all of the pictures on my wall. Many contain myself with another. When I saw myself, I only saw a beautiful beacon of light. Before, I could not even stand to have my picture taken and I did not want to look at myself in any photos. I had so much resistance to "what is" that I could not release it. When I finally embraced me and stopped fighting against where I was in that moment, I opened myself up for change. I have enjoyed this growth experience. It has all been so beautiful to witness, to watch it unfold in the most magnificent ways.

The next experience was when I took Xander to get his haircut. We were sitting in the waiting area and a woman told me that she liked my blouse and asked me where I got it. I told her the name of the store and then she said "Do they have them in small sizes?" My only response was, "Yes, I believe they do." It was a wonderful opportunity for me to experience that I have truly shifted my thoughts about myself. Before this would have been a trigger point for me. I would have immediately gone to thoughts of – am I that huge? Instead I was able to receive it exactly as it was intended. She was indeed a small woman, much smaller than myself. Her question came from genuine interest and that was it. The energy I had held onto for so long had been released and no longer acted as a trigger point for me. I am grateful to this woman for her participation in my process.

I also recently went shopping for some new clothes. The last time I went long ago, I cried when I tried on the clothes. This time, not only did I find a lot of outfits that I loved, they all fit perfectly and I thought I looked beautiful in them. Had my physical body changed since the last shopping spree? Not a bit. It was only my perception of it that had shifted.

The Role of Another

A friend of mine asked me about what role Jan had played in my life. And what conclusions did I come to that helped me reach this decision. I had previously explained that he had helped me process through a lot of physical body and intimacy issues and that there was a lot of growth for us. My friend still didn't quite understand how that occurred.

I told him that it all has to do with our trigger points and having someone who is willing to walk though them with you for the experience and growth of it. Jan was and is willing to "walk through" anything with me. By "walk through" I mean that he is in it, fully present, open and chooses to acknowledge and embrace the experience and desires to explore the growth in the process with me.

He does not get defensive, angry, or run from what may appear to be a "problem" or something unpleasant that would lead many people to an argument. But if there were anger or defensiveness, it would simply be a trigger point to be discussed. For us, we just talk it through and share. So what does this have to do with my body and intimacy you ask? Well, for one, although I knew I desired to release those old patterns of congested energy, it was the experience of walking through it that helped me to release them and experiences that confirmed for me that I was free.

My friend used the words "conclusion" and "decision" when asking me about this situation. I made a conscious choice that I desired change but a conclusion or decision is not so relevant here. I was consciously aware when I left my husband that I was holding onto these body/intimacy issues. And even though I was living my joy every day, I would occasionally have trigger points hit in which I would feel blah about my body. Or I would have triggers that led to feeling rejection. I chose to change this. I desired to embrace myself as I am and I welcomed the experiences in my life that would facilitate in the creation of this. And even though I chose to change, it is the experiences that can create a shift to occur.

The important thing here is to be able to recognize the opportunities in an experience when they show up. Because I chose to recognize them, I utilized what they were offering me. I was able to release the congested energy, experience growth in the process and set myself free of those issues. I also experienced joy in the entire process from the observer standpoint. There was great joy in witnessing myself shift from feeling confused to having a greater understanding and love of self.

Are You in Love?

A friend of mine heard that I was in love with Jan and wanted to know if there was any truth to that. This was my response: We like to say that we are rising in love together. Being "in love" might refer to something more traditional and our relationship is anything but that. We have something incredible but we both know we are not currently a match as long-term partners. We desire different things. We are, however, a perfect match for the right now. There has been tremendous growth and healing and we are showing each other what is possible. It has been an incredible experience.

It is hard to explain how you can be so-called in love, enjoying every moment, while at the same time know that you do not intend to spend your life together. It works for us because we are both on the same page. Now in acknowledging and discussing what we want for our long-term desires, we are not focused on the future. It's only relevance is how we interact with each other in the now. We enter the relationship knowing exactly where we are and what we desire. Of course, these desires are ever changing and we will continue to share where we are, as it will guide us in every moment. We do not need to define the future. It will unfold in the most magnificent ways when we stop blocking the path by trying to secure everything in place.

There are so many avenues in which things can flow into our life experience but often we may only see one and focus on that. We lock it in for security and then feel our future is set. But then when unexpected things occur, it can set our systems into an upheaval mode. When we let go and allow our life to be what it is, the ease of life emerges. Jan and I are continually living in the moment together with the conscious awareness of where we both are in that moment. It has been a phenomenal experience. And as of this moment, it continues to be. This is where we are.

Judgment or Observation?

I was talking with a friend of mine about relationships and I shared with her the following email about my grandparents' relationship:

My grandparents had a wonderful relationship! Married fifty-five years. Laughed together. Had a deep respect for one another. I know it was wonderful for where they were. Yet, I do not recall hearing them say "I love you" or them ever saying it to me. I am not sure how much in touch they were with their feelings and emotions. Clearly it was a great relationship for them. One they enjoyed immensely. I used to want what they had. But now, compared to what I now know is possible for me, I no longer desire this.

The response I received from my friend was this:

Being in a newer generation, I think you are making a judgment about your grandparents' relationship. In those generations and even in my parents' generation, I don't think spouses were always open about expressing their feelings for each other in front of others. That does not mean they did not do so in private. The same way that an unmarried pregnancy in the family was often kept quiet and private vs. today. You say they laughed, had deep respect for each other, were married for fifty-five years, and yet you judge it to be not what it should be based on what you want to have. It appears your grandparents had a great relationship but it might not meet your criteria for what you want. That is okay, just don't judge them based on what you would like today.

My response to her is to follow. I would like to share that this is a very dear friend of mine. One who has offered me tremendous growth because the framework of where we are is so vastly different. We have had many conversations and it is delightful to communicate and share our different perspectives. I rejoice in this. My reply:

Read it again, my dear one. There is no judgment. None. Not a bit. This is only how you perceive it, your perspective. It is not mine and not what I was expressing. What I was sharing was very beautiful. It is you who chose to see it differently. Through the perspective of where you are. I understand this. So please, allow me to explain a little more from where I am. Let us grow together in this wonderful discussion.

From where I am, another's life experience is another's life experience and the only purpose it serves me is to offer me growth and help me gain clarity about what I choose to create for my own life experience. As I stated, they had a wonderful relationship. It clearly was wonderful for them and they enjoyed it immensely. What I think about their relationship is irrelevant to them. It is only relevant to me. I utilize the experience to help me determine what it is that I desire. And I am grateful to them for that gift. My desire to create something else in no way "detracts" from the beauty of their experience. It is perfection. And I understand that it was a different way of life.

That many were not open to expressing feelings then. It simply is what was. There is no judgment, only observation for growth in the now. Clearly this discussion has triggered something for you. What a wonderful opportunity to walk through it. I recall you stating on our phone call the other night that judging others was an issue for you in which you desired to create change. I shared with you then that experiences would continue to show up in your life in order for you to have the opportunity to respond differently. Well, here is one now, right before you. Do you see it? Acknowledge it? Do you see how this works? It is truly beautiful to consciously witness the process. This is where the power is. Awareness.

I would also like to clarify that I don't think my grandparents' relationship "should" have been anything other than what it was. I wasn't saying this is where I am and therefore I think they should have been different. In fact, it is quite the opposite. As I observed where they were, it gave me clarity to declare, this is where I am. Everyone is free to create and experience whatever life they choose. I honor that. I don't think anyone "should do" anything. I don't come from that space. I know you may not understand that. And it is okay if you don't. Just know that I will continue to communicate with you for greater clarity, understanding, and growth for as long as you choose. I love you!

Still in Wedlock

I know how shocking it once was for a woman to have a child out of wedlock. For some, it still is. What about the idea of still being in wedlock once a relationship has ended and new relationships form? Is this surprising as well? Unacceptable? Wrong? If so, why? What is the thought that creates that? I would like to share with you more about my life experience.

I had a funny conversation this past weekend. A friend of Jan's said that she was concerned about his relationship with me. When I asked why he said it was about him getting involved with a married woman. I immediately said "but I'm not married" and he started laughing and said "Yes you are!" We both laughed hysterically about the fact that I forgot I was. I knew he knew this in the beginning about me so I hadn't thought about it since. My former husband and I are indeed still legally married. (I guess the word "former" seems silly in that sentence, but it makes perfect sense to us.)

I do not consider myself to be a married woman. To me it is just a legal technicality. For us, the marriage ended the moment we had the talk and agreed that we would be happier apart. We knew our purpose, our growth together, had been fulfilled. In that moment, there was an overwhelming sense of peace that filled the room and I could feel the energy around our relationship dissipate. That was the end of it for us. We have both moved on. We are dating and experiencing new relationships. Those involved are fine with the situation.

To be honest, I hadn't given the legal thing a second thought. To me, I am free as my former husband and I have chosen it to be. There will be those who say, "but you are still married." It is a piece of paper that has no relevance to the life I live. It is only relevant if I choose to make it so. Things only have the meaning we give them.

Now as of this moment, we have no plans for getting a legal divorce, only because we are not planning our future but allowing it to unfold. Should the moment arise when it becomes relevant to us, for example my former husband wanting to re-marry at some point, then we will create change. I know there are those who are thinking, why not just do it now then? Many have asked me this. My only response to that is because it is irrelevant to both of us. There is currently no purpose for us to create change in that. When the moment arises that we feel there is, we will. My question is, why is it so important to others how I choose to experience my relationships? I say this but I already have an answer, at least from my perspective. It is just part of the process. Where we are, watching, observing, sometimes judging as we decide what we want for ourselves, what we feel is right, or how we think things should be. So have at it! Let those thoughts popping up for you lead you to more clarity and a greater awareness of self.

Marriage/Relationships

Who defines what a relationship is or what it should be? There will always be a different answer to this question based on where we are. For those of you who have chosen the experience of marriage, I honor that. I rejoice in that experience for you. I chose it once myself. I am also aware that we are all having a different experience of what marriage is based on the thought we hold about it. I love weddings. I love to experience that expression of unity. But there are many ways in which we can experience this. I am just sharing my own personal experience and what I now choose for me based on the experiences I have had and the thoughts I now hold that have led me here.

Many have asked me if I desire a more committed relationship with Jan such as marriage, one that would be more meaningful or deep. My only response is that I already have it. Jan and I use the term "All In." We are fully present with each other and committed to sharing all of ourselves with each other in this moment of now. We are continually choosing in every moment. The idea that marriage will offer something "more" than what we already have or will somehow make it "better" or more "meaningful" is no longer a thought that I hold. I once did, but then I realized that my relationship is what I create it to be and is not defined by a ceremony, a document, or others. My partner and I only define it.

And to be quite frank, the idea of choosing something in this moment for the rest of the many moments of my life just seems so absurd to me now. These are just my thoughts. You can think them just as ridiculous, or not. I am aware that a lifetime promise is a promise I could not possibly make because I cannot know how I will feel at any other time except for this moment of now. That's all there is. I am living for right now. I can only ever choose in my now.

Well, I could actually make choices for my future, but then I might spend the rest of my moments struggling to live up to a choice while I suppress my true desires in the moment as things shift and change for me. To me, that just creates limitations. I do not choose to place myself in a box. As Jacob says, suppression of self creates congested energy (dis-ease) which can manifest in the form of what people refer to as mental illness or physical ailments.

As far as choosing for my future, I have already experienced that. And those experiences guided me here, to a different thought. Allowing myself to be in the moment creates a wonderful space for freedom of full expression. There is nothing so joyful as full expression of self. It is sheer bliss and Jacob says full expression of self IS the joy we feel. In this life experience, we are continually shifting, growing and expanding and how wonderful it is to let things shift and flow with EASE.

I have discovered just how easy everything is when I do not try to control it, figure it out, understand the "how," or have things planned out. When I just let go and allow things to show up for me, the universe does its magic and my life unfolds in the most magnificent ways. Not only is it easy, it's really fun. It's like a new surprise every day of what will show up next.

Now if this discussion (or anything else you have read here) has brought up any feelings of discomfort for you, this is a great opportunity to ask yourself why. If so, there is a trigger point being activated and I would tell you to get excited, as this is a powerful moment in which you can come to a greater awareness of self and where you are in your life experience.

Understanding why we react or respond in certain ways to others can tell us so much about ourselves. In coming to a greater awareness of what the source of our feelings is, our source thought about something, growth is offered. Continue to ask yourself what this is really about for you. Clarity will come, and a shift in consciousness will be created as you open yourself to receiving it.

If you were just reading along with no trigger activated whatsoever, then you can get excited about that as well. This too will tell you more about where you are. Now exactly what it is telling you is only for you to come to know and have a greater awareness about. You decide what the meaning is for you. It is in that thought process that the growth occurs. Utilize the experience of this moment to your greatest benefit.

Authenticity

When I shared the "still married" thing with a friend of mine, instead of a laugh, I got a lecture. He told me that now that I was going to be coming out with a book and developing a website, that I needed to think about my "public persona" and issues that may be created by remaining married. He told me that many people would judge me if I am still married while pursuing a new relationship. I told him that if I got divorced for my public persona, then I would be living for others and conforming to what they state is appropriate, which varies depending with whom you are speaking. I choose to live for me, to be free.

And this would also completely go against the message of Jacob which is to create your life experience as you desire. What message would I be sending by conforming? This would be very conflicting indeed. If others want to judge me, so be it. It will only tell me more about where they are. It does not define me. It is just the framework through which they are currently experiencing the world. And it is beautiful no matter what frame that is. It is just helpful to me to recognize where others are in their framing in order to have a greater understanding of their experience. This enables me to easily connect with them.

Perhaps my current marital situation will help those concerned to consider the possibility that no judgment is necessary of anyone and that we can honor everyone's choices for the life experiences they desire. Again, just another option, another choice of experience.

Stillness in the Store

Let me tell you about an amazing experience I had today. I was shopping in the grocery store and feeling so connected. I could feel my light energy radiating from me. All of the sudden, I looked at all of the people and there was a stillness. It was like in the movies where you are the only one moving and everyone else is frozen. I was aware in that moment that this was MY reality, that I was creating it, and that all of the people were just IN it. It was a wild moment. As if time stood still. I don't know how long it lasted. It was long enough for me to think about how incredible it was, to notice the stillness, and to be aware of my reality in that moment. There was a glow around me. It was incredible. I know that this was just a glimmer of what I now know to be so.

We Are One

Although I may speak of Neale and Esther and Jerry Hicks as having played an important role in my life experience, I want to be clear that everyone plays an important role. Everyone I come in contact with is offering me an experience. Everyone who shows up in my life is a part of this co-creative process. Not one is more important than another. Growth is growth. Expansion is expansion. I look at everyone as just another divine part of me. I am aware that I am interacting with myself in what appears to be a separate physical form. We are all divine as we are all one. I rejoice in knowing this is so.

Thanking Whom?

If we are all one, then whom exactly am I thanking when I say "Thank you for this gift"? I am thanking another divine part of me for choosing to participate in my process and offer me growth in what I would call this individual physical life experience. The idea of individualism serves the purpose for us to grow in our own life experience. Ultimately it is growth for the whole but there is much to be offered with this illusion. As I rejoice in others, I rejoice in who I am as they ARE me. It is beautiful.

Enjoy the Process

What a journey this has been and continues to be. In this moment, I asked myself what I would like to share with you from where I am now? I rejoice that I will forever be growing and expanding. And it is occurring whether we are consciously aware of it or not. We are all contributing. It is inevitable. I simply choose to be consciously aware and I choose to enjoy the process. It is beautiful to witness. As I choose to enjoy the process, choose to take notice of the growth opportunities that appear as experiences in my life, I experience great joy for how divine my life experience really is.

The only person who needs to hear me IS me, and the only person who needs to hear you IS you. This is your life experience. Create it, as you desire it to be. Go for it! Live it up! Experience whatever it is that you want to experience. Feel the joy and freedom in that. In my most terrifying moment, I walked through my fear. And when I arrived on the other side, I was embraced by the love and joy that had been there all along.

I looked back only to discover that the fear was just an illusion, that the fear had been my very own creation. As I awakened to this, I stepped out of my ordinary life and stepped into the extraordinary life that was awaiting me. Now when I say this,

I am in no way implying my ordinary life was somehow "less" than the life I live now. There is no "less," no "better" or "worse." It is all just a different experience. I describe it as "ordinary" because that is how I viewed my life at the time. I was just another person in the world, working, caring for my son and getting by. I was normal so to speak, at least what society might consider normal (again, my perspective here). The life I have stepped into has opened up a whole new world to me – one that I did not know existed before.

The beauty and magnificence of it goes beyond where, at one point, what I ever thought possible. And therefore, from my perspective, I have indeed stepped into an Extraordinary Life.

So What Was That Message in the Clouds?

As I mentioned earlier on, I had looked up the meaning of the animal totems long ago in my mother's book but didn't think too much of it at the time. After all that has since transpired, I decided to go back and read it again. It is all magnificently divine. It's just another grand event in my transition that I knew was pretty amazing at the time but had no idea just how much it was revealing to me about what was to come. The following is from the book *Animal Speak* by Ted Andrews. There was a lot of information and I am sharing the parts that stood out to me:

It says that the wolf represents guardianship, ritual, loyalty and spirit. The wolf teaches you to know who you are and to develop strength, confidence and surety in that so you do not have to demonstrate and prove yourself to all. The wolf is a reminder to listen to your own inner thoughts, as the intuition will be strong. And when a wolf shows up, it is time to breathe new life into your life rituals. Find a new path, take a new journey and take control of your life.

The leopard is about renewal of vision and vitality. Those with any leopard totem usually have strong intuitive faculties and heightened sensibilities. When a snow leopard reveals itself, it hints of divine protection and a reawakening of one's own spark of divinity. The snow leopard holds the promise of new life, new perception and a renewed perspective on life.

The panther, part of the leopard family, is a very powerful and ancient totem. Those aligning with the panther begin to develop a greater depth of vision of their life, events, or other people. This is more than just psychic insight; it is an inner knowing. To those with whom the panther links comes the ability to develop clairaudience, to hear the communications of other dimensions and other life forms. The panther often signals a time of rebirth after a period of suffering and death on some level. It also symbolizes a time of moving from mere poles of existence to new life without poles or barriers. The panther awakens the unconscious urges and abilities that have been closed down.

It signals a time of imminent awakening. The panther is a symbol of awakening to the heroic quest. And there either already exists or will soon arrive upon the scene an individual who will serve as teacher and nurturer and guide upon the heroic path. Alternate realities will open up to those with panther totems. These alternate realities, the beings within them, all have powerful ties to sexual energies. It may reflect a time of resolving old sexual issues. The panther is the promise that whatever is lost will be replaced by that which is greater, stronger and more beneficial. The panther marks a new turn in the heroic path of those to whom it comes. It gives an ability to go beyond what has been imagined.

I do not know what the vision of the woman with the headpiece was about. But I am sure there are those of you reading this now that would love to enlighten me on its meaning as you know it to be. What I do know is that I'm here now, choosing to enjoy every moment. And that I now take full notice of the wonderful message that appeared to me in the sky that day. Thank you for this gift.

All Is Perfection

I wanted to ask Jacob for some final words of wisdom as we are nearing the conclusion of this book. So I asked the following questions:

How do we live a joyful life?

Joy is experienced with full expression of self. You can consciously choose to be aware that every experience is an expression of self and experience the joy in allowing full expression and consciously observing it. This is awareness. In every situation ask yourself – What is the growth in this for me? What is the experience offering me? What thoughts do I hold about this situation that have caused me to respond the way that I have? How do I feel about what I am feeling about this experience? What possibilities can I open myself up to in order to expand my thoughts to experience this differently? – Continue to ask questions, it is an expression of self.

The joy is in the seeking, the asking, the coming to know and understand what these experiences are about for you. Be the observer of your life and experience the joy in consciously observing many expressions of source, which is you. Remember that you are not here to cross this finish line. Enjoy observing the race from the sidelines while you are also in it, running along, experiencing life at your own glorious pace.

What is enlightenment? How does one get there?

Enlightenment is growth and expansion and therefore you are all experiencing it in some form. It is not a place that you reach or get to. It is a process. This is life.

Someone recently asked me if I felt enlightened by this process. Absolutely. I have come to a greater understanding about my own life, a deeper connection with others, and a great love for all of humanity. Does this mean that I am an enlightened person? As Jacob has said, we all are. There will always be more for me to experience, grow and expand from. So the process of enlightenment will always continue. I embrace where I am in this moment. I feel great to be where I am. If others call it enlightenment, so be it. But it is no different than where you are. I may have a different awareness, perspective of life, but we all do. I am expanding right along with all of you. Expansion is just occurring from different experiences. That is all it is.

Is there anything else you would like to share with those who are asking, seeking to know more about who they are?

We often say to look within, that the answer is within you. By this we are referring to the awareness of the magnificent being that you are and the power that you wield to create and experience the life that you desire. There are no real answers. It is not the answers that you seek but the experience of seeking the answers. This is the growth. Explore, observe, create, experience, express, expand. Enjoy the process of your life experience. Our connection with you in this moment is your divine creation. You are seeking to know more about who you are and this desire has led you to us.

We invite you to look within your self, connect with the source of who you are, and experience your world from a greater perspective of where you are. And what we mean by this is that we invite you to consciously choose to expand the framework of your perspective. How does one do that you ask?

Your perspective is like a picture frame. Envision a small picture frame in front of you. This is the framework through which you view and experience your world. This is just where you are. It is perfection. Everything outside of that frame is not a part of your current life experience. There are endless possibilities available to you. You have access to all that is. And by consciously choosing to expand your framework, you will invite experiences into your life that will offer you the opportunity to create a shift to expand your current frame. From this expanded perspective, you will experience your world from a greater perspective. And this will now be where you are. It is not who you are but where you are in this life experience. Everything is filtered through this framework. Your view of another is through your own framework. Their view of themselves is through their own framework.

Misunderstandings arise because you are experiencing something entirely different. Many of you feel frustration when others do not view your world the way you do but they do not have your frame. It cannot be. They will always have their frame. And it is never about comparing one frame to another's. It is only ever about the growth and expansion of your own framework. The purpose of life is growth and expansion. You desire the growth and every experience offers you the opportunity to gain clarity about where you are in order to grow and expand your framing. You are continually growing and expanding. It is for you to enjoy the process. Rejoice in where you are. It is perfection.

My Perspective Now

So what is my perspective of my childhood, my relationships and my past experiences now? I love and rejoice in them all for the divine creations they are. I can see the perfection in all of it. My childhood wasn't actually stifled at all but a wonderful opportunity for me to grow. It created a foundation that caused me to desire to know more about my life and who I was. My mother and father provided so many experiences for me to expand my frame. I am incredibly grateful for their many gifts.

My father has not yet spoken to Jacob and I no longer feel a draw for this to occur. I feel that the growth with my father has been fulfilled. This is only my feeling in this moment and what is so for me now. It feels good to me. I sense there is much more for me to experience with my mother. I also know that even the lack of communication we have experienced has offered me much growth and clarity about where I am, and that, too, is perfection. Our relationship is continually unfolding and I am enjoying the process.

My relationship with my former husband was also a wonderful growth experience. I came to understand so much about myself. I gained clarity about the types of relationships I choose to create now and how I choose to participate and experience them. I am so grateful for his many gifts.

I understand that no one has ever done anything "to me." It may have felt that way at the time, but I am now clear that I created all of it and that others were offering me experiences for growth. They were actually doing something "for me." But I did not know how to consciously utilize these experiences then. And the process of me coming to this understanding was all expanding my frame.

So even though I did not consciously utilize the experience, my frame was expanding from my experiences anyway. Just in smaller bits and pieces. It has been an incredible process that was occurring all along but I was completely unaware of it. It is delightful to look back and experience my journey through the framework of where I am now. When memories are triggered by something or someone, I get to experience the event in a whole new way. I love to talk about all the many glorious experiences I remember because I experience great joy as I come to greater clarity and a deeper understanding of their purpose in my life.

And what do I think now about the many moments I had wished I were dead, the days I could not get out of bed? I rejoice in them because these experiences provided me the extreme contrast to what I am living now.

The reason I am filled with such joy at experiencing simple pleasures is because I have the comparison from experiencing great struggle in my life where everthing felt like it was so hard. I could not possibly know and experience the tremendous joy and freedom I feel as life flows with ease had I not first known what it felt like to be suppressed in a box with my own shackles in place.

Of course, I could experience something, but it would not be the same. These experiences give us a foundation and we grow and expand from there. We are continually shifting and changing our foundation and expanding our frame using that current foundation as a comparison for growth. I rejoice in all that has unfolded and continues to unfold to create my foundation. How delightful it is! I am grateful.

And if that little caterpillar were to crawl on my foot again, I would gladly welcome it and bring it forth to snuggle in my hands. I would say hello and thank that glorious creature for choosing to visit me. I would love to just sit on the bench and speak with this other divine part of me for hours. I know I would experience the oneness that we are and that it would be a most delightful experience. Perhaps I will get another chance to do just that!

All In

So where did Jan and I end up? We are still beautifully flowing, communicating, sharing, laughing, playing and enjoying life together. We continue to feel a big draw to one another as growth continues to be offered in our experiences. We still continue to talk for many hours every night. It is in this interaction that I find myself captivated. I feel uplifted in sharing the joys of our day, discussing the glorious process of life, and talking about all the many beautiful things we wish to create.

We continue to walk together through all of the activated triggers that surface for us in order to create change. This is my favorite part. I always get so excited to delve into the deeper meaning of our reactions. Sometimes there is a big reaction and I think, wow, what is the source of THAT? Now that's fun! It is so much fun to explore ourselves and come to a greater understanding about why we respond the way that we do, the source of our current thoughts, and how we choose to express ourselves. Sharing this exploration with Jan has been phenomenal.

Do we know where our relationship is going or what the future holds for us? Honestly, we haven't a clue. But we know where we are now. A place of awareness, presence, and deep connection with one another. And that is powerful! We continue to choose to live in the moment and enjoy the journey together as it beautifully shifts and changes. As we have done so, things have unfolded in the most magnificent ways. Ways we would never have thought possible at the beginning of our adventure together, yet when we opened the door to allow for greater possibilities by just being with one another moment to moment, so much flowed in. It allowed for more than either of us ever imagined. Where we will end up next is a continual adventure and I am excited to see what will be revealed. As for this moment, I am delighted to say that in this glorious moment of now, we are "All In."

Embracing the Magnificent Variety

How wonderful it is that we all see the world through a different framework of where we are. And this is continually ever-changing. This is the growth. People have told me, "We're just too different," as if there were something wrong with that. It is our variety that makes our interactions so pleasurable. If everyone felt the same as I did, where is the growth in that? I rejoice in our differences and utilize it for the greater benefit of my own growth.

Another person commented that we live in two different worlds. Yes! Yes! I agree. But it is not just the two of us who live in different worlds. It is every single one of us. Because each and every one of us is viewing the world through the framework of his or her own unique perspective based on the experiences we have had and where we are in the moment. Isn't that wonderful? And in knowing this, I have no desire to try to conform anyone to my own personal beliefs or views. It's just where I am.

Why then have I been sharing my journey? I have been sharing where I am with you for the purpose of offering you the opportunity to declare where you are, to gain clarity about how you feel about what you observe in my life experience.

This is its only relevance to you. You can choose to view it as uplifting and consciously choose to create change in your own life experience or you can choose to see it as the contrast and have clarity about what you do not want. Either way, it is beneficial to you. Utilize it.

What Do You Choose?

In this moment, as you have come to the end of this book, you too have been on a journey, a journey of clarity about where you are. This is not about making a comparison to my life as a place to get to.

I say this only because I have had numerous people make the comment to me, "I'm not where you're at yet." It is not about me and there is no place to get to. There is only what you want to experience. It is about you, opening up to greater possibilities from where you are. Whatever that might be to you. Welcome experiences that offer you the opportunity to grow and expand your frame beyond the current limits, limits that only you have set in place for yourself. Open yourself up to a new way of life, one where anything is possible.

This is your moment. Right here, right now. Allow yourself to expand your thoughts and bring into your life experience more than you once ever thought possible. YOU are what you have been waiting for. Awaken to your own magnificence. What do you choose? I rejoice in whatever life experience that you choose for you. Just by choosing to consciously choose, *you ARE Awakening to the Extraordinary YOU!* Explore it, however you desire!

*Be the observer of your life.
It is a powerful view.*

For more information
please visit the author's website:
www.AwakeningToYou.com

About the Author

My name is Kayite Ashcraft and I am the mother of a delightful five-year old boy. I grew up in Richmond, Virginia, and experienced what I perceived at the time to be a very rough childhood. I spent most of my life thinking I was not good enough or worthy of anything. There were many days I no longer wanted to live.

This carried into my early adult life. But in going to that deep place of despair, it caused me to ask many questions – questions about life, what was the purpose, and why was I here? As I opened myself up and desired to know more, things began to shift for me. Experiences showed up in my life to give me the opportunity to create change. And change I did.

On the eve of my 34th birthday, I began channeling and communicating with a group of spiritual beings known by the name of Jacob. It was an incredible experience that completely changed my whole life. I experienced the world from an entirely different perspective. I understood we are all one. Not just one with others but one with everything. I also understood what a wonderful experience my childhood had been. It was a tremendous opportunity for growth and I am grateful to those who participated and offered me such glorious gifts. I now live my life knowing that no one is ever doing anything "to me" but rather "for me" and that every experience is offering me an opportunity to grow and expand. From this space, I enjoy life.

Some people call me the Soul Whisperer, but I am really just another divine part of you. I am usually able to connect with people on a deep level very quickly because I am aware of this. I can often move past the barriers and connect with the soul essence that is here in this life experience. Others seem to know this.

Because I am open, they are drawn to me and seem to know that I am someone who will listen. They just come up to me and begin sharing their struggles and life story. And of course I listen, I share and I am here to love them. I may hold their hand or give them a hug. I love to look into their eyes and see the moment that tears well up for them as they experience a moment of knowing that I am not a stranger. They see it in my eyes, and I know they know me, they recognize me. It is beautiful.

The most glorious part is that this connection is available to all of us. We are one magnificent source of energy expressed in different forms – connected, intertwined, beautifully flowing together. All it takes is allowing yourself to be vulnerable and open. I know this is something that can be a scary thing to do, and it certainly was for me. But in doing so, you open yourself up to wielding the most magnificent power there is, YOU.

I currently live in the beautiful mountains in Charlottesville, Virginia. I intend to create a retreat center here and it will be open to all those who wish to experience it. My life is about people and connecting with others. I am here to offer myself and where I am in my life experience. I am here to interact with you in a beautiful co-creative process. I want you to know that I love you. I love you just as you are. You are perfection. My love is not conditional. No matter what you are choosing to experience in this life, it does not change who you are. You are divine. Perfect in every way.

With Great Love for All
Kayite

*Please visit our website at
www.JimSamInc.com
to order additional copies.*

JimSam Inc. Publishing
P.O. Box 3363
Riverview, FL 33568
813.748.9523